NORTHERN CALIFORNIA
CHEAP SLEEPS

Recommendations for the Budget Traveler

Rebecca Poole Forée

SASQUATCH BOOKS
SEATTLE

Associate editor: Nancy Leson
Copy editor: Cynthia Rubin
Proofreader: Sherri Schultz
Researcher: Erika Lenkert
Cover design: Elizabeth Watson
Cover illustration: Laura Cook
Interior design: Lynne Faulk
Interior map illustrations: Karen McClinchy
Composition: Fay Bartels

Library of Congress Cataloging in Publication Data
Northern California cheap sleeps: recommendations for the budget traveler/edited by Rebecca Poole Forée.
    p. cm.
    Includes index.
    ISBN 1-57061-025-8
    1. Hotels—California, Northern—Guidebooks. I. Forée, Rebecca Poole.
TX907.3.C22N678 1995
647.9479401—dc20   95-23606

Sasquatch Books
1008 Western Avenue
Seattle, Washington 98104
(206)467-4300

CONTENTS

Sierra Nevada

Gold Country

Central Coast

Indexes

INTRODUCTION

I grew up with a father who never understood why anyone in their right mind would pay $200 for a night in a hotel when you could get a clean bed in a motel for only 30 bucks. As he sees it, you're better off spending the extra cash on the things you can enjoy while you're awake—like German beer and a good fishing pole. After publishing more than 30 travel books that have covered both the priciest and the cheapest accommodations this world has to offer, I must confess that Dad has a good point. Although I can thoroughly appreciate the luxury of slumbering under a goose-down comforter in a ritzy resort overlooking the sea, I find it more satisfying to pay the bill for my budget bed knowing I'll have enough change in my pocket to extend my vacation for a few more days or splurge on a horseback-riding trip through the redwoods. I have also learned that traveling on the cheap inevitably leads to a richer range of experiences and closer encounters with the locals—perks that often merit renting a room with a shared bath or even a slightly sagging bed.

Of course, what's considered an acceptable cheap sleep for one penny-pincher may not be up to snuff for another, so we've done our best to offer a variety of places that will suit everyone in search of a good deal—from free campsites in the woods overlooking San Francisco Bay to quaint Wine Country hotels with private baths, swimming pools, and hot tubs. Unlike most guidebooks to budget lodgings, this one gives you a candid summary of each cheap sleep. That way, you won't be surprised to discover that an inn allows smoking in every room, or that the "beautiful Olympic-size swimming pool" advertised in the hotel brochure resembles an algae experiment in your high-school biology class.

Northern California Cheap Sleeps is also packed with hundreds of great, inexpensive places to eat and tips on how to get the most bang for your buck at Northern California's top attractions. And you can rest assured that this book has no advertisers, sponsors, or other sources who have paid or bribed us for a plug. Just like the authors of the top-rated *Best Places* guidebooks, the *Cheap Sleeps* writers always travel anonymously and pay in full. So use this trustworthy guide as your ticket to a bargain bed, and as my father would say, save your hard-earned cash for the suds and the sites.

ACKNOWLEDGMENTS

If it weren't for the biggest cheapskate I know, **Matthew Richard Poole**, this guide to the best cheap lodgings and activities in Northern California wouldn't be nearly as good. Matthew (who happens to be my brother and travel-writing partner) is a native Californian who taught scuba-diving in Hawaii and downhill skiing in Switzerland before I talked him into working with me for longer hours and less pay. He has since contributed to a half-dozen guidebooks on California, Hawaii, and skiing, and is the author of *Northern California Coast Best Places* (Sasquatch Books, Spring 1996).

Two other major contributors to this first edition of *Northern California Cheap Sleeps* are **Mary Anne Moore**, who frequently travels the globe in search of great getaways, idyllic jogging trails, and the world's best bookstores—when she isn't busy advising the political hot-shots in the California State Capitol—and **Maurice Read**, a Sacramento-based lobbyist who tours Northern California with his Australian shepherd, hunting for dog-friendly lodgings, great fly-fishing spots, and memorable meals that don't cost much more than a box of Milk-Bones.

A heartfelt thanks to **Nancy Leson**, a terrific editor and project manager, not to mention a fantastic eating, drinking, and sunbathing partner. And hats off to wordsmith **Cynthia Rubin**, who made a good book even better, and researcher **Erika Lenkert**, who has more energy than a pack of stevedores and always manages to get the job done quickly and expertly.

I am also grateful to the folks at Sasquatch Books: publisher Chad Haight, senior editor Stephanie Irving, managing editor Joan Gregory, art director Nancy Deahl, sales associate Gary Sarozek, and the mighty marketing team of Linda Stark, Kate Rogers, and Elise Annes.

—Rebecca Poole Forée

WHAT'S CHEAP?

We did our darndest to review only lodgings that charge less than $70 per night for two. Occasionally prices crept above the limit (usually during peak traveling seasons), and sometimes they remained well below, but they were always a great deal for the area. Many establishments offer only one or two rooms at budget prices, so it pays to reserve these far in advance. Bear in mind that rates are subject to change, so ask before you book.

Discounts

Prices for off-season visits, weeknights, and stays of three or more nights are usually discounted (and some places require a two-night minimum stay on weekends and holidays). Ask for the corporate rate, which is always less than the standard rate. You don't need to be on a business trip or even look corporate; just drop the name of your company, and you'll usually be rewarded. Have a AAA card? An AARP membership? A student ID? Don't forget to flash it for a possible discount. For even greater savings, travel with four or more people and ask for a group rate.

Children

In general, most of the lodgings listed welcome children. We make note of those that do not. To be sure, call ahead.

Smoking

Many places offer a choice of either a smoking or a nonsmoking room, but some permit smoking in every unit and others ban smoking altogether. If we discovered an inn is all-smoking, we pointed it out. If you smoke and don't want to be relegated to puffing in the parking lot, ask about the smoking policy before you make your reservation.

Wheelchair Accessible

Several of the cheap sleeps are wheelchair accessible, but some of the older motels and remote cabins are not. If you have special needs, please call ahead.

Pets

Some of the lodgings listed allow pets, usually only small dogs. Whenever possible, we've specified those establishments. In cases where the proprietors were lukewarm, charged a steep fee, or attached too many qualifications, we did not mention pet policy.

Reader Report

At the end of the book is a report form. Every year, we receive hundreds of reports from readers of the *Cheap Sleeps* and *Best Places* guidebooks suggesting new places or agreeing or disagreeing with our assessments. They are a great help in our evaluations, and we encourage you to respond.

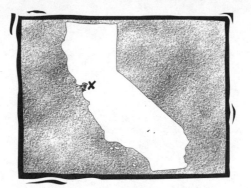

SAN FRANCISCO BAY AREA

San Francisco

Marin County

Berkeley

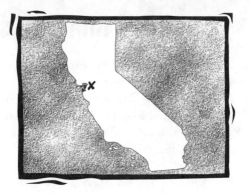

San Francisco

San Franciscans know they are uniquely blessed. In no other city in the country is the meeting of land and sea so spectacular. The late-afternoon sun flashes off the dark-blue bay and lights up the orange towers of the Golden Gate Bridge, and the magnificent sails of boats and wind surfers add color in brilliant flashes. Almost every evening the fog pours in from the Pacific, spilling over the towers of downtown like a white wave. Lovers of all persuasions kiss on street corners. Poets still scribble in coffee shops. No wonder this is one of the world's favorite cities.

Over the years, however, San Franciscans have begun to view this magnetism as something of a liability. Drawn by the city's fabled beauty, cuisine, art, and culture, newcomers from around the globe have poured into this hilly, 46-square-mile oasis. Housing prices have soared, forcing many middle-class families to move to distant suburbs. On bad days, it seems the city is populated entirely by frazzled workaholic singles, weary long-distance commuters, and legions of the homeless. But even on those days, most people are still smiling.

ON THE ROAD

San Francisco, like Paris, is a great walking town, and one of the city's most spectacular and scenic walks is along the **Golden Gate Promenade**, a 4-mile stretch from **Aquatic Park** in front of the Cannery, through the beautiful **Marina Green** and **Crissy Field**, to the historic **Fort Point**, a four-level fortification built in 1861 that's nestled under the south end of the Golden Gate Bridge. (If you're not too winded at this point, continue your tour with a walk across the blustery, and usually chilly, bridge for a breathtaking view of the Bay Area.) Another gorgeous waterfront stroll follows the **Embarcadero** north from Market Street, past the landmark **Ferry Building** to the handsome pier just south of Broadway, where you'll get a good look at **Treasure Island** and the yachts and freighters sailing beneath the Bay Bridge. Heartier souls should continue up the Embarcadero to touristy **Pier 39** to see the hundreds of silly sea lions playing, barking, and basking in the sun on the pier's west side. The third-most-visited amusement attraction in the nation, Pier 39 is packed with kitschy shops and bad restaurants, but it boasts beautiful views of Angel Island, Alcatraz, and the bay, and has great entertainment for kids with its Venetian Carousel, jugglers, mimes, the "motion theater" Turbo Ride, and an arcade stocked with every gizmo and quarter-sucking machine the young-at-heart could dream of.

Once you've had enough of the pier, hop aboard a ferry for the surprisingly interesting audiocassette tour of **Alcatraz**, a San Francisco Bay cruise, or a scenic trip to the pretty little rich towns across the bay, Sausalito and Tiburon (highlights of these sister cities are outlined in the Marin County chapter); for tour information and ferry schedules, call the Blue & Gold Fleet (at Pier 39) at (415)705-5444 (recording) or (415)705-5555, or the Red & White Fleet (at Piers 41 and 43½) at (800)229-2784 (California only) or (415)546-2700.

Theme Park Thrills

If you've set aside a chunk of cash for a day of amusement-park rides, go to Paramount's Great America, Northern California's largest family entertainment center. Expect to pay at least $27 a head for general admission (which gives unlimited access to all the rides). Great America is located off Highway 101 in Santa Clara, 45 miles south of San Francisco; call (408)988-1776 for more details.

The Best-Dressed List

Years of propaganda about sunny California have left millions of tourists freezing in the City by the Bay. Although San Francisco's weather is usually mild and temperatures don't change drastically throughout the year (they rarely rise above 70°F or fall below 40°F), it's seldom warm enough to go without a coat or sweater. Spring and fall are the warmest, and summer is usually foggy, except at midday. Locals beat the summer-morning chills by dressing in layers.

Just a short jaunt west of Pier 39 are the world-famous **Fisherman's Wharf**, **The Cannery**, and **Ghirardelli Square**. They're always mobbed with tourists, but they offer some interesting shops and are riddled with witty, wisecracking, watch-me-pull-a-rabbit-out-of-my-shoe street entertainers. And from mid-November through June, this is also where you'll see the city's highly touted (and delicious) Dungeness crabs boiling in large metal pots on the sidewalks; all three attractions are located side by side on the waterfront at the north end of the Embarcadero and next to Aquatic Park.

While tourists flock to Fisherman's Wharf and Pier 39, locals often head to Golden Gate Park to visit the extraordinary **California Academy of Sciences**. Under one roof you'll find the **Natural History Museum**, **Morrison Planetarium**, the **Laserium**, and the superb **Steinhart Aquarium**, offering one of the most diverse collections of aquatic life in the world, including the popular seals, dolphins, and alligators (in Golden Gate Park off Middle Drive East, between John F. Kennedy and Martin Luther King, Jr., Drives, (415)750-7145). Another San Francisco favorite is the **Exploratorium**, a unique interactive

Dazed and Confused?

The friendly folks at San Francisco's Visitor Information Center are available every day to answer questions and help you find your way around the city streets. Stop by the office at 900 Market Street at Powell (near the Union Square cable-car turntable), or call (415)391-2000. For an up-to-date listing of San Francisco's hottest activities and events (some are even free), call the center's 24-hour recorded hotline at (415)391-2001.

Golden Gate Park Perks

Now you can see five top attractions at San Francisco's famed Golden Gate Park for only $12.50 with an Explorer Pass. Just flash your pass at the entrances to the California Academy of Sciences (home of the Steinhart Aquarium), Japanese Tea Garden, Asian Art Museum, de Young Museum, and the Conservatory of Flowers and walk on in. You'll save 25 to 30 percent off the cost of regular adult admissions. The pass allows a one-time entry to each venue and is valid for up to a year. Purchase your Explorer Pass at the Visitor Information Center at 900 Market Street at Powell (near the Union Square cable-car turntable) or at any of the five participating attractions. Call (415)750-7459 or (415)391-2000 for more details.

museum that brings scientific concepts to vivid life—it's a blast at any age. The marvelous **Tactile Dome**, where visitors must feel their way through a maze of hurdles in total darkness, requires reservations and a certain amount of nerve. The Exploratorium is housed within the magnificent **Palace of Fine Arts**, designed by the renowned Bernard Maybeck for the 1915 Panama-Pacific International Exposition. The palace is surrounded by a natural lagoon—an ideal spot for a picnic and for tossing your leftovers to the grateful swans, pigeons, and sea gulls (3601 Lyon Street, between Jefferson and Bay, near the on-ramp to the Golden Gate Bridge, (415)561-0360 (recording); Exploratorium, (415) 563-7337; Tactile Dome, (415)561-0362).

Golden Gate Park, 1,017 acres of beautiful, lush grounds dotted with magnificent museums, lakes, and ponds, is a masterpiece of design. For a good introduction, join one of the free guided walking tours held every weekend from May through October; call the Friends of Recreation and Parks for more information at (415)221-1311. Park highlights include the **Strybing Arboretum**, which boasts more than 6,000 species of trees and plants (near 9th Avenue and Lincoln Way; (415)661-1316). Right next door is the lovely but often crowded **Japanese Tea Garden** (to avoid the hordes, visit when it's raining). And nearby is the spectacular **Conservatory**, a Victorian fairyland hothouse full of tropical flora, which was erected in 1879 and is the oldest operating conservatory in the country (on John F. Kennedy Drive near Conservatory Drive; (415)641-7978). The **Children's Playground** features a dazzling, restored Golden Age carousel that's guaranteed to make every child's heart go pitter-patter (at the intersection of Martin Luther King, Jr., and Kezar Drives). Every

🚲 *Presidio Pointers*

After years of congressional debates and other political squabbles, the U.S. Army finally handed over the beautiful 1,480-acre San Francisco Presidio, one of the nation's oldest military installations, to the National Park Service in 1995. Established by Spanish colonists in 1776, the Presidio offers 14 miles of biking trails, 11 miles of hiking routes (including the spectacular Coastal Trail and Lover's Lane/Ecology Trail), picnic areas, lookout points, historic buildings, and even the last free-flowing stream in San Francisco. For a free guide about the Presidio's history and a detailed map, call (415)561-4323 or stop by the Presidio Visitor Information Center (on Montgomery Street in the Presidio) or the Presidio Museum (on the corner of Lincoln Boulevard and Funston Avenue). Or send your request to Golden Gate National Recreation Area– Presidio, Fort Mason, Building 201, San Francisco, CA 94123.

Sunday, Golden Gate Park's main drag is closed to auto traffic, so skaters and joggers can let loose on the tree-lined street (skate rentals are available on Fulton Street and on Haight Street).

The city's northwest corner is part of the **Golden Gate National Recreation Area** (GGNRA), the largest urban park in the world. Take a hike along its glorious wildflower-laced **Coastal Trail**, which hugs the headlands for more than 10 miles and offers fantastic views of the bay; start at Point Lobos (at the end of Point Lobos Avenue, near the Sutro Baths) and wind your way to the Golden Gate. **The Presidio**, formerly a 1,480-acre parklike military base, is now part of GGNRA and offers superb views to hikers and bicyclists. Nearby are **Crissy Field**, a fabulous wind-surfing spot (and a great place to hang out and watch the surfing dudes and dudettes), and the **Marina Green**, prime kite-flying and jogging territory (both are located off Marina Boulevard, near the Golden Gate Bridge on-ramp). Riptide-ridden **Ocean Beach** doesn't offer any water sports, but the long, sandy shore is a popular place for blustery walks and picnics (off the Great Highway). On warm days, sun worshipers bask at **Baker Beach** while gazing at the view of the Golden Gate (as at most of the city's beaches, however, swimming is unsafe here). The east side of the beach is a popular gay hangout, where sunbathers bare all (take 25th Avenue to the end, bear right, then look for signs to Baker Beach). Other scenic spots include **Glen Canyon Park**, which has a playground (on Bosworth Street at O'Shaughnessy Boulevard); the lush

7

Stern Grove (on Sloat Boulevard at 19th Avenue); and **Lake Merced**, where you can rent a rowboat, canoe, or paddleboat and fish for trout (off Harding Road, between Highway 35 and Sloat Boulevard, near the zoo; call (415)753-1101 for boat rental information).

On the other side of the city, near the ocean, is the **San Francisco Zoo**, a delight for animal lovers of all ages. Don't miss the famed Primate Discovery Center, where several species of apes and monkeys live in glass-walled condos. The zoo also boasts one of the world's largest gorilla habitats and a children's petting zoo, and it's one of the few in the nation that houses koalas (on 45th Avenue and Sloat Boulevard; (415)753-7061).

City dwellers and their habitats are as fascinating to observe as the critters in zoo cages. For an up-close-and-personal look at San Francisco's multiethnic neighborhoods and architectural masterpieces, strap on your heavy-duty walking shoes and—starting in the **Russian Hill** neighborhood, at the top of the crookedest street in the world, **Lombard Street** (at Hyde)—wind your way down those multiple, red-brick, flower-lined curves, continuing east until Lombard intersects with Columbus Avenue. Then turn right and stay on Columbus for a tour of charming **North**

I Can See Clearly Now

San Francisco is famous for its beautiful, sweeping views, and you'll find some of the city's best at the following locations:

Alamo Square • On the square's south side, on Hayes Street between Pierce and Steiner

Alcatraz Island

Angel Island

Baker Beach • On Gibson Road, off Lincoln Boulevard via 25th Avenue

Coit Tower • On Telegraph Hill, at the east end of Lombard Street

Fort Point • Under the southern end of the Golden Gate Bridge, at the end of Long Avenue, off Lincoln Boulevard

Golden Gate Bridge

Mission Dolores Park • On the park's south side, on 20th Street, between Dolores and Church

Pier 39 • At the north end of the Embarcadero

Point Lobos • The westernmost tip of San Francisco; follow the trails from the parking lot at El Camino del Mar and Point Lobos Avenue

Twin Peaks • On Twin Peaks Boulevard, in the center of the city

Beach—a predominantly Italian and Chinese neighborhood where residents practice tai chi in Washington Square or sip espresso as they peruse Proust or the *Bay Guardian*'s really racy personal ads (guaranteed to make you blush—or send you running for the nearest phone). You can extend this tour by turning right off Columbus onto Grant Avenue, which will take you through the heart of the ever-bustling and fascinating **Chinatown**—the only part of the city where vendors sell live, 3-foot-long slippery eels next to X-rated fortune cookies and herbs meant to cure whatever ails you.

For those in need of an aerobic workout, take this tour: instead of turning off Lombard onto Columbus, keep following Lombard east all the way up to **Coit Tower** on the top of **Telegraph Hill**—then reward yourself for making the steep ascent with a trip (in an elevator, *gasp, gasp*) to the top of the tower for a panoramic view of the Bay Area; (415)362-0808. And for those who'd rather ride than walk the hills, an outside perch on one of the city's famed **cable cars** is always a kick. The three cable-car routes are named after the streets they run on (you can take them in either direction): the Powell-Mason line starts at Powell and Market Streets and terminates at Bay Street near Fisherman's Wharf; the Powell-Hyde line also begins at Powell and Market, but ends at Victorian Park near Aquatic Park and the bay; and the California line runs from California and Market Streets to Van Ness Avenue, the widest street in the city. For cable car information, call (415)391-2000.

⭐ *Don't Rain on Our Parade*

Every winter, the two-week-long Chinese New Year celebration culminates with an electrifying parade led by a 150-foot-long dragon that winds through downtown, Union Square, and Chinatown; call (415)982-3000. In summer and spring, street fairs that typify their neighborhoods pop up from upscale Union Street to the still-hairy Haight; a St. Patrick's Day parade marches through downtown in March, (415)587-1452; Japantown launches its Cherry Blossom Festival with a parade in April, (415)563-2313; the Mission District draws crowds with its Cinco de Mayo Parade in late April or early May, (415)826-1401, and the Carnaval Parade on Memorial Day weekend, (415)826-1401; the San Francisco Lesbian and Gay Freedom Day Parade draws up to half a million revelers every June, (415)864-3733; and in October the Italian community in North Beach kicks off Columbus Day celebrations with a big parade, (415)434-1492.

Top Ten Tourist Attractions

Too much to see and too little time? Here's the short list (in alphabetical order) of visitors' favorite San Francisco Bay Area attractions:

Alcatraz	Golden Gate Park
Cable car rides	Muir Woods
Chinatown	Museums and art galleries
Fisherman's Wharf/Pier 39	Sausalito
Golden Gate Bridge	Union Square

A tour of the town wouldn't be complete without walking through one of San Francisco's main attractions: the shops. The famous and oh-so-trendy **Union Square** district and the nearby **San Francisco Shopping Centre** (at Market and 5th Streets) boast half a dozen major department stores (including Macy's, Nordstrom, and Neiman Marcus) and more specialty shops than Imelda Marcos has shoes. A short walk away is the chichi **Crocker Galleria**, a 67-foot-high, glass-dome, tri-level shopping mall modeled after Milan's 1867 Galleria Vittoria Emmanuelle (bounded by Post, Kearny, Sutter, and Montgomery Streets; (415)393-1505). The vast **Embarcadero Center** is a sophisticated triple-level, open-air neo-mall well worth a spree (bounded by Clay, Sacramento, Battery, and Drumm Streets; (415)772-0585). Many big-name fashion firms have factory outlets south of Market Street, including Esprit (499 Illinois Street off 3rd Street; (415)957-2500) and Gunne Sax (35 Stanford Street, between 2nd and 3rd Streets; (415)495-3326).

Stroll down Sacramento Street (between Lyon and Locust) for elegant clothing and furnishings. For vintage, cutting-edge, and folksy fashions and crafts, shop on Noe Valley's 24th Street (between Castro and Church), Castro Street (between Market and 19th), Fillmore Street (between Jackson and Sutter), Haight Street (between Masonic and Shrader), and Union Street (between Gough and Steiner). The 5-acre

What's Pink and Black and Read All Over?

The *San Francisco Chronicle's* "Datebook," which is more commonly known as the "pink section" because part of it is printed on pink paper, appears in the Sunday newspaper and is the best Bay Area guide to current art events and other entertainment.

Open House

Architecture and history buffs should get their hands on the 31-page booklet *Bay Area Historic House Museums*. A guide to 27 historic homes spread throughout the Bay Area, it features maps, photos, descriptions, hours, and admission fees (many allow visitors for free). For a copy, send a request and $3 to Bay Area Historic House Museums Association, 22701 Main Street, Hayward, CA 94541. For more information, call (510)581-0223.

Japan Center houses several shops selling Japanese crafts, housewares, and books, with numerous sushi bars sandwiched in between (on Post Street, between Laguna and Fillmore; (415)922-6776).

Cosmopolitan cooks can stock up on Asian foodstuffs in Chinatown along Stockton Street (between California and Broadway) or in New Chinatown on Clement Street (between Arguello and 10th Avenue, and 18th and 25th Avenues). North Beach sells Italian treats along Columbus Avenue (between Broadway and Bay), while the Mission offers Latin specialties on 24th Street (between Mission and Potrero). Good bookstores include **City Lights**, still Beat after all these years (261 Columbus Avenue at Broadway, (415)362-8193); **A Clean Well-Lighted Place for Books** (601 Van Ness Avenue, in Opera Plaza, between Golden Gate Avenue and Turk Street, (415)441-6670); the city's largest bookstore, **Borders Books and Music** (400 Post Street at Powell in Union Square, (415)399-1633); **Stacey's** (581 Market Street at 2nd, (415)421-4687); and **Green Apple** (506 Clement Street at 6th, (415)387-2272).

While San Francisco's visual art scene isn't New York's, it still holds its own and continues to get raves from critics around the nation. Some of the not-to-be-missed highlights include the **M. H. de Young Memorial Museum**, which showcases American art from colonial times to the 20th century and hosts many traveling international exhibits (in Golden Gate Park, off John F. Kennedy Drive; (415)863-3330). In the de Young's west wing is the **Asian Art Museum**, site of a world-famous collection of Far East art, including many masterpieces from the Avery Brundage collection; (415)668-8921. The **San Francisco Museum of Modern Art**, now housed in an impressive contemporary red-brick building designed by internationally acclaimed Swiss architect Mario Botta, offers works by Picasso, Matisse, O'Keeffe, Pollock, Warhol, and Lichtenstein, to name just a few (in Yerba Buena Gardens, 151 3rd Street, between Mission and Howard; (415)357-4000). The city also has several

All the Fun at Half the Price

For a sweet deal on opera, theater, dance, and concert tickets, stop by **TIX Bay Area**, which sells half-price, day-of-performance tickets. Discount info is not available by phone, so get in line early at 251 Stockton Street, between Post and Geary, in Union Square. Half-price tickets are sold—for cash only—Tuesday through Thursday, from 11am to 6pm, and Friday and Saturday, from 11am to 7pm (Sunday and Monday tickets are sold on Saturdays).

terrific, small folk-art museums, most notably the **Mexican Museum** (at Fort Mason Center, Building D, on Marina Boulevard at Buchanan; (415)441-0404).

Vibrant murals decorate many public spaces in the city, particularly in the **Mission District**; for maps outlining self-guided walks ($1 fee) or for two-hour guided tours ($4 per adult), contact the Precita Eyes Mural Arts Center (348 Precita Avenue at Folsom Street; (415)285-2287). For free guided walking tours of the Mission's murals, call City Guides; (415)557-4266. Galleries for established artists are located primarily on Grant Avenue near Market and in the vicinity of Union Square; up-and-coming artists tend to exhibit in SOMA (the area south of Market Street). For current art listings, check the *San Francisco Chronicle's* "Datebook" in the Sunday paper.

While Los Angeles still reigns as the nation's movie capital, the Bay Area's motion-picture industry has garnered an international reputation, and San Francisco offers several highly regarded events for film buffs, including the **San Francisco International Film Festival**, held for a fortnight every spring (various venues, (415)931-3456); the **San Francisco International Lesbian and Gay Film Festival**, which takes place in June, (415)703-8650; and **Spike and Mike's Festival of Animation**, held in April at the Palace of Fine Arts (3601 Lyon Street, between Jefferson and Bay; call (619)459-8707 for more information). For rare revivals and premieres, check the palatial **Castro Theatre**, a flamboyant Spanish baroque-style movie palace designed by Timothy Pflueger in 1923 (429 Castro Street off Market, (415)621-6120); the funky (but finely programmed) **Roxie Cinema** (3117 16th Street at Valencia, (415)863-1087); and the homey **Red Vic Movie House** (1727 Haight Street, between Cole and Shrader, (415)668-3994).

The world-class **San Francisco Opera**, led by Lotfi Mansouri, alternates war-horses with rarities in May and June and from September through December at the beautiful **War Memorial Opera House**, which was modeled on Garnier's Paris Opera and first opened in 1932 (it closes in January 1996 for seismic renovations and reopens in June 1997; call the opera for information on its temporary venue). Subscribers grab up most seats, but fans with smaller bankrolls can line up early on performance mornings to buy standing-room tickets (box office (415)864-3330; general information (415)861-4008). The **San Francisco Symphony** performs from September through July at the modern **Louise M. Davies Symphony Hall**, a gorgeous $38 million concert hall with a wraparound glass façade (201 Van Ness Avenue at Grove; (415)431-5400). Other classical groups include the **Lamplighters Music Theatre**, performing Gilbert and Sullivan's comic operas (Lindland Theatre, at Archbishop Riordan High School, 175 Phelan Avenue, (415)227-0331); the **Women's Philharmonic** (First Congregational Church, at Post and Mason, (415)543-2297); and the **San Francisco Early Music Society** (Meadowlands Assembly Hall, Dominican College in San Rafael, (510)528-1725).

For 10 successive Sundays starting in June, families tote blankets and picnic baskets to the oldest continuous free summer music festival in America. The free outdoor performances—everything from jazz to opera—are held at 2pm at the pleasant **Stern Grove** (Sloat Boulevard and 19th Avenue; (415)252-6252). The **San Francisco Jazz Festival**, one of the largest in the country, toots its horn every fall; call (415)864-5449 for information.

American Conservatory Theater (ACT), the city's best-known theater company, presents solid productions of new works and classics from late September to mid-June in the Geary, Stage Door, and Marines Memorial Theaters; call (415)749-2ACT for program information.

Free Tours of the Town

There's no better way to discover the City by the Bay than by following the footsteps of a savvy guide. City Guides offers more than two dozen different guided walking tours for free. You'll see everything from San Francisco's old brothels and Chinatown shops to its rooftop gardens, art deco architecture, and Haight-Ashbury haunts. The two-hour tours are offered year-round (rain or shine) and reservations are not required. For a list of topics and schedules, call (415)557-4266 or send a business-size SASE to City Guides, Friends of the Library, Main Library–Civic Center, San Francisco, CA 94102.

Broadway shows on tour are performed at the Golden Gate, Curran, and Orpheum Theaters; call (415)474-3800 for the current lineup and ticket information. For off-Broadway acts, contact the Theatre on the Square (TOTS), (415)433-9500, and Marines Memorial Theatre, (415)771-6900.

Summer and early fall bring free outdoor performances by America's oldest political musical-comedy theater group, the **San Francisco Mime Troupe** (call (415)285-1717 for performance locations) and by the more serious **Shakespeare in the Park** theater group (in Golden Gate Park at Liberty Tree Meadow, off John F. Kennedy Drive near Conservatory Drive, (415)666-2221 or (415)666-2222). The long-running *Beach Blanket Babylon*, a cabaret-style show full of silly jokes and famous for its wild costumes and humongous hats, remains a favorite of residents and visitors alike, although tickets are pricey and you need to reserve weeks in advance (Club Fugazi, 678 Green Street near Powell, (415)421-4222).

San Francisco has launched many comedians' careers, including those of the nation's reigning king and queen of comedy, Robin Williams and Whoopi Goldberg. See the latest talents at the **Punchline** (444 Battery Street, 2nd floor, between Clay and Washington, (415)397-7573) and **Cobb's Comedy Club** (in the Cannery, 2801 Leavenworth Street, Building S, courtyard entrance at Beach Street, (415)928-4320).

The internationally renowned **San Francisco Ballet**, led by artistic director Helgi Tomasson, kicks off the season in mid-December with the classic *Nutcracker* and dances to more contemporary pieces beginning in February; tickets (415)865-2000, general information (415)861-5600. Ethnic dance troupes abound in the Bay Area, and they come together in June for the **San Francisco Ethnic Dance Festival**, (415)474-3916. Fans of modern and contemporary dance shouldn't miss the **ODC/San Francisco** dance troupe; call (415)863-6606 for more information.

If *your* feet were made for dancing, San Francisco offers dozens of

The Car-Potato's Guide to San Francisco

Introduce yourself to all sides of San Francisco by cruising in your automobile along the 49-Mile Scenic Drive—a four-hour journey along the city's prettiest streets and past its most scenic sites. The route is marked by blue-and-white signs with pictures of sea gulls—but don't follow the birdie during the rush hours unless you also enjoy staring at lots of license plates. Free detailed maps outlining the course are available at the San Francisco Visitor Information Center at 900 Market Street at Powell (near the Union Square cable-car turntable); call (415)391-2000.

Coming to a Street Corner Near You

The question most frequently asked by visitors to San Francisco is, alas, "Where's the rest room?" Well, soon tourists and residents won't have to travel far to find a public potty. The city's first self-cleaning, French-designed Decaux toilet was installed at the corner of Market and Powell Streets in the summer of 1995—a celebrated event christened (literally) by the mayor himself. Nineteen more of the forest-green commodes will be erected on select corners. The cost of admission is only 25 cents, which may be the best bargain seat in town. Caveat emptor: You must do your duty within 20 minutes or the door will open automatically—and stay open till you deposit another quarter.

great nightclubs. For live blues, jazz, and rock, **Slim's** (co-owned by Boz Scaggs) can't be beat (333 11th Street, between Folsom and Harrison; (415)621-3330). Those who prefer hip-hop, rock, purple hair, and nipple rings should venture into the **DNA Lounge** (375 11th Street at Harrison; (415)626-1409). You can dance among the masses at **The House of 1015** (formerly Club Dakota; 1015 Folsom Street at 6th, (415)431-1200) and the wild **Club DV8** (540 Howard Street, between 1st and 2nd; (415)777-1419). For a mix of live music, the trendy set kicks up its heels at **Cafe Du Nord** (2170 Market Street, between Church and Sanchez, (415)861-5016); **Harry Denton's** (in the Harbor Court Hotel, 161 Steuart Street, between Mission and Howard, (415)882-1333); **Johnny Love's** (1500 Broadway at Polk, (415)931-6053); and the rowdy **Last Day Saloon** (406 Clement Street at 5th, (415)387-6343). Shake, rattle, and roll with the high-fashion crowd at **Club 181** (it's in an unsavory neighborhood, so take a cab or use the valet parking services; 181 Eddy Street, between Taylor and Mason, (415)673-8181).

To hear the sounds of the city's new bands, stroll **Haight Street**. Numerous venues line both sides of this famous strip, still populated by drugged youth, the homeless, and various eccentrics. Over in the Tenderloin area, the ornate **Great American Music Hall** attracts the over-30 crowd with its mix of Motown, rock, and jazz bands (859 O'Farrell Street, between Polk and Larkin, (415)885-0750). For a blast of the blues, go to the Marina and visit the dimly lit **Blues** club (2125 Lombard Street at Fillmore, (415)771-BLUE), or head south to **Jack's Bar**, which has hosted the likes of John Lee Hooker and James Cotton (1601 Fillmore Street at Geary, (415)567-3227). Great jazz joints include

Kimball's (300 Grove Street at Franklin, (415)861-5555) and **Rasselas** (2801 California Street at Divisadero, (415)567-5010). Most of the city's clubs offer up-to-date recorded listings if you call ahead.

San Franciscans need to have something to cut the chill of those long foggy nights, so many head to North Beach, which has more than its share of popular watering holes, including **Little City**, a great spot for flirting over drinks and plates of antipasti (673 Union Street, near Washington Square, (415)434-2900); the pleasant (and semisecret) **Spec's**, an old Beat-generation hangout (on tiny Saroyan Alley off Columbus, south of Broadway, (415)421-4112); the charming but rough-around-the-edges **Savoy Tivoli** (1434 Grant Avenue, between Union and Green, (415)362-7023); and **Tosca Cafe**, where locals and celebs hang out and sip the house specialty: coffee-less cappuccino made with brandy, milk, and chocolate (242 Columbus Avenue, near Pacific, (415)391-1244).

When the fog burns off and the weather heats up, grab a chair on the patio of **Cafe Flore** and order a latte or a glass of wine (2298 Market Street at Noe, (415)621-8579), or get the full array of spirits on the outdoor decks of such funky local favorites as **The Ramp** (855 China Basin Street off 3rd, (415)621-2378) and **Pier 23** (on the Embarcadero near the end of Lombard, (415)362-5125). For a more romantic retreat, splurge on a cocktail at the gorgeous **Redwood Room** in the Clift Hotel (495 Geary Street at Taylor, (415)775-4700); the lounge of the Carnelian Room restaurant, which, perched at the top of the 52-story Bank of America skyscraper, offers a spectacular panoramic city view when the sky is clear (555 California Street at Kearny, (415)433-7500); or the **Equinox**, the unique revolving rooftop lounge and restaurant at the Hyatt Regency in Embarcadero Center that gives patrons a 360-degree view of San Francisco and the bay (5 Embarcadero Center, (415)788-1234). Union Square's best bustling bar is at **Kuleto's** restaurant (221 Powell Street,

Prized Produce and the Bay's Best Bread

Even if you don't have a place to store any farm-fresh fruits and veggies, stroll through the fantastic Ferry Plaza Farmers Market and sample some of Northern California's finest bounty. From award-winning homemade salami and Berkeley's famous Acme bread to delicious organically grown produce and sheep's-milk cheese, you'll find the makings for a great meal right here. There's free live entertainment, too. Held year-round (rain or shine) on Saturdays from 8am to 1:30pm in front of the Ferry Building on San Francisco's Embarcadero; call (415)981-3004.

Sports Roundup

Fans of the **San Francisco 49ers** are justly proud of their championship football team, but many are less enthusiastic about their windswept, bone-chilling home stadium, Candlestick Park (nicknamed "The Stick"). Bring your jacket if you're going to watch the Super Bowl stars strut their stuff. Individual 49er tickets cost the same no matter where you sit; call (415)468-2249 for prices and ticket availability. The **San Francisco Giants** take over the Stick during baseball season, and you can buy bleacher-seat tickets (on the day of the game only) for less than the price of a movie; call (415)467-8000.

Held in July, the **San Francisco Marathon** attracts about 5,000 athletes who run from the north end of the Golden Gate Bridge to Kezar Stadium in Golden Gate Park; call (415)391-2123 for information. If you'd rather race against two-legged Brillo boxes, centipedes, Snow White and the Seven Dwarfs, and a Whitney Houston clone in drag, sign up for the wild and wacky 7.5-mile **Bay to Breakers** race (and walk), held in mid-May—it's the largest footrace in the world; call (415)808-5000, ext. 2222. In the South Bay you'll find the **San Jose Sharks** duking it out with their ice-hockey sticks in the San Jose Arena from October through April; call (510)762-BASS for ticket information. If you're a fan of the Oakland As, Oakland Raiders, or Golden State Warriors, see the "Oakland" box in the Berkeley chapter.

between Geary and O'Farrell, (415)397-7720), and for the best Irish coffee in town, the **Buena Vista** takes top honors (2765 Hyde Street at Beach, (415)474-5044).

San Francisco abounds with cheap eats, and you'll find cafes serving great sandwiches, salads, and snacks at nearly every turn. Some local favorites for breakfast include the homey **Sears Fine Foods** (439 Powell Street at Sutter, (415)986-1160); **Home Plate**, for fat omelets and pancakes smothered in fresh fruit (2274 Lombard Street at Pierce, (415)922-4663); **Patio Cafe**—don't get there too late or they'll sell out of the giant, gooey cinnamon rolls, served on weekends only (531 Castro Street, between 18th and 19th, (415)621-4640); and the **Pork Store Cafe**, a former butcher shop now known for its flapjacks and other traditional American fare (1451 Haight Street, between Ashbury and Masonic, (415)864-6981). For lunch and dinner, your good fortune won't cost you a fortune at one of the city's best (and least expensive) Chinese restaurants: **House of Nanking** (919 Kearny Street, between Jackson and Pacific, (415)421-1429). Or sink your teeth into some dim sum at one of several restaurants that line the streets of Chinatown. **Yank Sing** serves some of the best of these sweet or savory Chinese snacks in its elegant dining room and adjoining to-go stand (427 Battery Street, between Clay and Washington, (415)781-1111; and 49 Stevenson Street, off 1st Street, (415)541-4949). For good sushi at good prices, dine in Japantown at **Sanppo** (1702 Post Street at Buchanan, (415)346-3486).

There are great beans and rice and other Mexican specialties at **La Taqueria** (2889 Mission Street at 25th, (415)285-7117) and **La Canasta** (2219 Filbert Street at Fillmore, (415)921-3003, and 3006 Buchanan Street at Union, (415)474-2627). Fantastic fish tacos can be had at **Pozole** (2337 Market Street, between Noe and Castro, (415)626-2666) and at Sweet Heat (3324 Steiner Street, between Chestnut and Lombard, (415)474-9191). Assuage your burger craving at **Barney's Gourmet Hamburgers** (3344 Steiner Street, between Lombard and Chestnut, (415)563-0307) or **Hamburger Mary's**, which also offers cheap strong drinks and free eats during its happy hour (4pm to 7pm Tuesday through Friday) and drag shows and other live acts on Sunday nights (1582 Folsom Street at 12th, (415)626-5767). Hearty bowls of soup and freshly tossed green salads are served nightly till midnight at the popular **Radio Valencia** (1199 Valencia Street at 23rd, (415)826-1199), and hidden in Union Square in the basement of Macy's men's department store is **Fresh Choice**, where you can get all the soup and greens you want for one reasonable price (on Stockton Street at O'Farrell, (415)989-6861). For a hot, sloppy, finger-lickin'-good meatball or eggplant focaccia sandwich (and one of the best cappuccinos in town), head for **Mario's Bohemian Cigar Store Cafe** (566 Columbus Avenue, at Union and Powell, (415)362-0536; and 2209 Polk Street, between Green and Vallejo, (415)776-8226). If you're looking for terrific coffee, muffins, sandwiches, and ceasars, check the phone book for the nearest **Pasqua**—more than two dozen dot the streets of San Francisco.

CHEAP SLEEPS

The average daily room rate of a San Francisco hotel is $100, although a surprisingly large number of establishments offer rooms for much less. The following are some of the best. Prices range from $12 to $70 per night, and all are in relatively safe areas. If the budget-priced rooms are full, contact the Visitor Information Center (900 Market Street at Powell, near the Union Square cable-car turntable,

(415)391-2000) and ask for their free "San Francisco Lodging Guide," which lists hundreds of accommodations and their room rates. Beware: Several of the city's budget beds (including those listed in that lodging guide) are in questionable neighborhoods; ask the center to recommend a safe place to stay. In a pinch, try one of the many motels along Lombard Street between Van Ness and Lyon.

Free parking in San Francisco is as rare as a royal flush in Las Vegas, so don't expect to find it at the following establishments unless otherwise noted.

Pension San Francisco
1668 Market Street (between Gough and Franklin),
San Francisco, CA 94102 • (800)886-1271 or (415)864-1271
District: Civic Center

Nestled between several storefront windows on bustling Market Street is the handsome Pension San Francisco—just look for the forest-green awning emblazoned with the words "Tourist Hotel." This is the kind of budget lodging even your fastidious mother would appreciate. The 36 small, tidy rooms have bright white walls, carpeting that doesn't look too trampled, glossy pine dressers, small basins and closets, and phones. Most have double beds with a view of the Civic Center skyscrapers. The tiny but clean bathrooms are shared, and there's a small, comfortable sitting room on each of the four floors. None of the rooms are designated for nonsmokers, and the scent of cigarettes often lingers in the air, but the windows usually provide plenty of ventilation. Zuni Cafe, one of San Francisco's best restaurants, is just steps away, and although a meal there would probably cost more than your room, the bar is a great place to get a nightcap and watch the locals in action. Be careful about roaming too far from the hotel at night, though—the Tenderloin and the Western Addition, two unsafe neighborhoods, are a few blocks away. Small pets are welcome.

The Adelaide Inn
5 Isadora Duncan (off Taylor Street, between Post and Geary),
San Francisco, CA 94102 • (415)441-2261
District: Union Square

This European-style pensione is hidden on a street so small it's rarely—if ever—shown on a San Francisco map. Once you arrive, however, you'll feel as if you've stumbled on a cluttered country inn that would be right at home in an old French village. The 18-room inn was originally an apartment building and has a lot of steep stairs (but no elevator). Unfortunately, the Adelaide has lost a lot of its former grace and style. The wallpaper in the halls must have looked quite elegant in earlier years, but now its age is starting to show, and the hodgepodge of photos and prints

19

doesn't quite hide the rips and tears. The rooms are poorly lit and can be lackluster or garish, the queen-size or double bed sometimes sags a little, and the tiny black-and-white TV has poor reception. However, the bathrooms are clean (there's a 10-minute time limit in the shower), each room is equipped with a small basin, and guests have access to a large kitchen with a refrigerator, microwave, and several small tables. A breakfast of coffee and rolls is included in the low rates, and the amiable innkeeper will be happy to tell you how to get around the nearby theater district and Union Square.

The Amsterdam Hotel
749 Taylor Street (between Sutter and Bush), San Francisco, CA 94108 •
(800)637-3444 or (415)673-3277
District: Union Square

This 1909 Victorian offers 30 handsome rooms, each with a four-poster bed, matching armoire holding a cable TV, and a table with cushy chairs by a bay window. The private baths have tub showers and niceties such as blow dryers and boxes of tissue that aren't usually offered in budget hotels. If you tire of sitting in your room gazing at Taylor Street, you can relax on the cream satin couches in the large lounge or take a short walk to the Union Square shops or the top of Nob Hill. A continental breakfast is included.

Brady Acres
649 Jones Street (between Post and Geary), San Francisco, CA 94102 •
(800)6-BRADY-6 or (415)929-8033
District: Union Square

Most of this hotel's 25 studio rooms are rented by the week starting at $300, and for that great price you get all the creature comforts: a room with a twin bed; a private, newly tiled bathroom with tub shower and towels; a dining area equipped with everything from microwave to flatware, as well as TV and radio/cassette player; and a private phone line complete with answering machine. Units usually have a wet bar with a sink, and there's a coin-operated washer-dryer downstairs, with free laundry soap to boot. The hosts of Brady Acres can even get you a good rate on an Alamo Car rental as well as discounted parking at the garage around the corner. With this kind of deal—and a prime locale in Union Square—you may never want to go home. Ask about package deals like stay-six-nights-and-get-one-free. A few studios are rented by the day in summer only.

Golden Gate Hotel
775 Bush Street (between Powell and Mason), San Francisco, CA 94108 •
(800)835-1118 or (415)392-3702
District: Union Square

Quick! Book a room here before the owners realize what a bargain they're offering for their lovely little rooms bathed in Laura Ashley fabrics and wallpaper. This turn-of-the-century bed-and-breakfast inn couldn't be more pleasant: light, airy rooms are furnished with antique dressers, white wicker chairs, pedestal sinks, cable TV, phone, twin reading lights, and pots of beautiful, bright flowers in each room's sunlit window. Some of the "shared bath" units even have a private shower stall in the room. The Golden Gate is nowhere near its namesake bridge, but it is just a couple of blocks from Union Square and the top of Nob Hill.

Herbert Hotel
161 Powell Street (at O'Farrell), San Francisco, CA 94102 • (415)362-1600
District: Union Square

You can't get much closer to the *square* in the Union Square district without paying top dollar, but you'll be hard-pressed to find a duller room in the city than what you'll get at Herbert's. Still, the weekly rates for a spacious room with private (and clean) bath start at $110 a week, and only $90 a week for a unit with a shared bath. Folks, these are better than dorm rates! The furniture in the bare-walled rooms looks like garage-sale specials, but at least the pieces match, and if you tape a couple of pictures to the bare walls, perhaps they won't look so grim. Smoking is permitted in all 90 units—and it smells like it, too. Ask for a room overlooking Powell Street, and expect to hear a lot of cable-car bells ringing. The boarded-up interior of the elevator looks as if it suffered from a bomb blast, but don't let that scare you away.

Hostel at Union Square
312 Mason Street (at O'Farrell), San Francisco, CA 94102 • (415)788-5604 ✳
District: Union Square

Set on a prime lot next to fashionable Union Square, this terrific new hostel (formerly the Hotel Virginia) has 230 beds—40 of them in private rooms for couples. The rates are hard to beat ($14 a night for an American Youth Hostel member, $17 for a nonmember), and you don't have to worry about curfews, chores, or bringing sleeping bags or sheets. The rooms are equipped with either bunk beds (complete with little ladders), twins, or doubles. The couple's rooms are first-come, first-served; if they're full, ask about the four- or five-person rooms for men or women. Bathrooms are shared, of course, but there are plenty of them, so lines shouldn't be a problem. The large furnished kitchen area is very pleasant and tidy and is equipped with the essentials, from microwaves to flatware. Coffee and tea are free, as is the movie shown in the TV room every night. If you forgot your earplugs or money holster, you can buy them and other supplies at the hostel's nonprofit Travel Center next door. Another plus: Free guided city walking tours are offered regularly to all guests.

Grant Plaza Hotel

465 Grant Avenue (at Pine), San Francisco, CA 94108 •
(800)472-6899 or (415)434-3883

District: Chinatown

The word is out about this terrific hotel in the busy heart of San Francisco, so make your reservations early. The small, pleasant rooms were recently renovated and are available at great prices (particularly if you're traveling in a group of four and need only two beds). Many of them boast a terrific view of the Financial District skyscrapers, and if you peer down at the street below, you'll see vendors galore hawking their backscratchers, calendars, and live chickens. It's a prime location for exploring the most fascinating parts of Chinatown (the Chinatown Gate is a few yards south), and Union Square and the cable cars are only a short jaunt away. In the glitzy lobby, crystal chandeliers hang over plum leather couches, and the large storefront windows are perfect for looking out at all the passersby. The hotel's 72 compact rooms are contemporary in decor, and each has a tiny bath with a gleaming white shower as well as a TV and phone. The rooms over Grant Avenue have the best views, but they're also the noisiest. Ask about the "Super Saver Package," which includes free parking and breakfast.

Hotel Astoria

510 Bush Street (at Grant), San Francisco, CA 94104 •
(800)666-6696 or (415)434-8889

District: Chinatown

If the Astoria were any closer to the ornate Chinatown Gate, it'd be sitting on top of it. And like its neighbor, the Grant Plaza, this seven-story hotel is smack-dab in the center of one of the city's best shopping districts. About half of the 75 rooms have private baths, and although they're larger than the Grant Plaza's, they're not as attractive. The quite ordinary furnishings are color-coordinated in shades of tan and cream, and, perhaps in an effort to spruce things up, an angular high-tech light hangs incongruously over the queen-size bed. The TV is on a dresser alongside the bed, requiring you to either crane your neck or lie sideways to see the screen. The rates are very reasonable—particularly if you go for the shared bath.

22

Pacific Tradewinds Guest House

680 Sacramento Street (between Kearny and Montgomery),
San Francisco, CA 94111 • (415)433-7970

District: Chinatown/Financial District

Sleeping in a bunk at the Pacific Tradewinds is like sharing a small room in a college dorm—the atmosphere is relaxed, the rooms are a little disheveled (but clean), and you can swap stories with your new roommates before falling asleep. This little guest house, tucked between the Financial District skyscrapers and the bustling Chinatown shops, caters to the overseas backpacking set, but Americans (especially students) are also welcome. For the same $14-a-night you'd pay at the local AYH, you can stay in this more-intimate 31-bed facility run by friendly folks eager to help you plan your city forays. Bedding is provided, and you won't have to do chores (but you *will* need to stand in line to use one of the two bathrooms). Other perks include a free safe-deposit box, a telephone, international fax service, luggage storage, kitchen use, laundry service (for only $2), and—something you certainly won't find in *any* other lodging in town—free sock washing. There's no curfew, but guests must check in between 8am and midnight (reservations are guaranteed only with a deposit in cash or traveler's check). And six nights' payment gets you the seventh night free—bringing the rate down to $12 a night, the *best* deal in San Francisco.

Temple Hotel

469 Pine Street (between Montgomery and Kearny),
San Francisco, CA 94104 • (415)781-2565

District: Chinatown/Financial District

The one feature that saves the Temple from being a basic bed-in-a-box is the pretty floor-to-ceiling print drapes that elegantly frame the windows. Ask for a room facing Pine Street so you'll have a view of the 52-story Bank of America World Headquarters building across the way, one of the best (and tallest) skyscrapers in San Francisco. And thanks to B of A's gardening team, your view includes the perfectly maintained trees and flower gardens on the high rise's grounds. The rooms are furnished comfortably, with a double bed, an old white-marble pedestal table, and comfortable Naugahyde chairs, though the rabbit-ear antenna on top of the black-and-white TV doesn't do what it's supposed to. Still, the Temple is in a great part of town for shopping and sightseeing, and literally a few steps from the front door is the popular Belden Square alley, where Financial District drones take their coffee and lunch breaks. Better yet, the room rates are dirt cheap, and if you share a bath and stay more than four nights, you'll pay only $25 a night; weekly rates are even lower.

San Remo Hotel

2237 Mason Street (between Francisco and Chestnut),

✳ *San Francisco, CA 94133 • (800)352-REMO or (415)776-8688*

District: North Beach

Hidden in a quiet section of North Beach between Fisherman's Wharf and bustling Washington Square, the San Remo is within easy walking distance of San Francisco's main attractions, including Chinatown, the Embarcadero, Pier 39, and one of the main cable-car stations. Combine that with the inexpensive rates, and you have one of the best bargains in town. This charming, well-preserved, three-story Italianate Victorian originally served as a boardinghouse for dockworkers displaced by the great fire of 1906, so the 62 rooms are rather small, bathrooms are shared, and walls are thin. If you can live with these minor inconveniences, however, you're in for a treat. The rooms are reminiscent of a European pensione, modestly decorated with brass or iron beds, porcelain sinks, and white wicker furniture; most have ceiling fans. Those on the second floor, particularly numbers 36, 43, and 45, which overlook Mason Street and have views of Coit Tower, are favorites. The old-fashioned bathrooms, spotlessly clean and restored to their original luster, have brass pull-chain toilets with oak tanks, claw-footed tubs, and showers. In the lobby and hallways, antiques and plants are bathed by sunlight filtering through leaded-glass skylights. There's even a laundry room with vending machines stocked with detergent, sodas, and snacks. And you can count on the friendly, city-savvy staff to help you plan your day on the town.

Van Ness Motel

2850 Van Ness Avenue (at Chestnut), San Francisco, CA 94019 •
(415)776-3220

District: The Marina/Russian Hill

Although this two-story 42-room motel faces the major artery of Van Ness Avenue, it's just steps from such popular attractions as Ghirardelli Square, the Cannery, Aquatic Park, and Fisherman's Wharf, attracting many German, French, and Japanese tourists. The rooms are nothing special, but they're tidy and include a comfortable queen-size bed and a small private bath with shower, TV, and phone. Be sure to ask for a unit located off the busy street. The loquacious manager has been working here for nearly 20 years and goes out of his way to provide travel tips. Nearby Polk Street and the west end of Chestnut Street are great shopping areas lined with several popular cafes, coffeehouses, boutiques, and some of the locals' favorite watering holes. The rooms get pricey on summer weekends, but they're reasonable the rest of the year, and free parking (practically unheard of in the city) is an added plus.

Hostel at Fort Mason

Fort Mason (enter via Franklin Street at Bay Street), Building 240
(at Funston and Pope), San Francisco, CA 94123 •
(415)771-7277 or (415)771-3645 (reservations only)

District: The Marina

One can only imagine what the Hyatt Regency's top brass would pay to get their hands on this fantastic piece of real estate. The Hostel at Fort Mason has the best locale of *any* lodging—cheap or expensive—on the north side of San Francisco, if not in the entire city. Perched on a grassy bluff above the bay, this 150-bed hostel offers views of the Golden Gate Bridge and practically sits on the scenic Golden Gate Promenade—an ideal stretch of land for strolling, jogging, skating, and bicycling. And Ghiradelli Sqare and Fisherman's Wharf are an easy walk away. Combine that with its $14-per-person rate (no hostel membership required) *and* free parking, and it's almost too good to be true. There's one small catch: You have to pitch in with a simple chore such as sweeping, vacuuming, or emptying the trash (don't worry, toilet cleaning is not on the list). In exchange for the help and low rates, you get bedding and towels; clean bathrooms and hot showers; a massive, fully stocked kitchen; lockers for storing your gear; and 24-hour hostel access. Other pluses: a laundry room, jukebox, first-rate pool table, old piano, redwood deck with picnic tables, and a lounge with couches, books, and fireplace. A free movie or live entertainment is offered nightly, and there are free city tours and organized events such as baseball games and museum trips. No smokes or booze allowed.

Marina Motel

2576 Lombard Street (between Broderick and Divisadero),
San Francisco, CA 92123 • (800)346-6118 or (415)921-9406

District: The Marina

Tucked among the scores of characterless motels lining busy Lombard Steet is the pretty Spanish-style Marina Motel. Pink fuchsias and bougainvillea and brilliant purple and red petunias grow along the stucco exterior, and behind each polished-wood door are handsome rooms with queen-size beds, twin brass reading lights, TVs, phones, and a clean tile bathroom with a large shower. The reasonable rates vary with the seasons, but for only five dollars extra you can get a fully equipped kitchen (available in about half of the 40 rooms). This family-run motel also offers a precious commodity: your own private parking garage, gratis, right on the premises. Such favored attractions as the Marina Yacht Harbor, trendy Union Street, the Palace of Fine Arts, and the Exploratorium are only a few blocks away, and the Golden Gate Bridge is a mile to the north. It's also quite easy to catch a bus on Lombard to other parts of town and even to Marin County. Ask for a room set far back from the street.

The Red Victorian Bed & Breakfast Inn

1665 Haight Street (at Cole), San Francisco, CA 94117 • (415)864-1978

District: The Haight

To say that the Red Vic is not a typical tourist hotel is putting it a tad mildly. About 20 years ago, owner Sami Sunchild (her real name) sort of accidentally acquired this sprawling 1904 Victorian hotel in the heart of the Haight, world capital of '60s hippiedom. The 18 upstairs guest rooms have sinks and telephones, but most share New Age bathrooms: one is lined with mirrors and strips of twinkling lights and another has a fish tank suspended over the toilet plus a sunken tub. The rooms are equally intriguing, with fanciful decor ranging from feline-inspired artwork and tie-dye canopies to bright ceiling and wall murals of rainbows, clouds, and the sun. Unfortunately, the Vic's immense popularity has prompted Sunchild to practically double her rates, and now there's only one bargain bed in the house: the small Butterfly Room, with a canopied double bed and soft-colored lights, rents for about $69 a night *if* you stay for at least three nights. Four other rooms run about ten bucks more (some rates are reduced if you're sleeping alone). In the morning, you're encouraged to hang loose with other guests at breakfast in the Gallery of Meditative Art.

Twin Peaks

2160 Market Street (between Church and Sanchez),
San Francisco, CA 94114 • (415)621-9467

District: The Castro

In an area where lodgings tend to be pretty pricey, you'll be relieved to find some great rates at the 60-room Twin Peaks, in the heart of San Francisco's gay and lesbian neighborhood. For about $50 you can get a comfortable room with private bath, TV, and a bay window overlooking the hustle and bustle of Market Street; the price drops by $10 if you're willing to share one of the clean baths down the hall. Rent by the week and rates go down to less than $25 a night, but the weekly units are small and cramped, with battered furniture, tiny black-and-white TVs, shared bath, and no view (ask for a peek before you pay). The hip Cafe Du Nord bar and nightclub is three doors up the street, and the heart of the Castro is only 2 blocks away.

ACCESS

Parking in San Francisco can be an ordeal. Many neighborhoods limit nonresidents to only two hours of parking, and most downtown meters have a maddening maximum time limit of 30 minutes—about the time it takes to get change for the meter. To make matters even more frustrating, traffic cops are quick, ruthless, and in abundance. Whenever you see a tow-away warning, take it *very* seriously. Public parking garages abound, however, and if you look hard enough (or ask a local), you'll find a garage or park-and-pay lot that doesn't charge Manhattan rates. San Francisco taxis usually cruise only the most populated streets, so if you need a cab, call one.

Public transportation serves every neighborhood, but grows sparse after midnight. San Francisco Municipal Railway (**MUNI**)—aptly nicknamed "Muniserable Railway" by *San Francisco Chronicle* columnist Herb Caen—comprises buses, over- and underground streetcars, and cable cars. Exact change is required, and free transfers (except for cable cars) grant two more rides within the next 1½ to 2 hours. One-, three-, and seven-day MUNI passes are available at the San Francisco Visitor Information Center (900 Market Street at Powell Street, near the Union Square cable-car turntable; (415)391-2000) and in the lobby of the War Memorial Veteran's Building (401 Van Ness Avenue at McAllister Street; no phone). For route, ticket, and bus-pass information, call (415)673-MUNI (and expect to be put on hold for a long time). Bay Area Rapid Transit (**BART**) is a clean, reliable underground commuter train that runs through the southeastern side of the city, with routes to Daly City and the East Bay; for schedule and ticket information, call (415)992-BART.

The **San Francisco International Airport** (SFO), (415)876-7809, is about 15 miles south of San Francisco on Highway 101 (the Bayshore Freeway); allow 30 to 40 minutes to drive there from the city and at least an hour during commute times. If you need transportation to or from SFO, reserve a seat with one of the fast, reliable shuttle services, such as Super Shuttle, (415)558-8500, or catch a ride on one of the two Sam Trans buses, (800)660-4BUS, that travel between SFO and San Francisco's Transbay Transit Terminal at Mission and 1st Streets (one Sam Trans bus permits passengers to bring luggage, but the other allows only one carry-on bag per person). The **Oakland International Airport** (OAK), located about 5 miles south of downtown Oakland, often offers less expensive flights (and parking) than SFO, and it doesn't take much more time to drive there from San Francisco if you avoid the rush hours (off Hegenberger Road via Highway 880 South, Oakland; (510)577-4015 or (510)577-4000).

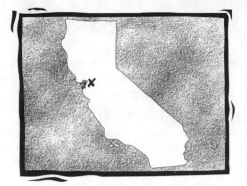

Marin County

If you listened to all the ballyhoo, you'd believe everyone in Marin drives a BMW (or "Boring Marin Wagon," as San Francisco Chronicle columnist Herb Caen dubs the ubiquitous vehicles), soaks in a hot tub under the stars every night, and smokes two joints in the morning. Granted, these portrayals characterize some local residents, but certainly not all of them, as Marinites are quick to point out. Nonetheless, this North Bay community, the wealthiest county in California, does boast a Little League team coached by rock star Huey Lewis, and proud parents do sit in the bleachers munching designer popcorn and yelling, "We got money, we got stocks, don't need no credit cards to clean your clocks!"

What they've also got—much to the envy of the rest of Northern California—is a home surrounded by thousands of acres of public parkland, wilderness, redwood canyons, mountain meadows, and pristine beaches, not to mention sunny weather practically year-round. As a result, Marin is a mecca for hikers, bicyclists, bird-watchers, sunbathers, and beachcombers. Although the beautiful hillside and waterfront towns of Sausalito, Tiburon, and Mill Valley aren't exactly rich in inexpensive lodgings, they do have numerous attractions and recreational offerings for the *budget traveler, and their incredible natural beauty alone is worth the trip over the Golden Gate.*

ON THE ROAD

To get to those alluring rolling hills and seacoast towns on the north side of the bay, drive, walk, or bike across the 4,200-foot-long Golden Gate Bridge, which at midspan hangs 249 feet above the water—an awesome height requested by the Navy so its big battleships could pass underneath. About three-quarters of the way over, you will have crossed the Marin County line. Before you descend into Marin, take a moment to admire the breathtaking view of San Francisco at **Vista Point**, the first exit off the bridge.

The bridge's next turnoff is Alexander Avenue, and if you head west up Conzelman Road (follow the signs), you'll reach the **Marin Headlands**, 12,000 acres of undeveloped, windswept land that served as a military camp in the late 19th and early 20th centuries. Several miles of trails wind along the rolling hills, and many are littered with old battle-gun sites and bunkers. The vistas from the trails are mesmerizing. Hike down the steep, ¾-mile-long road (not accessible by car) leading to Kirby Cove (park in the small lot at Battery Spencer) and you'll find a quiet little beach where you can gaze at the belly of the bridge.

The **Marin Headlands Visitor Center**, in the former post chapel, offers a wealth of information, including free trail maps outlining where you can take your dog, horse, and bike; handouts on free campsites in the area; free workshops and nature programs (see the quarterly "Park Events" newsletter); intriguing exhibits on the history of the region's

No-Cost Camping

Fifteen rustic tent-camping sites are available for free in various locations in the lush Marin Headlands. Camping permits must be picked up in person at the Marin Headlands Visitor Center, and reservations are accepted no more than 90 days in advance; take the Alexander Avenue exit off the Golden Gate Bridge, make an immediate left, and follow the "Marin Headlands" signs. The visitor center is at Fort Barry, at the intersection of Field and Bunker Roads; (415)331–1540.

Where the Wild Things Are

You can get splashed by magnificent killer whales, feed the gentle giraffes, play tug-of-war with a 5-ton elephant, and watch Bengal tigers swim with their trainers at Marine World Africa USA, a one-of-a-kind wildlife park and oceanarium with 160 acres of creatures great and small. Open year-round, the park is located in Vallejo, a 30- to 40-minute drive from Marin and San Francisco, and 15 minutes from Napa. From Highway 101 north, take Highway 37 east to Marine World Parkway; (707)643-ORCA.

Coast Miwok Indians and Portuguese dairies; and a large selection of guidebooks and maps. (Open daily. Take the Alexander Avenue exit off the Golden Gate Bridge, make an immediate left, follow the "Marin Headlands" signs leading up the hill—it turns into a one-way road at the top—and then down; keep bearing right, and you'll find the center at Fort Barry, at the intersection of Field and Bunker Roads; (415)331-1540.)

Follow Alexander Avenue toward the east side of Marin, and you'll reach the pretty little town of **Sausalito**, a former Portuguese fishing village that's now home to the well-heeled owners of many spectacular hillside mansions. Stay on Alexander, which eventually turns into Bridgeway, the main drag through the center of town. Pricey boutiques and waterfront restaurants line this street, and a paved promenade offers an unobstructed view of Angel Island, Alcatraz, and the San Francisco skyline. To best appreciate Sausalito, park your car (you may have to hit a municipal lot or a side street to find a spot) and walk along the promenade and through the tiny village. For the perfect perch on the bay, walk through the touristy (and pricey) **Horizons** restaurant and grab a seat on the wind-sheltered deck, where you can sip the spirit of your choice and wave at the yachters sailing just a few feet under your nose (558 Bridgeway, Sausalito; (415)331-3232).

There aren't many good restaurants in Sausalito (not even the most expensive are comparable to what you'll find in San Francisco), and the dining scene is particularly bleak on Bridgeway. The only place worth a stop is a little hamburger stand called simply **Hamburgers** (don't confuse it with a similar spot a couple of blocks north that sells burgers and Lappert's ice cream). For $4 and some change, you'll get one of the best burgers in Marin; the fresh grilled chicken burgers are about five bucks (737 Bridgeway, Sausalito; (415)332-9471).

The **No Name Bar** is probably the only place on Bridgeway where you'll find a local resident. Don't try looking for the name, because it's marked only by a small, handsome wooden sign that says "Bar" in gold letters. The No Name's free jazz and R&B concerts (held Friday and Saturday nights) draw crowds (757 Bridgeway, Sausalito; (415)332-1392). Stroll across the street and you'll see the pier, where you can catch a ferry to San Francisco; (415)546-2896. Nearby is the tiny **Plaza Viña del Mar**, graced by a pair of elephant statues and a fountain from the Panama-Pacific Exposition of 1915. One of the highlights of Sausalito is its gorgeous yachts—walk down the wooden planks and try to guess how many greenbacks it takes to own (and maintain) one of these glistening beauties.

The four-story **Village Fair**, on the west side of Bridgeway, is a quaint shopping mall honeycombed with shops and flowers and even a little waterfall. Don't expect to find any bargains here, but it's worth a quick look (777 Bridgeway, Sausalito; (415)332-1902). You'll see many folks licking **Lappert's** ice cream in freshly made waffle cones, which is dished out in two spots on either side of Village Fair (689 Bridgeway, Sausalito; (415)332-3019; 813 Bridgeway, Sausalito; (415)332-8175). If you prefer gelato, try **Caffe Trieste** farther north (1000 Bridgeway, Sausalito; (415)332-7770). Across from Trieste is Caledonia Street, where the locals hang out. Stop for breakfast or lunch at tiny **Cafe Soleil**— a BLT is only $3.50 and a salad with a baguette is a buck more. Soleil also whips up great smoothies (37 Caledonia Street, Sausalito; (415)331-9355). There are plenty of magazines, newspapers, and paperbacks at **The Newstand** (33 Caledonia Street, Sausalito; (415)332-3640), just steps away from the town barbershop with its red-white-and-blue spiral pole. On the north end of Caledonia is the **Caledonia Kitchen**, which tosses great salads and makes sandwiches with fresh herbs and freshly baked bread (400 Caledonia Street, Sausalito; (415)331-0220).

Friends of the Sea

Since 1975, veterinarians and hundreds of volunteers at the nonprofit Marine Mammal Center have been rescuing distressed seals, sea lions, dolphins, porpoises, whales, and sea otters on the Northern and Central California coast. Every year, hundreds of marine mammals are taken to the center, nursed back to health, and then returned to the sea for a second chance at life. Public visiting hours are 10am to 4pm daily, and admission is free. The center is located in the Marin Headlands at Fort Cronkhite, between the Marin Headlands Visitor Center and Rodeo Beach; (415)289-SEAL.

A couple of other popular and inexpensive breakfast spots are the **Lighthouse Cafe** (1311 Bridgeway, Sausalito; (415)331-3034) and, at the north end of town, **Fred's Place**, which has been making terrific French toast and other belly-packing fare since 1966 (1917 Bridgeway, Sausalito; (415)332-4575). Across the street and down the hill from Fred's is the **Bay Model**, a gigantic working hydraulic model of the San Francisco Bay and the Delta region used by the U.S. Army Corps of Engineers to study the tides and various bay problems. The Bay Model also offers interactive exhibits and a World War II shipyard display; admission is free (Marinship Way, off the east side of Bridgeway, Sausalito; (415)332-3871). Just before Bridgeway merges with the freeway, you'll find Sausalito's community of houseboat dwellers. Take a gander at the **floating homes**, which vary from funky little wooden abodes covered with pots of bright flowers to swanky houseboats with helipads (park at the Waldo Point Harbor Houseboat Marina at the north end of Bridgeway).

Before you say so long to Sausalito, take a spin through the lush, landscaped hills, zigzagging your way from one end to the other to get a taste of how the rich really live. It's hard to get too lost—all of the streets eventually wind down to Bridgeway—just don't get distracted by the magnificent mansions as you navigate the twisting roads. For a tour of tiny Tiburon and Belvedere, the waterfront towns directly across the bay, head north on Bridgeway until it hooks up with Highway 101, then follow the signs to Tiburon Boulevard and downtown Tiburon (about a 15-minute drive).

Formerly a railroad town and until 1963 the terminus of the Northwestern Pacific Railroad, **Tiburon** (Spanish for "shark") is now a quaint New England–style coastal village. Its short Main Street is packed with

Go Ahead, Make Their Day

Kids will get a kick out of the Bay Area Discovery Museum, where they can sing and dance in the Discovery Theater, "pump" gas into a Model T in the Transportation Building, create a clay sculpture or paint a picture in the Art Spot, build a skyscraper in the Architecture & Design Building, dissect a squid in the Science Lab, and much more. This unique hands-on interactive learning center is designed for children ages 1 through 12—and it's a guaranteed kid-pleaser. Located at Fort Baker, under the north end of the Golden Gate Bridge, in Sausalito; call (415)487-4398 for directions and more information.

Escape to Angel Island

Hikers, mountain bikers, and sun worshipers hop aboard the ferries to Angel Island every sunny weekend to escape the city crowds and admire panoramic views of the Bay Area. This heavily wooded 740-acre island, the San Francisco Bay's largest, is only a mile from the Tiburon peninsula, but it feels as if it's far from civilization, particularly if you hike to the top of 781-foot Mount Livermore. The island is known as the "Ellis Island of the West," having once served as an immigration station for millions entering the United States. Angel Island has also been a native American settlement, a Civil War fort, a prisoner-of-war camp, and a Nike missile site. Now it's all been set aside as a state park and wildlife preserve, home to deer, raccoons, birds, and harbor seals.

Mountain-bike rentals and one-hour, open-air tram tours are available on the island; call (415)897-0715 for details. Free docent-led tours are offered on weekends from May through October; for more information call (415)435-3522. To pitch your tent at one of the island's nine environmental campsites, call Mistix at (800)444-7275 for a reservation. Pick up an informational Angel Island map ($1) on the island, or send $2 to PO Box 866, Tiburon, CA 94920. Ferry service to the island is offered by the Red & White Fleet at Pier 43½ in San Francisco's Fisherman's Wharf, (800)229-2784 or (415)435-2131, and by the Angel Island–Tiburon Ferry, located at the pier on Main Street in downtown Tiburon, (415)435-2131. For more information on Angel Island, call (415)435-1915.

expensive antique and specialty shops, as well as restaurants with incredible bay views. You can leave your car on the outskirts and walk to the village, or park in the large pay-lot off Main Street. (An even better way to get here is by bicycle or by taking the ferry from San Francisco; it drops off passengers at the edge of town.) At the tip of the Tiburon peninsula is a small grassy park with benches, and on sunny days people flock here with picnics to admire the panoramic view of San Francisco and Angel Island.

If you're willing to splurge on a very good, moderately priced meal with a view, ask for a seat on the patio of **Guaymas** (you'll likely need reservations), and indulge in the classic Mexican fare and a frothy margarita (5 Main Street, at the ferry landing, Tiburon; (415)435-6300). You can get lesser-quality fare but equally spectacular views at the ever-popular

☕ Armchair Travel

No matter where you plan to journey next, you'll undoubtedly find a book and a map on your upcoming destination at Book Passage, Marin County's premier bookstore specializing in guidebooks and travel literature. And when you tire of flipping through the hundreds of travel tomes, you can take a seat at Book Passage's small corner cafe, sip an espresso, and snack on a sweet until you're ready to plunge into the shelves again. The store is located about 10 miles north of the Golden Gate Bridge, at 51 Tamal Vista Boulevard, in the Market Place Shopping Center, Corte Madera; (800)999-7909 or (415)927-0960.

Sam's restaurant, where Bay Area residents crowd the huge outdoor deck on sunny weekends for beer, burgers, and big baskets of fries (27 Main Street, Tiburon; (415)435-4527). For breakfast or a healthy bowl of soup and a sandwich, sit at one of the checkered-clothed tables at the pleasant **New Morning Cafe**, which serves the morning meal all day long (1696 Tiburon Boulevard, near Main Street, Tiburon; (415)435-4315).

Stroll west on Main Street and you'll bump into the intimate **Tiburon Deli**, which offers Bud's ice cream, frozen yogurt, and $4 sandwiches (110 Main Street, Tiburon; (415)435-4888). The deli is part of Tiburon's historic **Ark Row**, an assembly of charming 100-year-old restored arks that now house several shops. Follow Main beyond the shops to Beach Road for another amazing view of the bay, one that includes the prized yachts docked in front of the members-only San Francisco Yacht Club. This is where Tiburon blends into **Belvedere** (Italian for "beautiful view"), an ultra-exclusive community that makes Sausalito look like a poor cousin. The entire city comprises only one-half of a square mile of land—but this is one tony piece of real estate. Drive up Belvedere's steep, narrow roads for a glimpse of the highly protected, well-shielded multimillion-dollar homes where international celebs like Elton John have been known to hide out. After your hillside cruise, drive along San Rafael Avenue, which hugs Richardson Bay on the north side of Tiburon, for another great view of the water. You can't tell from the street, but behind a stretch of houses on the east side of San Rafael Avenue is **Belvedere Lagoon**, where residents sail, canoe, kayak, and mingle with their neighbors basking on their sunny waterside decks (you can get a peek at the lagoon just steps from the intersection of San Rafael Avenue and Windward Road).

Message to Mountain Bikers

Mount Tamalpais offers fantastic scenic trails for mountain bikers, but some trails are restricted to pedestrians only—and they're fiercely guarded. If you don't want to get slapped with a $200 fine for pedaling up the wrong path, ask a ranger for a list of legal bike routes, or look them up on a trail map.

San Rafael Avenue winds its way north to Tiburon Boulevard, which leads back to Highway 101. If you stay on Tiburon Boulevard and follow it past the highway on-ramps, it turns into East Blithedale Avenue and leads directly into the center of the lovely, sleepy town of **Mill Valley**. This is where many millionaires have forsaken bayside plots of land for the highly coveted real estate nestled in the redwoods. Introduce yourself to the town by walking along Throckmorton Avenue, the main shopping strip off Blithedale. Visit the popular **Depot Bookstore & Cafe**, where you can purchase some good reads and enjoy them with a glass of wine and a sandwich on the patio facing the town's central plaza (87 Throckmorton Avenue, Mill Valley; (415)383-2665). Hard-core coffee drinkers in search of the best cup in town should cross the street to **Peet's** (88 Throckmorton Avenue, Mill Valley; (415)381-8227). In the evening, stop by **Sweetwater** for great live jazz, R&B, and rock 'n' roll (153 Throckmorton Avenue, Mill Valley; (415)388-2820).

Mill Valley's best cheap eats are spread out along its west side, most notably **Jennie Low's Chinese Cuisine** (38 Miller Avenue, near Sunnyside Street, Mill Valley; (415)388-8868) and **Joe's Taco Lounge**, an exuberant place with a cherry-red counter that sells soft tacos in sets of two for only $3.50 (382 Miller Avenue at Montford/La Goma Streets, Mill Valley; (415)383-8164). Next door to Joe's is the landmark, white-and-red **2AM Club**, a big, crowded bar where you can chug the specially priced shot of the day and play a game of pool (380 Miller Avenue, Mill Valley; (415)388-6036). Drive south on Miller Avenue to the major intersection known as Tam Junction, and you can get a good Thai lunch or dinner for less than $10 a plate at pretty **Chariya Reun Thai Cafe** (252 Almonte Boulevard, Mill Valley; (415)389-8759). Farther south is one of Mill Valley's most popular breakfast and lunch spots, the **Dipsea Cafe**, which flips huge, delicious buttermilk and whole-wheat blueberry pancakes every day of the week (200 Shoreline Highway (Highway 1), near Tam Junction, Mill Valley; (415)381-0298).

No visit to Marin would be complete without a journey up **Mount**

🚲 *The Two-Wheel Route*

The hilly, scenic bike trails of Marin are a haven for amateur and professional cyclists alike. A favorite not-too-strenuous route takes you north across the Golden Gate Bridge, then follows the bike trail under the bridge and down a steep hill to downtown Sausalito. The paved trail hugs Sausalito's waterfront, leading past houseboats and marshes to Bayfront Park in Mill Valley; the ride takes about two to three hours. To avoid riding (or pushing) your bike uphill to the bridge for the return trip, coast onto a ferry in Sausalito or Tiburon and sail back to San Francisco's Fisherman's Wharf (Red & White Fleet ferry; (800)229-2784 or (415)546-2628).

The Marin Headlands and Mount Tamalpais are the bicycling hot spots for diehards, although you don't need Stallone-size thighs to make it up all the trails. Maps to the numerous bike paths are available at many Marin and Bay Area bike stores and bookstores, the Pan Toll Camp/Mount Tamalpais Ranger Station, (415)388-2070, and the Marin Headlands Visitor Center, (415)331-1540.

Recommended bicycle rental shops include American Bicycle Rental (2715 Hyde Street, in Fisherman's Wharf, San Francisco; (415)931-0234); Marina Cyclery (3330 Steiner Street, San Francisco; (415)929-7135); Wheel Escapes (30 Liberty Ship Way, Suite 210, off the east side of Bridgeway, Sausalito; (415)332-0218); and Bike Sport (1735 Tiburon Boulevard, Tiburon; (415)435-5064).

Tamalpais (tam-ul-*pie*-us), commonly referred to as Mount Tam. You can drive to the top of this 2,586-foot peak (Marin's highest) and get an amazing bird's-eye view of the entire Bay Area, as well as the **Farallon Islands** 25 miles out at sea and the Sierra Nevada mountain range nearly 200 miles away; follow Highway 1 (also called the Shoreline Highway) to the Panoramic Highway, turn right on Pan Toll Road, then right again on East Ridgecrest Boulevard, which leads to the mountain's east peak (it costs $5 to park in the lot, but you can park on any turnout in the road as long as you stay behind the white street line). To best appreciate the 6,400-acre Mount Tamalpais State Park, with its redwood groves, streams, grassland, chaparral, deer, and even mountain lions, follow one of the 50 miles of well-maintained hiking and bicycling trails. If you don't have a map of the mountain (available in many Marin bookstores), invest a dollar in the trail map sold at the Pan Toll Camp/Mount Tamalpais Ranger Station (from Highway 101 north, take the Stinson

Beach/Highway 1 exit, follow Highway 1 for 3 miles, make a sharp right onto Panoramic Highway, and follow this two-lane road until you reach a sign that says "Stinson Beach 4 miles, Mt. Tamalpais 4 miles"; the station is on the left side of the intersection; (415)388-2070).

You can pick up free photocopies of Mount Tam trail maps at the **Mill Valley Chamber of Commerce** (85 Throckmorton Avenue, next to the Depot Bookstore, Mill Valley; (415)388-9700). The Mount Tamalpais Interpretive Association offers free guided walks of Mount Tam (ranging from 4 to 12 miles) every weekend starting at 9:30am, moonlight hikes on full-moon nights, and interesting astronomy programs on new-moon nights at Mount Tam's Mountain Theater; call (415)388-2070 or (415)258-2410 for more details or stop by the Mount Tamalpais Ranger Station. Another must-see in Marin is Muir Woods National Monument, the Bay Area's last remaining old-growth redwood forest. (For more information on Muir Woods and Marin's coastal areas, including Stinson Beach, see the North Coast section of this book).

CHEAP SLEEPS

Compared to San Francisco's vast array of inexpensive lodgings, it's surprising Marin County has so few. You also won't get as much bang for your buck at the budget lodgings in Marin's inland cities, so consider slumbering in San Francisco or along the Pacific coast instead. (Cheap sleeps in Marin's coastal towns are listed in the North Coast section of this book.) The following accommodations are the only budget lodgings in Mill Valley and Sausalito (Tiburon has only one hotel, and it's definitely not cheap). If you're looking for an inexpensive sleep north of Mill Valley, you'll find a handful of dull chain hotels off Highway 101, particularly around San Rafael.

If you're interested in renting a room for one or more nights in a Marin resident's home, contact Suellen Lamorte at Bed & Breakfast Exchange of Marin, a referral and reservation service specializing in noncommercial "homestays." Rates range from $55 to $150 per night (45 Entrata Avenue, San Anselmo, CA 94960; (415)485-1971).

Marin Headlands Hostel
Fort Barry, Building 941, Sausalito, CA 94965 •
(800)444-6111 or (415)331-2777

Formerly known as the Golden Gate Hostel, the Marin Headlands Hostel sits high on a hill covered with evergreen trees and pink wildflowers and is an ideal hideaway if you prefer slumbering to the sounds of crickets and birds rather than to the hooting cars and night owls of city streets. The remote locale is gorgeous, but a car is really a necessity here. Building 941 was constructed in 1907 and served as the U.S. Army infirmary; now the aging complex has 66 bunks, a fully equipped kitchen, a spacious lounge with a piano and stereo, a laundry room, and a rather weathered rec room with a pool table, Ping-Pong table, TV, and VCR (videos available at no extra charge). In the summer of 1995 the hostel opened the doors of its recent acquisition, neighboring Building 937, formerly a private residence. This beautiful new addition is spiffier than its neighbor, with its newly polished hardwood floors, Oriental carpets, plush couches, four carved-oak fireplaces, and 37 bunks in rooms with views of the hills and, in some cases, the Pacific. (Expect the hostel's $10-per-night rates—no membership required—to increase as word gets out about the new building.) Both buildings are closed from 9:30am to 3:30pm (so you must spend the day elsewhere), linens are rented for $1, and guests are expected to help with light chores. Rodeo Beach is only a short drive or a 15-minute walk away, and numerous trails wind throughout the scenic Marin Headlands. There are a few different ways to get to the hostel, which is about 5 to 10 minutes from the Golden Gate Bridge, so call for directions. Arriving before sunset? Be sure to ask for the scenic route.

Fireside Motel ✳

115 Shoreline Highway (Highway 1), Mill Valley, CA 94941 • (415)332-6906

The rates at the crescent-shaped Fireside are comparable to what you'd pay at the Tamalpais (see below), but they seem to change hourly, depending on the mood of the flippant manager (or perhaps on whether or not she likes your shirt?). Some of the 25 rooms are ragged and stained, with mildew in the lime-green tiled showers and ancient heaters that look as if they must violate some safety code, but others have been remodeled and sport sparkling showers, big bathroom sinks, and color-coordinated bedspreads and drapes. Ask for room 20 if you want a queen-size bed, and try for room 5 if you prefer two doubles. El Rebozo, a pricey Mexican restaurant with an adjoining workingman's bar, sits in front of the Fireside's parking lot, but doesn't do much to buffer the highway noise. Perhaps the motel's best attribute is that it's steps away from the popular Buckeye Roadhouse, which doesn't have food at budget prices, but does have a beautiful bar where you can mingle with the locals.

Fountain Motel

155 Shoreline Highway (Highway 1), Mill Valley, CA 94941 • (415)332-1732

If you're not interested in staying in a hostel and the Travelodge (see below) is booked, here's the runner-up. For about the same rate as a

Travelodge room, the Fountain Motel offers a spacious room (in fact, larger than the rooms at the Travelodge) with a king- or queen-size bed, an electric-blue tiled bathroom with a tub shower, a phone, and a 25-inch TV with cable. There are also a table and a couple of chairs in each unit, or if you'd rather be outdoors, you can sit on one of the old white picnic benches and gaze at Mount Tam. Like the rest of the area's motels, the Fountain suffers from the hustle and bustle of the highway. And yes, the motel does have a fountain gracing the entryway, but it rarely seems to work.

✕ Tamalpais Motel
680 Redwood Highway (Highway 101), Mill Valley, CA 94941 •
(415)381-4775

This is Marin's only-if-you're-desperate cheap sleep. As you zip along the Redwood Highway and glance over at the motel's light-pink exterior, baby-blue doors, and Spanish tile roof, you might think it looks like a respectable roadside stop. But look again. Perhaps in better hands this could be a cute little place, but it's been neglected over the years, and the $45 to $55 nightly rate is rather steep for a room with mildew on the bathroom walls. In addition, the motel hugs the side of the highway, so if you're not a super-sound sleeper, you might prefer a nice campsite in the woods. To get there, exit Highway 101 on Seminary Drive and head north.

Travelodge ✕
707 Redwood Highway (Highway 101), Mill Valley, CA 94941 •
(800)255-3050 or (415)383-0340

There's no competition between the Travelodge and Mill Valley's other budget motels—this one wins by a long shot. The 55 guest rooms have white walls and steel-blue carpeting, with color-coordinated bedspreads and comfortable, contemporary furnishings. Each unit also has air conditioning and cable TV with a built-in alarm clock and radio. Reading lights are mounted on the wall on either side of the queen-size bed, and there are a couple of cushioned chairs, a desk, a phone, and a bathroom with a shower stall. Unfortunately, the Travelodge sits alongside a very busy highway, but that's true of every Marin cheap sleep; if you can't fall asleep to the sound of speeding cars, bring earplugs. To reach the Travelodge, exit Highway 101 on Seminary Drive and head south.

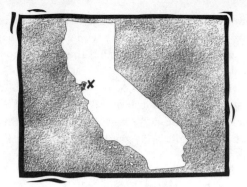

Berkeley

You can still buy tie-dyed "Berserkley" T-shirts from vendors on Telegraph Avenue, but the wild days of this now-middle-aged, upper-middle-class burg are gone. There's nary a whiff of tear gas in the air; these days most UC Berkeley students seem more interested in cramming for exams than in organizing sit-ins. Thanks to the much-disputed People's Park (owned by the university, occupied by the homeless), occasional street battles still rattle Telegraph Avenue, though pillage, not protest, seems to be the order of the day. On the other hand, the city still has an official Peace and Justice Commission and sister cities in every politically correct corner of the globe.

Although PC politics still reign in Berkeley's city government, many of its well-heeled citizens seem more concerned about the plight of their palates than the plight of the poor. Lucky for them, Berkeley continues to hold its own as one of California's culinary hot spots. Alice Waters, owner-chef of Northern California's most famous restaurant, Chez Panisse, has been at the forefront of the California cuisine revolution since 1971, when she started cooking simple French meals for groups of friends, then opened her legendary restaurant. The crowds still come to Chez Panisse, as well as to the numerous wannabes nearby (and not all of them *require dipping into your life savings to settle the tab). Even San Franciscans cross the Bay Bridge from time to time to indulge in a big Berkeley breakfast or lunch, followed by a tour of the city's terrific bookstores and unique shops.*

ON THE ROAD

If you're a newcomer to Berkeley, start your tour of the town at the world-renowned **University of California at Berkeley** (also known as UC Berkeley and Cal), the oldest and second-largest of the nine campuses comprising the UC system. Driving through the campus is virtually impossible, so park on a side street and set out on foot. The university isn't so huge that you'd get hopelessly lost if you wandered around on your own, but without a guide you might miss some of the highlights. So pick up a self-guided walking packet at the UC Berkeley Visitor Information Center, or attend one of the free 1½-hour tours held every Monday, Wednesday, and Friday at 10am and 1pm and on selected Saturdays (open Monday through Friday; 2200 University Avenue at Oxford, University Hall, Room 101, Berkeley; (510)642-5215 (recording) or (510)642-INFO).

A few paces north of the intersection of Telegraph Avenue and Bancroft Way is the university's legendary **Sproul Plaza**, where the Free Speech Movement began in 1964. Walk up the famous steps of Sproul Hall, where many demonstrators stood (and still stand) to speak their piece; pass through the double doors, and just beyond the entrance you'll see a display of photos commemorating those exciting times. Several hundred feet north of Sproul Plaza is the pretty bronzed-metal and white-granite **Sather Gate**, originally the main campus entrance until the university was expanded in the sixties. If you head northeast toward the center of things you'll spot the **Campanile** (officially named Sather Tower, though nobody calls it that), a 307-foot clock tower modeled after St. Mark's Campanile in Venice, Italy. Built in 1914, this is Cal's best-known landmark; for only 50 cents you can take the elevator to the top for a stunning view of the Bay Area. The only original building still standing on campus is just southwest of the Campanile: **South Hall**, built in 1873. Walk north past the tower and turn east on University Drive, and you'll eventually see, on your left, the Beaux Arts beauty known as the **Hearst Mining Building**. Continue east on University Drive, and at the top of the hill in a eucalyptus grove is the **Greek Theatre**, which

This Bread's for You

Most Berkeley residents go to Steve Sullivan's famous **Acme Bread Company** to stock up on the Bay Area's best loaves (1601 San Pablo Avenue at Cedar, Berkeley; (510)524-1327). When Acme sells out of its goods (and it always does), they head over to the **Cheeseboard**, a collectively owned bakery and vast gourmet cheese shop (1504 Shattuck Avenue at Vine, Berkeley; (510)549-3183). Two Berkeley bagel shops rival Brooklyn's best: **Brothers' Bagels** (1281 Gilman Street at Santa Fe, Berkeley; (510)524-3104) and **Noah's Bagels**, a wildly popular chain that started in Berkeley on College Avenue in 1989 and now has branches as far south as LA (3170 College Avenue at Alcatraz, (510)654-0944; 2344 Telegraph Avenue at Durant, (510)849-9951; and 1883 Solano Avenue at The Alameda, (510)525-4447).

architect Juila Morgan (of Hearst Castle fame) modeled after the amphitheater in Epidaurus, Greece. The popular theater was presented in 1903 as a gift by newspaper publisher William Randolph Hearst.

A visit to Berkeley wouldn't be complete without a stroll down bustling **Telegraph Avenue**, still the haunt of students, street people, runaways, hipsters, professors, and tarot readers. If you want a cup of joe before you go, head east on Bancroft to **Caffè Strada** (Bancroft Way at College, Berkeley; (510)843-5282) and nab a seat on the sunny patio, where all the architecture students get their caffeine blasts before disappearing inside the gray monstrosity across the street known as Wurster Hall. If you prefer classical music with your coffee, go to the nearby **Musical Offering** (2430 Bancroft Way, west of Telegraph Avenue, Berkeley; (510)849-0211), which also sells sandwiches, soup, CDs, and tapes. Start your trek down Telegraph at Bancroft, and make a loop around all the friendly street vendors hawking everything from top-quality tie-dyed shirts, dresses, and boxer shorts to handmade earrings and hand-painted ties. Along this street are some great bookstores (including Cody's Books) and dozens of cheap eats ranging from food carts selling burritos and hot dogs for a little more than a dollar to pizza stands like the loud, raucous, and ever-popular **Blondie's**, where you can get a giant slice of greasy pizza from a purple-haired, tongue-pierced college student for only a couple of bucks (2340 Telegraph Avenue, between Bancroft and Durant, Berkeley; (510)548-1129).

For more substantive fare that won't blow your budget, go to **Café**

Intermezzo for a salad the size of your head and some fresh honey-wheat bread (2442 Telegraph Avenue at Haste, Berkeley; (510)849-4592), or cross the street and take a seat at **Caffé Mediterraneum**, which made its film debut in *The Graduate*. "The Med" captures the bohemian flavor of Telegraph, and churns out excellent cappuccinos as well as burgers, pastas, and desserts (2475 Telegraph Avenue, between Haste and Dwight, Berkeley; (510)549-1128). A block south is **Ann's Soup Kitchen**, where you can get terrific whole-wheat pancakes for breakfast, soup for less than $2, and sandwiches for about $3 (2498 Telegraph Avenue at Dwight, Berkeley; (510)548-8885).

On Dwight Way, between Telegraph and Bowditch, is **People's Park**, famous as a site of student riots, which first flared in 1969 when the university wanted to replace the park with a dormitory (the National Guard was called in by then-governor Ronald Reagan). The university never got its dorm, but in 1991 UC officials succeeded in placing a few sand volleyball courts and basketball courts in the park, although even that incited several protests.

Farther south in Berkeley, near the Berkeley/Oakland border, is the small **Elmwood** neighborhood shopping district, which stretches along College Avenue and crosses over Ashby Avenue. Poke your head into the tiny **Tail of the Yak** boutique for a look at the fabulous (though pricey) displays of Central American and other art treasures (2632 Ashby Avenue, west of College, Berkeley; (510)841-9891), then stroll along College, where you can pet the lop-eared baby bunnies and squawk back at the beautiful parrots at **Your Basic Bird** (2940 College Avenue, north of Ashby, Berkeley; (510)841-7617); dip into the huge candy jars at **Sweet Dreams** (2901 College Avenue at Russell, Berkeley; (510)549-1211); munch on fantastic fresh-fruit cheese danish at **Nabolom Bakery** (2708 Russell Street at College, Berkeley; (510)845-BAKE); shop for clothes at numerous boutiques; and indulge in one of **Bott's** freshly made ice creams (2975 College Avenue, south of Ashby, Berkeley; (510)845-4545). For fresh pasta salads and sandwiches, try **Ultra Lucca Delicatessen** (2905 College Avenue, north of Ashby, Berkeley; (510)849-2701), or **Espresso Roma**, where you can sip strong coffee drinks, teas (try a jolt of chai), fresh lemonade, beer on tap, or wine by the glass, and eat some great calzones and sandwiches (2960 College Avenue at Ashby, Berkeley; (510)644-3773).

Rick & Ann's Pantry (cheaper than their adjoining restaurant) serves breakfast sandwiches and oatmeal for less than $2 and gourmet sandwiches for less than a fiver (2922 Domingo Avenue, in front of the Claremont Hotel, off Ashby, Berkeley; (510)649-0869). At **Viva! Taqueria**—where they slap together great burritos (including a low-fat version called "El Suave") for about $4—you can dine on the sunny deck or indoors under the ceiling fans (2984 Russell Street at Claremont Avenue, off Ashby, Berkeley; (510)843-5565).

On the opposite side of Berkeley, just northwest of Cal on **Shattuck Avenue**, is the area well-known as the **Gourmet Ghetto**, thanks to the international reputation of **Chez Panisse** and other terrific neighborhood restaurants. Spend some time browsing through the upscale shops, most of which are concentrated on Shattuck between Virginia and Rose Streets and in **Walnut Square** on Vine Street. If all the hoopla about Chez Panisse has you wondering if it's worth a splurge, first consider Alice Waters's much less expensive (but also wonderful) Café Fanny in West Berkeley (see below). Other favored retreats in this neighborhood are **Chester's Cafe**, which serves breakfast all day, lunch, and weekend brunch—search for a seat on the upstairs deck, where you can look out at the bay and the Golden Gate (1508B Walnut Square, off Vine Street, Berkeley; (510)849-9995); **Saul's** old-fashioned deli, which serves breakfast from sunrise to sunset as well as classic "regular or full-figured" sandwiches (1734 Shattuck Avenue at Vine, Berkeley; (510)848-DELI); **Cha Am**, for good, reasonably priced Thai food served on a glassed-in patio under towering palm trees (1543 Shattuck Avenue at Cedar, Berkeley; (510)848-9664); and **New Phnom-Penh**, a Cambodian restaurant with more than twenty $4 lunch specials (1600 Shattuck Avenue at Cedar, Berkeley; (510)841-9405).

When Berkeley carnivores hear the call of the wild and nothing but a big, rare burger will do, they head for **FatApple's**, just a few blocks northwest of the famous Shattuck strip. A prime contender in the ongoing Berkeley burger wars, FatApple's makes its burgers of exceptionally lean, high-quality ground beef and serves them on home-made wheat rolls. Don't miss the flaky olallieberry or pecan pie, thick jumbo shakes, or the ethereal cheese puffs (1346 Martin Luther King, Jr., Way at Rose, Berkeley; (510)526-2260). For a hot dog and a good brewski, head south on Shattuck to the **Triple Rock Brewery** and order the specialty beer of the day (1920 Shattuck Avenue between Berkeley and Hearst, Berkeley; (510)843-2739), then go way up the hill on Hearst to **Top**

🍷 *Sake It to Me!*

For free sips of sake and plum wine, visit the tasting room of Takara Sake, the largest sake brewery in America. It's located at 708 Addison Street, off University Avenue, in Berkeley, and open daily; (510)540-8250.

Buy the Book

As any local bookworm will tell you, most of the Bay Area's best bookstores are in Berkeley. Top of the list is **Cody's Books**, and most locals agree that if you can't find a book at Cody's, it probably isn't worth reading (2454 Telegraph Avenue at Haste; (510)845-7852). Almost every night, nationally known literary and political writers appear at Cody's and at **Black Oak Books**, a popular purveyor of new and used titles (1491 Shattuck Avenue at Vine; (510)486-0698). The four-story **Moe's Books** specializes in used books and remainders (2476 Telegraph Avenue, next to Cody's; (510)849-2087), and a **Barnes & Noble** megastore, complete with park benches for on-the-spot reading, offers discounts on *New York Times* bestsellers and stocks hundred of periodicals (2352 Shattuck Avenue at Durant; (510)644-0861).

Dog, a cheap, kinda grungy Berkeley institution that's been serving good dogs for years (2503 Hearst Avenue at Euclid, Berkeley; (510)843-1241).

Tucked away near the bay in West Berkeley is the **Fourth Street** shopping area, where you can find bargains galore at the **Crate & Barrel Outlet Store** (1785 4th Street, between Hearst and Virginia, Berkeley; (510)528-5500). Several purveyors of high-quality, high-priced gardening gadgets line this street, along with eclectic boutiques that are fun to browse. Get a bite to eat at **Bette's-to-Go** (BTG) or, better yet, plan on indulging in a big breakfast here at the adjoining **Bette's Oceanview Diner**, a small, nouveau-'40s diner that doesn't have an ocean view (or any view, for that matter) but does have red booths, chrome stools, a checkerboard tile floor, hip waitresses, the best jukebox around, and damn good breakfasts. On weekends, bring the newspaper or a good book and expect a 45-minute, stomach-growling wait, but consider the payoff: enormous, soufflé-style pancakes stuffed with pecans and ripe berries, farm-fresh eggs scrambled with prosciutto and Parmesan, outstanding omelets, corned beef hash, and the quintessential huevos rancheros (1807A 4th Street, between Hearst and Virginia, Berkeley; (510)644-3230). For lunch, dinner, or an inexpensive drink, belly up to the bar-and-hofbrau at **Brennan's**, a Berkeley landmark that's been serving hand-carved roasted-meat sandwiches with mashed potatoes and gravy since 1959. Brennan's handsome dark-wood bar serves great Irish coffee and pints of beer for as little as $1.50 (4th Street and University Avenue, under the overpass, Berkeley; (510)841-0960).

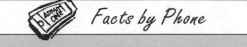

Facts by Phone

Want to know what time the museums open? Or where to take your fidgety four-year-old? Or who's playing at the Greek Theatre next week? Call Berkeley's 24-hour information hotline, an up-to-date recording with all the answers to these questions and much, much more.

Berkeley's Information Hotline: (510)549-8710

Press: 101   This Week in Berkeley
102   Accommodations
103   Museums
104   Performing Arts
105   Theaters and Events by Facility
106   Places of Interest
107   Parks and Recreational Activities
108   Shops
109   Attractions for Kids
110   UC Berkeley Campus
111   Parking
112   Transportation

A short drive away is another very popular breakfast and lunch spot, Alice Waters' diminutive **Café Fanny** (1603 San Pablo Avenue, between Cedar and Virginia, Berkeley; (510)524-5447). This corner cafe, nestled next to the famous Acme Bread Company, can handle fewer than a dozen stand-up customers at once, but that doesn't deter anyone. On sunny weekend mornings the adjacent parking lot fills with the overflow, with the luckier customers snaring a seat at one of the few tiny outdoor tables. Named after Waters' daughter, this cafe recalls the neighborhood haunts so dear to the French. Breakfast on crunchy Café Fanny granola, jam-filled buckwheat crêpes, or perfect soft-boiled eggs served on sourdough toast with a side of home-made jam, and sip a café au lait from a big, authentically French, handleless bowl. For lunch, order a small pizza or one of the seductive sandwiches. You won't get trencherman portions, but you'll love every crumb.

Where the northwest border of Berkeley meets the little town of Albany is **Solano Avenue**, a popular mile-long street lined with shops and cafes. Solano is also home to one of the East Bay's best pizza joints, **Zachary's Chicago Pizza** (1853 Solano Avenue at Colusa, Berkeley; (510)525-5950). For years Bay Area transplants from the East Coast complained about the wretched local pizza. Then along came Zachary's with its tasty rendition of Chicago-style deep-dish: a deep-bottom crust packed with a choice of fillings, covered with a thin second crust, and topped with tomato sauce. (The bottom crust turns crisp in the oven; the top one melts into the filling.) Try the gooey spinach-cheese-and-mushroom, or the chicken and spinach in a whole-wheat crust.

There *is* more to Berkeley than great food and shops. Several museums grace this little city, including the highly regarded **University Art Museum**, which has a small permanent collection of modern art and frequently hosts unusual but riveting exhibitions by such artists as Robert Mapplethorpe (2626 Bancroft Way, between College and Bowditch, Berkeley; (510)642-0808). The **Judah L. Magnes Museum**, the third-largest Jewish museum in the West, offers numerous exhibitions (2911 Russell Street, off Claremont Avenue, Berkeley; (510)849-2710). A vast array of anthropological artifacts is showcased at the **Phoebe Hearst Museum of Anthropology** (in UC Berkeley's Kroeber Hall, at the corner of College Avenue and Bancroft Way, Berkeley; (510)643-7648). Hands-on exhibits exploring the world of lasers, holograms, and cutting-edge computers are featured at the **Lawrence Hall of Science**, and while you're there, duck outside to see (and hear) the giant, eerie wind chimes and take a peek at the Stonehenge-like solar observatory (on Centennial Drive, near Grizzly Peak Boulevard, in the hills above UC Berkeley; (510)642-5133).

Berkeley Repertory Theatre has a national reputation for innovative new works and experimental productions of the classics and other plays (2025 Addison Street, Berkeley; (510)845-4700). Every summer the **California Shakespeare Festival** performs in an outdoor theater (bundle up, it's usually quite cold) in the Berkeley hills near Orinda (100 Gateway Boulevard, Orinda; (510)548-3422). Movie mavens will appreciate the

They're Creepy and They're Crawly . . .

If you *really* want to impress the folks back home, leave the silly "I Left My Heart in San Francisco" souvenirs at the wharf and get your hands on a live 200-pound African rock python or a spider as big as a dinner plate. Thousands of snakes, lizards, spiders, and their vertebrate friends are crawling and slithering along the walls of **East Bay Vivarium**, an only-in-Berkeley shop boasting the largest selection of reptiles and amphibians in the nation. Take a peek at the cold-blooded critters at 1827 5th Street (at Hearst) in Berkeley. It's open daily; (510)841-1400.

UC **Theatre**, a revival movie house where the flicks change nightly (2036 University Avenue, between Milvia and Shattuck, Berkeley; (510)843-6267), and the **Pacific Film Archive**, which shows underground and avant-garde movies as well as the classics (2625 Durant Avenue, in the University Art Museum, Berkeley; (510)642-1412). For up-to-date listings of cultural events, pick up a free copy of *The Express*, the East Bay's alternative weekly, which is available at cafes and newsstands throughout the city.

For some toe-tappin' fun, visit **Pasand Lounge** for jazz and R&B (2284 Shattuck Avenue at Bancroft, Berkeley; (510)848-0260), or get blasted at **Blake's** with modern rock, funk, and acid jazz (2367 Telegraph Avenue at Durant, Berkeley; (510)848-0886). You can rock out to world beat and other ethnic music at **Ashkenaz** (1317 San Pablo Avenue, near Gilman Street, Berkeley; (510)525-5054), or mellow out at **Freight & Salvage**, the prime Euro-folkie hangout (1111 Addison Street, a half-block east of San Pablo, Berkeley; (510)548-1761). Live rock, jazz, folk, reggae, and other concerts are frequently held at UC

 *Emeryville*

Slivered between Berkeley, Oakland, and the bay, the tiny town of Emeryville was once a dowdy industrial area, but 10 years of manic redevelopment has turned it into one of the most intriguing urban centers in the Bay Area; computer jockeys, artists, and biotechies now abound here in their live-work spaces. Emeryville's town center is a nouveau ultramall called the **Emeryville Public Market** (5800 Shellmound Street, off Powell; (510)652-9300). The mall offers great inexpensive ethnic food stands, a huge **Borders Books and Music** store with a cafe and espresso bar, (510)654-1633, and the hot **Kimball's East**, (510)658-2555, a jazz and blues supper club with national headliners (cover charges range from $15 to $25).

If you're in the area, stop by **Carrara's Cafe and Gallery** for a good, hearty meal (1290 Powell Street, between Doyle and Beaudry; (510)547-6763). Carrara's has an airy warehouse environment with changing art shows and a bohemian clientele, and it's the perfect spot for people-watching, lingering conversations, or a late-night rendezvous. You'll feel completely comfortable dining solo at the counter. The Italian sandwiches and antipasto plate with exotic meats and cheeses are terrific.

Berkeley's intimate, open-air **Greek Theatre**, a particularly pleasant place for sitting beneath the stars and listening to music on warm summer nights (on Gayley Road off Hearst, Berkeley; (510)642-9988). **Cal Performances** presents up-and-coming and established artists of all kinds—from Sting and Seal to superstar mezzo Cecilia Bartoli (call (510)642-9988 for a schedule of events).

When you're ready for more pastoral (and free) diversions, stroll through the **Berkeley Rose Garden**, a terraced park with 3,000 rose-bushes (250 varieties) and a stellar view of San Francisco, particularly at sunset (on Euclid Avenue, between Bay View and Eunice), or walk through the 30-acre **University of California Botanical Garden**, where you'll see more than 12,000 plants, including a spectacular collection of cacti from around the world, a Mendocino pygmy forest, and a Miocene-era redwood grove; free guided tours are offered on weekends (in Strawberry Canyon on Centennial Drive, Berkeley; (510)642-3343). The 2,065-acre **Tilden Regional Park**, set high in the hills above town, offers picnic sites, forests, open meadows, and miles of hiking trails, plus a steam train, a pretty merry-go-round, and a farm and nature area for kids (off Wildcat Canyon Road, Berkeley; (510)843-2137). Tilden also boasts a beautiful **Botanical Garden** specializing in California native plants; (510)841-8732. For kite flying, frisbee throwing, and a very popular playground, drive to the west end of town to the **Berkeley Marina**, which extends 3,000 feet into the bay, providing a stunning view of the San Francisco skyline, the Bay Bridge, and the Golden Gate (at the foot of University Avenue, Berkeley; Adventure Playground, (510)644-8623).

CHEAP SLEEPS

Berkeley is a college town, so bear in mind that just about every accommodation has been booked three to four months in advance for May graduations; this guaranteed booking period also prompts most lodgings to jack up their rates for that month.

Campus Motel
1619 University Avenue (between McGee Avenue and California Street), Berkeley, CA 94703 • (510)841-3844

Located only 5 blocks from UC Berkeley, the Campus Motel is advertised as "squeaky clean"—and that's no lie. Many of the lodgings lining University Avenue charge a few bucks less a night, but a mildewy shower and worn-out furnishings are usually part of the package. This eggshell-white motel with red adobe roof offers 23 well-maintained rooms, each with a double or queen-size bed framed by a pine headboard; amenities such as TV, phone, and coffee maker; and a full bath with a gleaming tiled shower. The only thing the Campus Motel *doesn't* have is air conditioning, but it's still one of the best cheap sleeps near the university.

Flamingo Motel

1761 University Avenue (at Grant Street), Berkeley, CA 94703 •
(510)841-4242

Is there a city in California that doesn't have at least one ugly pink motel with a black flamingo spray-painted on its side? Berkeley is no exception, and to make matters worse, this motel is even lined with bright green indoor-outdoor carpeting, making the whole place look like an oddly reconstructed miniature-golf course. In each of the 29 rooms the drapes droop, ancient yellow carpeting covers the floors, tacky art hangs lopsidedly over the beds, and air conditioning is nonexistent. But you'll also find reasonably clean bathrooms with showers, as well as phones, TV, and proximity to the campus (only 4 blocks away). It may be worth suffering the dreadful decor.

The French Hotel

1538 Shattuck Avenue (between Cedar and Vine Streets),
Berkeley, CA 94709 • (510)548-9930

Because it's in the heart of Berkeley's famed Gourmet Ghetto, with a staggering array of specialty food purveyors on all sides, you could begin and end your trip to the Bay Area at the French Hotel. Simply haul an unending stream of goodies up to your room and stagger downstairs every now and then to quaff an espresso at the hotel's cafe, where you can relax at a sidewalk table while wondering what twist of fate turned a town from a hotbed of radicalism into a haven of haute cuisine in just a few short years. This North Berkeley hotel has 18 rooms, although unfortunately only one (Room 101) qualifies as a cheap sleep. That room is Berkeley's best bargain accommodation, with modern, comfortable furnishings, a very large bathroom, and a private patio with a table and chairs (smoking is permitted, too). And if you're a university or government employee or a member of the California Alumni Association, you'll get fantastic rates for most of the hotel's other rooms.

Golden Bear Motel

1620 San Pablo Avenue (between University Avenue and Cedar Street),
Berkeley, CA 94702 • (800)525-6770 or (510)525-6770

If the French Hotel's budget room is booked (see above), go to the 42-room, Spanish-style Golden Bear. For less than $50 you'll get a clean, comfortable room with full bath and, best of all, you can walk across the street in the morning and be first in line when the famed Acme Bread

Company and the adjoining Café Fanny open their doors. Golden Bear's beds are covered in shimmering Wizard-of-Oz-green bedspreads, and each room is equipped with TV and phone. The motel is 1½ miles from UC Berkeley, 8 blocks from a BART station, and very near the highway on-ramp leading to San Francisco. This part of town isn't the safest place to hang out at night, though, so beware.

Travel Inn

1461 University Avenue (between Sacramento and Acton Streets),
Berkeley, CA 94702 • (510)848-3840

Drive up at night and the first thing you'll see in the parking lot is a red neon sign that says "Quiet." Whether that's a command or an advertisement isn't quite clear, but given this lodging's location—on the edge of busy University Avenue—you should ask for a room in the back just to play it safe. The classic U-shaped pink stucco building (with turquoise doors, of course) looks somewhat dingy outside, but the 42 rooms are clean and the price is right: about $35 for two people. The furnishings are your basic flea-market specials—Naugahyde chairs and rickety nightstands—but each room has a color TV and phone. Ask for a nonsmoking room if the leftover smell of cigarettes makes you gag. Pricey but primo Andronico's supermarket is across the street, and a BART station is only 2 blocks away.

Travelodge

1820 University Avenue (at Martin Luther King, Jr., Way), Berkeley,
CA 94703 • (800)578-7878 or (510)843-4262

When the temperatures soar in the summer, most savvy Berkeley visitors book a room at the Travelodge, the only budget sleep in town with air conditioning. But that's not all this chain hotel has to offer. The 30 light, airy rooms are quite comfortable, the full bathrooms are sparkling clean, and there's even a table and a couple of chairs as well as TV, phone, and fax facilities. The Travelodge is within walking distance of the university and several cafes and ethnic restaurants. Ask for a room far from the street.

★★ Oakland

In an effort to help improve Oakland's image, Oakland Mayor Elihu Harris ordered the city to change all of the vaguely threatening "Entering Oakland" signs to read "Welcome to Oakland." Some folks scoffed at the action and said improving the city's wretched schools or cutting its alarming murder rate would be a better way to improve the city's reputation (something the mayor is also working on), but others appreciated the gesture. Most residents agree that Oakland has gotten a bad rap. While the media keeps close tabs on the body count, few seem to notice Oakland's peaceful, integrated neighborhoods and richly diverse cultural life.

Perhaps the only aspect of Oakland that gets as much publicity as its murder tally is its sports teams. This is the home of the tall guys of the **Golden State Warriors**, and you can watch them dribble the ball across the Oakland Coliseum Arena for as little as $10; (510)638-6300. Those hotshot boys of summer, the **Oakland A's**, offer bleacher seats for about $5 and better seating for a few bucks more; (510)638-0500 or (510)762-BASS). And, after abandoning Oakland for a 13-year stint in Los Angeles, the **Oakland Raiders** football team is back. Most of the Raiders tickets are sold to season-ticket holders a year in advance, but a small number are set aside and sold on a first-come, first-served basis on game days; (510)569-2121.

Oakland's less publicized but equally entertaining attractions include the **Oakland Museum**, a spectacular specimen of modern architecture with tiered Babylonian-style roof gardens and innovative displays of the art, history, and ecology of California (1000 Oak Street, between 10th and 12th Streets, Oakland; (510)238-3401); the **Paramount Theatre**, a restored art deco masterpiece offering dance performances, concerts, plays, and films from Hollywood's golden age (2025 Broadway, at 21st Street, downtown Oakland; (510)465-6400); the **Grand Lake Theatre**, a beautifully restored Egypto-deco movie palace where weekend screenings are kicked off by a live organist (3200 Grand Avenue, at Lake Park Avenue, downtown Oakland; (510)452-3556); and **Jack London Square**, a vast open-air shopping center on the Oakland port's waterfront where you can stroll the scenic boardwalk, catch a ferry to San Francisco, shop at the farmers market every Sunday from 10am to 2pm year-round, or listen to free live concerts on Thursday from 5:30pm to 7:30pm from May to mid-October (at Broadway and the Embarcadero, Oakland; (510)814-6000).

Berkeley

Oakland also has a happening music scene, and you can catch many of the best jazz acts in town at **Yoshi's Japanese Restaurant** (6030 Claremont Avenue near College, Oakland; (510)652-9200), and the bluest blues at **Eli's Mile High Club** (3629 Martin Luther King, Jr., Way, between 36th and 37th Streets, Oakland; (510)655-6661). The **Fifth Amendment** also offers live jazz and blues every night (3255 Lake Shore Avenue, Oakland; (510)832-3242).

Ethnic and other culinary traditions abound in Oakland at many excellent, inexpensive places such as **Asmara Restaurant and Bar**, where friendly folks often share tastes of their East African meals with fellow diners (5020 Telegraph Avenue at 51st, Oakland; (510)547-5100); **Flint's**, for a sinful serving of juicy barbecued ribs doused in a sinus-blasting sauce (open till 4am on weekends; 6609 Shattuck Avenue at 66th, Oakland, (510)653-0593, and 3114 San Pablo Avenue at 31st, Oakland, (510)658-9912); **Pho Anh Dao**, essentially a one-dish restaurant specializing in *pho*, the Vietnamese anise-scented beef-and-noodle soup (280 E 18th Street, between 2nd and 3rd, Oakland; (510)836-1566); **Sabina India Cuisine**, a gracious North Indian restaurant specializing in mildly spiced Indian comfort foods (1628 Webster Street at 17th, Oakland; (510)268-0170); and **Zza's Trattoria**, a bright, cramped, cheerful, and noisy spot where there's always a long line of people waiting for a dinner of thin, crisp-crust pizza and garlic-infused roast chicken (552 Grand Avenue near Euclid, Oakland; (510)839-9124).

If you're thinking about staying the night in Oakland, though, think again. While there are several pleasant, pricey places to stay, Oakland has a dearth of *safe* cheap sleeps. Most visitors to the East Bay get their bargain beds in Berkeley and make day trips here. You *can* find decent prices in the chain hotels by the Oakland International Airport if that fits your travel plans, but many of the city's other low-budget lodgings need an extended visit from Mr. Clean or are frequented by sweet painted ladies of the night who rent by the hour. An exception: The **Travelodge** in downtown Oakland, near Jack London Square, offers no-frills rooms for about $60 to $65 a night (423 7th Street at Broadway, Oakland; (800)578-7878 or (510)451-6316). For other suggestions, contact the **Oakland Convention and Visitors Authority** and ask them to recommend a safe place to stay (550 10th Street, Oakland; (800)2OAKLAND or (510)839-9000).

53

WINE COUNTRY

Sonoma Valley

Napa Valley

Sonoma Valley

Many California oenophiles would argue that when it comes to comparing Sonoma Valley with Napa Valley, less is definitely more: the Sonoma area is less congested, less developed, less commercial, and less glitzy than its rival. Smitten with the bucolic charm of the region, Sonomaphiles delight in wandering the valley's back roads, leisurely touring the wineries, and exploring the quaint towns along the way. Nestled between the Mayacama Mountains to the east and Sonoma Mountain to the west, the crescent-shaped valley is only 7 miles wide and 17 miles long. But what an impressive and historical stretch of land: after all, this is where California's world-renowned wine industry was born.

The town of Sonoma, designed by Mexican general Mariano Vallejo in 1834, is set up like a Mexican pueblo, with a massive tree-covered central plaza that's often hopping with fiestas and family gatherings. Several historic adobe buildings hug the perimeter of the plaza, most of them housing wine stores, specialty food shops, boutiques, and restaurants. The plaza's most famous structure is the Sonoma Mission, the last and northernmost California mission built by Father Junípero Serra. A short drive north of Sonoma is the tiny, sleepy town of Glen Ellen, where

Jack London spent the last years of his life. London fans flock here to peruse the famous author's Beauty Ranch, a vast expanse shaded by oaks, madrones, and redwoods.

ON THE ROAD

One of the joys of exploring the small city of Sonoma is that you can park your car and spend the day touring the shops and sites on foot. Begin your walk at the 8-acre Spanish-style **Sonoma Plaza**, a National Historic Landmark and the largest town square in California. In the mid-1800s the square was a dusty training ground for General Vallejo's troops, and at the turn of the century a women's club transformed it into the lush park you see today, with more than 200 trees, rose gardens (look for the salmon-colored bloom called the Sonoma Rose), picnic tables and benches, a playground, and a pond swarming with ducks and their far-from-ugly ducklings. Sitting squarely in the center of the plaza is **Sonoma City Hall**, a stone Mission Revival structure built by San Francisco architect A. C. Lutgens in 1908. Note that all four sides of it are identical—Lutgens didn't want to offend any of the plaza merchants, so he gave them all the same view of his building. The city hall should look familiar to fans of the former prime-time hit *Falcon Crest*, which featured it as the Tuscany County Courthouse.

Next to the city hall, on the plaza's east side, is the beautiful neoclassic brick building that houses the **Sonoma Valley Visitors Bureau**

Cheesy—But Free!

There may be no such thing as a free lunch, but in Sonoma there *are* free snacks. When you tour the historic plaza, amble over to the north side and step into the Sonoma Cheese Factory, where more than a dozen cheeses are made on the premises and set out for you to sample. Try their famous Sonoma Jack, creamy havarti, tender Teleme, and a variety of Jack cheeses spiked with hot peppers, onions, caraway, and pesto. The Viviani family has been making cheese here since 1931, and you can watch as workers in navy aprons and white hard hats whip up a batch in the 10,000-pound vats in the back. Call ahead for cheese-making schedules; 2 W Spain Street, Sonoma, (707)996-1931.

Maps by Mail

It pays to plan in advance. For a free guide to the Sonoma Valley—complete with maps to wineries, historical sites, and lodgings—just send your request to the Sonoma Valley Visitors Bureau, 453 1st Street E, Sonoma, CA 95476, or call (707)996-1090, and they'll send one to you. If you wait until you get to Sonoma to pick one up, it'll cost $1.50.

(open daily; 453 1st Street E, Sonoma; (707)996-1090). Stop here for info on special events such as the annual Ox Roast, held in June, and the Valley of the Moon Vintage Festival, held in September. For $3.50 you can also get the League for Historic Preservation's self-guided walking-tour map, which outlines a one-hour stroll to 59 historic plaza buildings.

Many people come to Sonoma simply to browse the dozens of shops and galleries circling the plaza. A couple of notable establishments are **Robin's Nest**, a small discount store that sells high-quality crockery, cooking utensils, and such oddities as decorative freeze-dried carrots and grapefruits (116 E Napa Street, Sonoma; (707)996-4169), and **Readers' Books**, a strangely configured but pleasant bookstore that stocks many of its tomes in two hard-to-find rooms in the back. This is the place to shop for best sellers, travel guides, and children's books (127 E Napa Street, on the plaza's southeast corner, Sonoma; (707)939-1779). For used books, stroll south of the plaza to **Chanticleer Books**, which has a table stacked with good reading material at prices ranging from 50 cents to $5 (552 Broadway, on the street's east side, Sonoma; (707)996-5364).

The town's beloved **Mission San Francisco Solano de Sonoma** (aka the Sonoma Mission) sits on the northeast corner of the plaza, and for a nominal fee you can tour the interior of this early 19th-century adobe structure (114 E Spain Street at 1st Street E, Sonoma; (707)938-9560). Your ticket into the mission also will give you access (provided you use it the same day) to the nearby **Sonoma Barracks**, a two-story adobe structure built between 1836 and 1840 to house Mexican army troops (1st Street E and E Spain Street, Sonoma; no phone), as well as to General Vallejo's well-preserved, yellow-and-white Victorian home, known as **Lachryma Montis**—Latin for "tears of the mountain," a reference to a mineral spring on the property (W Spain Street at 2nd Street W, Sonoma; (707)938-9559). Scattered locations notwithstanding, all of these historic structures are part of the **Sonoma State Historic Park**; (707)938-1519.

Franciscan fathers planted California's first vineyards at the Mission San Francisco Solano de Sonoma in 1823 and harvested the grapes to make their sacramental wines. Thirty-four years later, the state's first major vineyard was planted with European grape varietals by Hungarian Count Agoston Haraszthy at Sonoma's revered Buena Vista Winery. Little did the count know, however, that one day he would become widely hailed as the father of California wine—wine that is now consistently rated as some of the best in the world. Today more than 30 wineries dot the Sonoma Valley, most offering pretty picnic areas, free tours of their wine-making facilities, and, unlike many of their Napa Valley competitors, free tastings. Here's a roundup of some of Sonoma's best:

Buena Vista Winery • California's oldest premium winery (founded in 1857); a large estate set in a forest; picnic grounds and supplies; tours of the stone winery and the hillside tunnels; a gallery featuring locals' artwork. 18000 Old Winery Road, Sonoma, (707)938-1266.

Château St. Jean • Beautiful 250-acre estate with tastings in the mansion and stunning views from a faux medieval tower; self-guided tour; picnic area. 8555 Highway 12 (Sonoma Highway), Kenwood, (707)833-4134.

Ferrari-Carano Vineyards and Winery • Good chardonnay, fumé blanc, cabernet; cutting-edge facility. 8761 Dry Creek Road, Healdsburg, (707)433-6700.

Geyser Peak Winery • Stone winery covered with ivy; pleasant gewürztraminer and riesling; beautiful hiking trails; great picnic area available by reservation. 22281 Chianti Road, Geyserville, (707)857-9463.

Gloria Ferrer Champagne Caves • Interesting subterranean cellars; complimentary tapas served in the tasting room; excellent tour; Spanish cooking classes occasionally offered. 23555 Highway 121, Sonoma, (707)996-7256.

Gundlach-Bundschu Winery • Grand, historic building on impressive grounds; known primarily for its red wines; picnic facilities. 2000 Denmark Street, Sonoma, (707)938-5277.

Kenwood Vineyards • Renowned for its reds; quaint wooden barns. 9592 Highway 12 (Sonoma Highway), Kenwood, (707)833-5891.

Korbel Champagne Cellars • Ivy-covered brick building set in a redwood forest with a view of the Russian River; informative winery tours; extensive flower gardens open for tours May through September. 13250 River Road, Guerneville, (707)887-2294.

Kunde Estate Winery • Century-old winery set on 2,000 gorgeous acres of rolling hills; one of Sonoma County's largest grape suppliers; tasting room. 10155 Highway 12 (Sonoma Highway), Kenwood, (707)833-5501.

Matanzas Creek Winery • Beautiful drive to the winery; attractive facilities; outstanding chardonnay and merlot; guided tours; picnic tables. 6097 Bennett Valley Road, Santa Rosa, (707)528-6464.

Sebastiani Vineyards • Sonoma's largest premium-variety winery; tours of the redwood cellar featuring an interesting collection of carved-oak cask heads; tasting room; picnic tables. 389 4th Street E, Sonoma, (800)888-5532 or (707)938-5532.

Viansa Winery and Italian Marketplace • Buildings and grounds modeled after a Tuscan village; owned by the Sebastiani family; good sauvignon blanc, chardonnay, cabernet; gourmet Italian picnic fare and local delicacies; beautiful hillside picnic grounds. 25200 Highway 121, Sonoma, (707)935-4700.

For a list of highly recommended Napa wineries, see "Napa Valley Wineries" in the Napa Valley chapter.

The ever-popular **Sebastiani Vineyards** is only 4 blocks from the Sonoma Plaza (389 4th Street E, Sonoma; (800)888-5532 or (707)938-5532). After indulging in a few (or more) free sips of wine, walk or bicycle through the vineyards on the easy ¾-mile paved path that leads to General Vallejo's home.

As you pound the pavement around the plaza, you'll pass many of the city's terrific restaurants and cafes. Fortunately, Sonoma's cheap eats aren't as rare as its cheap sleeps. A longtime local favorite is the **Feed Store Cafe & Bakery**, which serves breakfast (ask about their $2.99 "Early Bird Specials" offered from 7am to 9am) and lunch indoors and outdoors on the flower-bedecked patio. Don't be surprised if you see a few hopeful ducks waddling around the grounds looking for snacks, or even some brave wild birds alighting on your table to snatch a few crumbs. The lunch menu offers a wide range of creative sandwiches, salads, and vegetarian dishes, as well as your standard burgers and fries. On your way out, stop by the adjoining bakery and indulge in one of the award-winning muffins or sinfully rich cookies (529 1st Street W, near the plaza's southwest corner, Sonoma; (707)938-2122). For a good cup of coffee or an iced espresso shake and a quick bite to eat, head over to the **Coffee Garden**, which has a pretty vine-laced patio hidden in back where you can relax to the sound of classical music (415 and 421 1st Street W, on the plaza's west side, Sonoma; (707)996-6645).

Belly-bustin' deli sandwiches are slapped together at the **Sonoma Cheese Factory**, where you can watch them make your cheese before they make your sandwich. Take your victuals to their covered patio, or even better, to a picnic table in the plaza (2 W Spain Street, on the plaza's north side, Sonoma; (707)996-1931). The **Old Sonoma Creamery** also makes hefty sandwiches, and its old-fashioned ice-cream parlor dishes out dozens of sweet treats—including fat-free shakes (400 1st Street E, across from the mission, Sonoma; (707)938-2938). On the east side of the plaza you can get $2 hot dogs and brie-on-a-baguette for only a few bucks at the tiny **First Street East Cafe** (408 1st Street E at E Spain Street, Sonoma; (707)996-0207), or seat yourself on a stool at **Basque Boulangerie Café's** handsome marble counter and order one of several fine wines by the glass, a caesar salad, and perhaps a French ham sandwich (460 1st Street E, Sonoma; (707)935-7687). A short walk west of the plaza is Northern California's ubiquitous **Chevy's Mexican Restaurant**—a chain restaurant, yes, but a good one for fajitas and margaritas on the cheap (136 W Napa Street, Sonoma; (707)938-8009).

When you're ready to venture beyond the town, drive north about 10 miles to Jack London territory. There are more places and things named after Jack London in Sonoma County than there are women

Find that Farm

Whether you want to buy garlic braids, a basket of fresh blackberries, or a Kashmir goat, the free Sonoma County Farm Trails map will point you in the right direction. The annually updated guide features more than 100 listings and brief descriptions of family farms and specialty growers that welcome visitors in search of farm-fresh foods, Christmas trees, nursery plants, herbs, or even exotic (and not so exotic) farm animals. Send your name, address, and 55 cents' worth of stamps (no envelope necessary) to: Sonoma County Farm Trails, P.O. Box 6032, Santa Rosa, CA 95406. For more farm facts, call (707)996-2154.

named María in Mexico, and this cult reaches its apex in **Glen Ellen**. This is where the author of *The Call of the Wild*, *The Sea Wolf*, and some 50 other books and numerous articles built his aptly named Beauty Ranch, an 800-acre spread now known as **Jack London State Historic Park** (2400 London Ranch Road, off Highway 12 and Arnold Drive, Glen Ellen; (707)938-5216). London's vineyards, piggery, horse stalls, and other ranch buildings are here, as well as the cottage where he wrote (and where he died) and a beautiful stone house-turned-museum called the House of Happy Walls. Lining those walls are pieces from London's interesting and worldly art collection and personal mementos, including some of the 600 rejection letters he received from publishers (such as a hotshot at the *San Francisco Chronicle*), who surely must have fallen over backwards in their cushy corporate chairs when London later became the highest-paid author of his time. There's a $5-per-car fee to enter the park (and it's worth spending an extra buck to get the informative park map), or you may hike or ride your bike or horse in for free. Your dog can come along, too ($1 fee), though canines are restricted to certain trails.

The park is a pretty place for a picnic, with tables and barbecues set out under the oak and eucalyptus trees (a short walk from the parking lot). Carry your lunch to London's cottage to find the park's best table: sitting next to a goldfish pond overlooking the grapevines. Hard-core hikers should plan to spend the day trekking to Bathhouse Lake and up Sonoma Mountain's steep slopes (carry water), which are blanketed with grassy meadows and forests of madrone, manzanita, redwood, and Douglas fir. Or consider letting the friendly folks at the Sonoma Cattle Company (based in the park) saddle up a horse for you. Call for the lowdown on their guided horseback trips (reservations are required; (707)996-8566).

Love Those Llamas

When's the last time you pet a Peruvian llama? Or fed a long-legged emu a snack? Here's your chance to mingle with the animals at World of Birds, a veritable petting zoo and the largest indoor breeding facility of exotic birds in the country. Cocky cockatoos, marvelous macaws, and their fine-feathered friends fill the bird hall with an ear-splitting cacophony, while a pair of pigs, a couple of emus, and dozens of llamas roam around the yard, just waiting for a friendly pat and a handout. And if you happen to find these critters irresistible, well, they're all for sale, even the lovely llamas and porky pigs. Open every day; free admission. Located at 23570 Highway 121 (Arnold Drive), across from Gloria Ferrer Champagne Caves in Sonoma; (707)996-1477.

A ticket to Jack London Park allows you free entrance (on the same day only) to the spectacular 2,700-acre **Sugarloaf Ridge State Park**, a 20-minute drive north. Sugarloaf has 25 miles of hiking and horseback-riding trails (with great views from the ridge), guided horseback rides, 50 tent campsites, and a horse corral (2605 Adobe Canyon Road, 3 miles east of Highway 12, Kenwood; camping reservations: (800)444-7275).

CHEAP SLEEPS

✓ Sonoma Hotel
110 W Spain Street (at 1st Street W), Sonoma, CA 95476 •
(800)468-6016 or (707)996-2996

Few Wine Country accommodations offer bargain rates, particularly in the tiny town of Sonoma, but this impressive vintage hotel rents more than half of its 17 elegant rooms for about $60 in the off season (summer rates jump up by $15). The Sonoma Hotel has a prime location on the northwest corner of the plaza. If you stay in room 20, you can peer out the window at the plaza's hustle and bustle, or perhaps you'd prefer room 21, where Maya Angelou wrote *Gather Together in My Name*. The least expensive rooms are on the third floor, and each has a window or two, a wash basin, and classy antique furnishings that might include a sleigh bed with hand-carved lions' feet or a marble-topped dresser and matching nightstand. Unfortunately, none of the hotel's rooms have air conditioning, which can be quite unpleasant when temperatures soar in the summer. Guests share two small but very clean gender-specific bathrooms. And there's a beautiful, century-old mahogany bar in the saloon downstairs if you'd like a nightcap before you retire.

Sonoma Valley Inn

550 2nd Street W (off W Napa Street), Sonoma, CA 95476 •
(800)334-5784 or (707)938-9200

This 75-room hotel is part of the Best Western chain and is located off a busy street across from a supermarket, but you won't care about all that once you see how spacious, tidy, and well appointed the rooms are. Standard features include a private bath, cable TV, air conditioning, mini-fridge, gift bottle of wine, continental breakfast delivered to your door, and a tiny enclosed patio. The floral bedspreads obviously didn't come from Sears, and even the art is more upscale than you'd expect in a chain hotel. In addition, most rooms have a wood-burning fireplace. The land-scaped courtyard with a swimming pool, fountain, and gazebo-covered Jacuzzi will prompt you to scratch your head and wonder if you can actually afford to stay here. Well, if you come in the off-season, it'll cost only about $50 to $60 a night (peak-season customers pay triple those rates).

Jack London Lodge

13740 Arnold Drive (P.O. Box 300), Glen Ellen, CA 95442 •
(707)938-8510

For those who really want to get away from the city scene, this white, two-story, wisteria-draped lodge offers 22 quiet rooms next to rippling, tree-lined Sonoma Creek. The lodge is a short drive from the town of Sonoma, near several wineries and the beautiful Jack London State Historic Park. The rates are reasonable, but as usual in the Wine Country, they creep over *Cheap Sleeps* price range in the summer. Ask for one of the upstairs rooms, with a view of the trees. The decor is simple if somewhat bland, and each unit has a brass bed (either one king-size or two queen-size), private bath, cable TV, a portable radiator, and air conditioning. A continental breakfast is included on weekends and holidays, and daily in the summer. The swimming pool sits alongside the creek, but its surrounding chain-link fence is an eyesore in spite of the vines of red roses planted all around. Next door is London's Grill, an attractive, moderately priced restaurant, and the wonderful Jack London Saloon, where you can admire London memorabilia and hoist a glass to the author's memory.

Mother Nature reigns supreme in Sonoma County's Russian River Valley, where folks prefer to sip their cabernets and chardonnays amidst the company of redwoods, fruit orchards, and sandy river beaches instead of chichi restaurants and wineries bustling with city slickers. Everything moves at a leisurely pace here, from the weekend revelers floating down the river in inner tubes to the cars cruising the winding roads. Pack a picnic and spend the day touring some of the 60 wineries sprinkled throughout the vast valley, or plunk down in a beach chair along the river and call it a day. If you decide you like this region so much you want to stay a night or two, you can get budget-lodging and campground referrals through the Russian River Region Visitor Information Center (14034 Armstrong Woods Road, Guerneville, CA 95446; (800)253-8800 or (707)869-9212) or the Sonoma County Convention & Visitors Bureau (5000 Roberts Lake Road, Suite A, Rohnert Park, CA 94928; (800)326-7666 or (707)586-8100). For a free copy of the excellent "Russian River Wine Road" map, which provides a summary of the valley's wineries, call (707)433-6782 or write to Russian River Wine Road, P.O. Box 46, Healdsburg, CA 95448.

Healdsburg is the heart of the Russian River Valley, and it's one tourist town whose charm seems completely unforced. Boutiques and bakeries surround a pretty, tree-lined plaza where you can sit and read the newspaper while munching on pastries from the marvelous Downtown Bakery & Creamery (308-A Center Street, Healdsburg; (707)431-2719). In summer, nothing beats paddling down the glorious Russian River past vineyards and secret swimming holes in a canoe or kayak rented from W. C. "Bob" Trowbridge Canoe Trips (20 Healdsburg Avenue, Healdsburg; (800)640-1386 or (707)433-7247). Come evening, catch a flick at the Raven Theater, the Wine Country's best movie house for new releases and art films (115 North Street, Healdsburg; (707)433-5448).

Southwest of Healdsburg is the Russian River Valley town of **Guerneville**, which was explored by the Russians in the 1840s and grew into one of the busiest logging centers in the West by the 1880s. More recently it was a haven for bikers (the leather, not the Lycra, sort), before becoming a hangout for hippies. Now it's a summer mecca for gays and lesbians and naturalists drawn by the beauty of the land. The town is a good place to kick off a nature expedition or a tour of the area's wineries. Armstrong Woods State Reserve boasts a peaceful grove of spectacular ancient redwoods and a variety of hiking trails (17000 Armstrong Woods Road, Guerneville; (707)869-2015). Equestrians should saddle up at Armstrong Woods Pack Station, which offers half- and full-day horseback rides with gourmet lunches (by reservation only); (707)579-1520. From May through October, you can rent canoes and paddleboats at Johnson's Beach, just under the main bridge; (707)869-2045. Johnson's Beach is also home to the wildly popular Russian River Jazz Festival, held every September; (707)869-3940. Another crowd-pleaser is the annual Stumptown Days Parade and Russian River Rodeo held on Father's Day weekend; (707)869-1959. For a good, simple meal, grab a bite at Burdon's (15405 River Road, Guerneville; (707)869-2615) or Sweet's River Grill (16521 Main Street, Guerneville; (707)869-3383).

Farther south on Highway 116 is **Forestville**, a tiny hamlet surrounded by redwoods. From here you can launch an all-day canoe trip down the gentle Russian River, where you'll see turtles, river otters, egrets, and great blue herons. Set forth from Burke's Canoe Trips from May through September, and someone there will pick you up 10 miles down the river and take you back to your car; (707)887-1222. While you're in the area, visit Koslowski Farms, a family farm that has turned into a gourmet-food business. Try their apple butter, jam, vinegar, and what they're most famous for, fresh berries (5566 Gravenstein Highway, Forestville; (707)887-1587).

Napa Valley

Despite the plethora of nouveau châteaus, fake French barns, and gimcrack stores selling cabernet-flavored jelly beans, Napa Valley is still one of Northern California's most magical spots. In early spring, the hills are a vibrant green, bright-yellow mustard blossoms poke up between the grapevines, and stands of fruit trees burst into showy flower. In summer, tourists flood the valley and its 250 wineries, cranking up the energy level a few notches and conferring a patina of glamour and excitement that some locals delight in and others deplore. Later, after the grape harvest, the vineyards turn a bright autumnal scarlet, and the region's quaint, Old West–style towns assume a more relaxed, homey atmosphere. At any time of year, the Napa Valley is a great area for wine tasting, hiking, picnicking, shopping, eating, exploring historic sites, and soaking in mud baths or hot springs—activities that won't leave you bankrupt as long as you bypass the ritzier resorts and restaurants.

The 35-mile-long valley is home to some of the most famous wineries in the world, and many of them are clustered along scenic Highway 29 and the verdant Silverado Trail, two parallel roads running the length of the region and through such quaint little towns as Yountville, Oakville, St. Helena, and Calistoga. The *valley is a zoo on weekends—especially in summer and early fall when traffic on narrow Highway 29 rivals rush hour in the Bay Area. Wise Wine Country visitors plan their trips here for weekdays, the misty months of winter, or early spring, when room rates are lower and everything's less crowded, but the valley is no less spectacular.*

ON THE ROAD

At the southernmost end of Napa Valley is the pretty, sprawling town of **Napa**, where about half the county's 114,800 residents live. Although its name is synonymous with wine, most of the wineries are actually several miles north of town. The city, founded in 1848, is well known for its imposing Victorian structures, many of them in the downtown area near the Napa River. Introduce yourself by taking a self-guided walking tour of downtown Napa's architectural gems. A detailed map highlighting everything from a Victorian gothic church to an art deco brewery and a Beaux-Arts bank is available for free at the **Napa Valley Conference and Visitors Bureau** (1310 Napa Town Center, between Pearl and Clay Streets, Napa, CA 94559; (707)226-7459), or you may choose from a half-dozen 25-cent walking-tour maps sold by Napa County Landmarks (1026 1st Street at Main Street, in the Community Preservation Center, Napa, CA 94559; (707)255-1836).

If you have time for only a quick tour, walk along Main Street, which crosses the river. At the south end of Main, adjacent to Veteran's Park on the river's west bank, is a handsome century-old building that's now home to **Downtown Joe's Restaurant and Brewery**. Joe's doesn't serve the cheapest food in town, but the covered outdoor patio is a pleasant place to sample a microbrew or two. For the best brew prices, come during happy hour: from 4pm to 6pm Monday through Friday, and 10pm to midnight nightly. Downtown Joe's even makes its own root beer and ginger ale (902 Main Street at 2nd Street, Napa; (707)258-2337). A couple of blocks north on Main the locals kick back at the **Napa Valley Coffee Roasting Company**, a great little spot for a cup of freshly brewed java (948 Main Street at 1st Street, Napa; (707)224-2233). Across the street at **Copperfield's**, you'll find new and used books at reasonable prices (1005 1st Street, Napa; (707)252-8002).

For a filling meal that won't cost more than a few bucks, order a big burrito at the nearby **Taqueria 3 Hermanos** (1122-A 1st Street, Napa;

Ever since Napa's wineries became world-renowned, millions of people from all over have journeyed here each year to see their favorite vintners in action. Most of the wine makers love the attention, although the onslaught of visitors has prompted many to charge a small wine-tasting fee. In addition, some wineries now require reservations for taking a tour (but don't be deterred—it's mainly to control the crowd and make sure someone's there to show you around).

As you whiz along the road past signs for some of the most famous wineries in the world, it's tempting to pull over at every one. But do yourself a favor and follow a tip from veteran tasters: pick out the four or five wineries you're most interested in visiting over a two-day period, and stick to your itinerary. Touring more than two or three a day will overwhelm and exhaust even the most intrepid connoisseur, although if you really want to cover several in a short period, skip the tours and stick to the tastings. If you're new to the wine-touring scene, rest assured that you won't ever be pressured to buy any of the wines you've sampled—the vintners are just delighted to expose you to their products (besides, you'll often find much better prices at some of the good wine stores in town). Here's a roster of some of Napa's most popular wineries, many of which offer free tours:

Beaulieu Vineyards • Historic estate (nicknamed "BV"); famous for its cabernet sauvignon. 1960 St. Helena Highway, Rutherford, (707)963-2411.

Beringer Vineyards • Napa Valley's oldest continuously operating winery; stately, old Rhineland-style mansion; good tours of the vineyards and caves; well known for its chardonnay and cabernet. 2000 Main Street, St. Helena, (707)963-7115.

Château Montelena Winery • A stunning French château-style winery built of stone; beautiful setting includes a lake with two islands; celebrated for its chardonnay; wonderful (though often-booked) picnic facilities by reservation only. 1429 Tubbs Lane, Calistoga, (707)942-5105.

Clos Pegase • Stunning, modern facility designed by architect Michael Graves; grand outdoor sculpture; "Wine in Art" slide show; interesting guided tours of the winery, caves, and art collection. 1060 Dunaweal Lane, Calistoga, (707)942-4982.

Domaine Chandon • Good sparkling wine; handsome building and location; four-star (expensive) dining room; fantastic guided tours. 1 California Drive, Yountville, (707)944-2280.

The Hess Collection Winery • Stone winery in a remote, scenic location; well known for its cabernet sauvignon and chardonnay; contemporary American and European art showcased in a dramatic building; good self-guided tour. 4411 Redwood Road, Napa, (707)255-1144.

Merryvale Vineyards • Historic stone building; daily tastings; informative and thorough tasting classes on Saturday mornings by appointment only; best known for its chardonnay. 1000 Main Street, St. Helena, (707)963-7777.

Robert Mondavi Winery • Huge, world-famous winery; Mission-style building; excellent tours; famous cooking school. 7801 St. Helena Highway, Oakville, (707)226-1335.

Schramsberg Vineyards • Attractive, historic facilities and extensive caves; first-rate sparkling wines; interesting, educational guided tours. 1400 Schramsberg Road, Calistoga, (707)942-4558.

Sterling Vineyards • Excellent self-guided tour through an impressive, white Mediterranean-style complex perched high on a hill; access via an aerial tramway (for a fee) offering splendid views; vast tasting room with panoramic views. 1111 Dunaweal Lane, Calistoga, (707)942-3300.

For a list of highly recommended Sonoma wineries, see "Sonoma Valley Wineries" in the Sonoma Valley chapter.

(707)224-6062) or **Taqueria Rosita** (1214 Main Street at Pearl Street, Napa; (707)253-9208). For terrific deli sandwiches, fresh vegetable juices, and smoothies, walk west on 1st Street to the **First Squeeze Deli & Juice Bar** (1149 1st Street at Coombs Street, Napa; (707)224-6762), or head north on Main and pick up a hefty sandwich and salad at **Andrews Meat Co. & Deli** (1245 Main Street, between Pearl and Clinton Streets, Napa; (707)253-8311). You'll have to drive to get to the best deli in town, **Genova Delicatessen**, which makes great sandwiches for less than $4, roasted chickens for about the same price, and a variety of salads and sweets. You can even sit at the espresso bar and order an Italian soda, gelato, or a great cup of joe (1550 Trancas Street, west of Jefferson Street, Napa; (707)253 8686). Another Napa favorite for breakfast, lunch, and early dinner is the **ABC/Alexis Baking Company and Cafe**, which is also a great place to pick up goodies-to-go like chocolate-caramel cake and pumpkin-spice muffins (1517 3rd Street at School Street, Napa; (707)258-1827).

About 9 miles north of Napa, just off Highway 29 where the hills are covered with grapevines, is the tiny town of **Yountville**, home of Moët et Chandon's Napa Valley–based winery, **Domaine Chandon**. Yountville was founded in the mid-19th century by pioneer George Clavert Yount, reportedly the first American to settle in Napa Valley, and it's now the site of some of the best (and priciest) restaurants in the Wine Country. Great cheap eats are rare here, with the exception of the ever-popular **Diner**. This is the place to go when you've brought the kids, want a tasty, informal meal, or have an uncontrollable urge for a butter-milk shake (that tastes just like cheesecake!). Terrific, belly-packing break-fasts (don't pass up the huevos rancheros) have secured the Diner's reputation for years, but lunches and dinners are good, too, with hearty,

When Only the Virgin Will Do

The family-run Napa Valley Olive Oil Manufacturing Company produces high-quality California olive oil (pure and extra-virgin) and sells it at bargain prices in a tiny, off-the-beaten-path shop in St. Helena. You'll also find a wealth of Italian gourmet foodstuffs ideal for a picnic in the park: salami, prosciutto, fresh mozzarella, dried fruit, fresh baked bread, biscotti, and more. Look for the white barn at the intersection of Charter Oak and Allison Avenues (at the end of the long block behind Ristorante Tra Vigne) in St. Helena. Open daily; (707)963-4173.

well-prepared Mexican dishes and seafood specialties supplementing the typical diner fare (6476 Washington Street, near Oak Street, Yountville; (707)944-2626).

In the heart of Yountville is the beautiful brick complex now known as **Vintage 1870**, a touristy mall with a few dozen overpriced shops and a handful of restaurants (6525 Washington Street, Yountville; (707)944-2451). The building was erected in 1870 as a winery, and now it's listed on the National Register of Historic Places. At the mall entrance is **Red Rock Grill**, (707)944-2614, a popular lunch spot for burger fans, and inside the complex is the **Yountville Pastry Shop**, (707)944-2138, which makes adequate sandwiches, pizzas, pastries, and cookies that you can enjoy outdoors on a redwood-and-red-brick patio decorated with bright flowers in terra-cotta pots.

Just up the highway from Yountville is the itsy-bitsy town of **Oakville**, which produces some of the best cabernet sauvignon in the world (as does its little nearby twin town, Rutherford). For eats, there's the popular (and expensive) **Stars Cafe**, a former stagecoach stop turned culinary hot spot (7848 St. Helena Hwy, Oakville; (707)944-8905); **Pometta's Deli**, where you can get good, reasonably priced whole-roasted barbecued chickens (7787 St. Helena Highway at the Oakville Grade, Oakville; (707)944-2365); and the famous **Oakville Grocery Co.**, a gourmet deli disguised as an old-fashioned country grocery store with a striking "Drink Coca-Cola" sign painted on the wall outside. Inside you'll find a fine variety of local wines (including a good selection of splits), a small espresso bar tucked in the corner, and pricey but delicious picnic supplies ranging from pâté and caviar to turkey sandwiches and freshly made sweets (7856 St. Helena Highway, Oakville; (707)944-8802).

If you continue north on this scenic stretch of Highway 29, you'll drive smack through the center of **St. Helena**, which has come a long way since its days as a rural Seventh-Day Adventist village. On St. Helena's Victorian Old West–style Main Street (aka Highway 29), farming-supply stores now sit stiffly next to chic women's-clothing boutiques and upscale home furnishings stores. It's a great place to shop—*if* you've got money to spare. If you don't, take a picnic lunch or supper to **Lyman Park**, and sit on the grass or in the beautiful white gazebo, where bands sometimes set up for free summer concerts (on Main Street, between Adams and Pine Streets, St. Helena). You can also rent bicycles for about $7 an hour (or $25 a day) at **St. Helena Cyclery** and pedal your way around the valley (open daily; 1156 Main Street, St. Helena; (707)963-7736).

For such a small, pricey town, St. Helena offers a number of inexpensive and reasonably priced places to eat. **Taylor's Refresher** has been

Mind Your Own Beeswax

Kids and candle collectors alike will get a kick out of a quick roadside stop at Hurd Beeswax Candles, where you can peer through a small window at thousands of honeybees working in their hive. Look for the little brown doors covering the hive in the center of the shop, and pull them open to let in the light and watch (the busybodies like to do their thing in the dark). On the other side of the store you can see how candle makers turn the beeswax into luminaries of all shapes and sizes. Open daily; 3020 St. Helena Highway (in the Freemark Abbey complex near Brava Terrace restaurant), 2 miles north of St. Helena; (707)963-7211.

serving bargain burgers, hot dogs, and shakes at its roadside stand since 1949 (933 Main Street, St. Helena; (707)963-3486). Tots in tow? Stop at the colorful, kid-friendly **Armadillo's** restaurant, where they'll have space to wiggle, crayons to color with, and a kids-only menu to choose from; in fact, there's such a large variety of California-Mexican dishes that youngsters *and* adults should be able to find something that pleases (1304 Main Street, St. Helena; (707)963-8082). For gourmet California-style fare at reasonable prices, take a seat at the pretty **Magnolia Cafe**, which serves a half-dozen sandwiches, soup, coffee drinks, and even peanut-butter-and-jelly sandwiches and bananas for the little ones (1118 Hunt Avenue, off Main Street, St. Helena; (707)963-0748). If you want to savor the famous fare of Ristorante Tra Vigne but don't have the bucks to pay for it, visit the adjoining **Cantinetta Tra Vigne**, whose beautiful patio is a great place to enjoy focaccia pizzas, Italian sandwiches, interesting soups and salads, pastas topped with smoked salmon and other delights, and a surfeit of sweets (1050 Charter Oak Avenue, off Main Street, St. Helena; (707)963-8888).

Leaving downtown St. Helena and heading north towards Calistoga, you'll pass under the **Tunnel of the Elms** (also called the Tree Tunnel), a fantastic row of dozens of elm trees arched across Main Street (Highway 29) in front of **Beringer Vineyards**. They were planted by the Beringer brothers more than 100 years ago, and their interlaced branches form a gorgeous canopy about a quarter of a mile long. Beyond Beringer are two parks popular for hiking and picnics. **Bale Grist Mill State Historic Park** holds a historic flour mill built in 1846 by a British surgeon named Bale. The 36-foot wooden waterwheel still grinds grain into meal and flour on weekends. If the park looks familiar, perhaps you saw it featured in the 1960 film *Pollyanna* (3369 Highway 29 at Bale Grist Mill Road, 3 miles north of St. Helena; (707)963-2236). Next door is the 1,800-acre **Bothe–Napa Valley State Park**, offering about 100 picnic spots with barbecues and tables, a swimming pool open from mid-June through Labor Day, and 50 campsites (call (707)942-4575 for general information and (800)444-PARK for camping reservations). You can even hike from one park to the other by following the moderately strenuous 1.2-mile History Trail.

Water-sports enthusiasts and anglers in search of trout, bass, crappie, catfish, and silver salmon should make the long haul east to Napa Valley's **Lake Berryessa**, the second-largest artificial lake in the state (after Shasta). The 21-mile-long, 3-mile-wide lake has boat launches, berths, picnic areas, campsites, 168 miles of shoreline, and marinas with boat and fishing rentals (on Berryessa Knoxville Road, via Steel Canyon Road or Pope Canyon Road, Napa Valley). For more details, call the Lake Berryessa Chamber of Commerce at (800)726-1256.

Sitting pretty at Napa Valley's northernmost end is the charming little spa town of **Calistoga**, where mud baths, mineral pools, and massages are still the main attractions. The city was founded in the mid-19th century by California's first millionaire, Sam Brannan, who had made a bundle of cash provisioning miners during the Gold Rush. Brannan quickly recognized the value of Calistoga's mineral-rich hot springs, and in 1859 he purchased 2,000 acres of the Wappo Indian hot springs land, built a first-class hotel and spa, named the region Calistoga (a combination of the words California and Saratoga), and watched his fortunes grow as affluent San Franciscans paraded in for a relaxing respite from city life. Generations later, spa-seeking city slickers are still doing that; these days, however, more than a dozen enterprises touting the magical restorative powers of mineral baths line the town's Old West–style streets. You'll see an odd combo of stressed-out CEOs and earthier types shelling out their dough for a chance to soak away their worries and get the kinks rubbed out of their necks. While Calistoga's spas and resorts are far from glamorous, many offer body treatments and mud baths you won't find anywhere else in this part of the state. If you decide to splurge on a spa treatment, first check for discount coupons in the town's free publications, such as "California Visitors Review" and "Inside Napa Valley," distributed in area hotels, businesses, and visitors bureaus.

After you've steamed or soaked, head over to the **Calistoga Inn**'s pretty outdoor patio for a tall, cool drink, or try one of their home-brewed beers and a sandwich from the grill (1250 Lincoln Avenue, at the bridge, Calistoga; (707)942-4101). Once you're rejuvenated, stroll down the main street and browse through the numerous quaint shops marketing

Hiding Out at Harbin Hot Springs

For a suntan without tan lines, head over to Harbin Hot Springs, a clothing-optional retreat nestled in a very secluded valley near Middletown, 30 minutes north of Calistoga. The nonprofit hot springs retreat has a sauna, two warm mineral pools, and a hot and a cold mineral pool, as well as dressing rooms, showers, and plenty of spacious redwood sun decks. You can come for the day or stay the night; the New Age resort offers clean, comfortable, and reasonably priced lodgings ranging from a dormitory with communal bathrooms to private cabins with full baths. Or camp out for about the same price as a day pass. The pretty 1,100-acre property is covered with meadows, spring-fed streams, and groves of oak and pine, with several hiking trails winding thoughout the terrain.

Guests have access to the communal Fern Kitchen, which has ample space and equipment but is vegetarian-only: no meat, poultry, or fish "in any form" is allowed inside. Harbin also offers free movies every evening, along with activities like meditations, moon ceremonies, and massages. Although the resort has a definite touchy-feely, aging-hippie flavor, it attracts plenty of more conventional types who just want to relax (albeit in the nude). The Harbin staff takes great pride in the tranquil environment it has created (telephones, TVs, and alarm clocks are purposely kept out of the rooms), and, indeed, it's so peaceful you're apt to see deer and their fawns lounging alongside guests on the lush lawns. If you're not comfortable around a lot of nudity, though, Harbin is not for you. For more information, call (800)622-2477 (Northern California only) or (707)987-2477.

everything from French soaps and antique armoires to silk-screened T-shirts and saltwater taffy. The **Calistoga Bookstore** carries a great selection of travel guides and kids' books, and provides a browser-friendly couch in back (1343 Lincoln Avenue, Calistoga; (707)942-4123). For a look back at Calistoga's pioneer past, stop by the **Sharpsteen Museum**, created by Walt Disney animator and Oscar-winning producer Ben Sharpsteen (1311 Washington Street, off Lincoln Avenue, Calistoga; (707)942-5911).

Along Calistoga's main drag are a number of fairly priced restaurants and cafes. Walk south to north on Lincoln Avenue and you'll find **Taqueria Santa Rosa**, which offers table service and all the Mexican standards (3150 Lincoln Avenue, Calistoga; (707)942-6468), followed by **Moreno's Burritos**, a tiny stand that sells burritos, all-beef dogs, sodas, and shaved ice (1428 Lincoln Avenue, Calistoga; (707)942-6964). Across the street, **Clearwater Cafe** serves breakfast, lunch, and a weekend brunch in a pleasant, airy brick building that's large enough to display a hot-air-balloon basket on the dining-room floor (1403 Lincoln Avenue at Washington Street, Calistoga; (707)942-9777). For California-style thin-crust pizza and calzone, check out **Checkers**, which also has an espresso bar, a children's menu, and fresh frozen yogurt with a variety of toppings (1414 Lincoln Avenue, Calistoga; (707)942-9300). At the north end of the town's shopping district, across from Nance's Hot Springs, is the **Calistoga Roastery**, a casual, cozy spot where you can get great coffee and iced-coffee drinks, as well as a $2.50 breakfast of poached eggs on toast or a lunchtime sandwich with potato salad for about $4 (1631 Lincoln Avenue, Calistoga; (707)942-5757).

Just outside of town you can marvel at the **Old Faithful Geyser**, which faithfully shoots a plume of 350-degree mineral water 60 feet into the air at regular intervals (open daily; 1299 Tubbs Lane, 2 miles north of Calistoga; (707)942-6463). Other natural wonders abound at the **Petrified Forest**, where towering redwoods were turned to stone by a volcanic eruption about three million years ago. You can read all about the fascinating event and the world's largest petrified trees at the museum in the gift shop (open daily; 4100 Petrified Forest Road, off Highway 128, 6 miles north of Calistoga; (707)942-6667).

For a splendid view of the entire valley, hike through the beautiful, rugged redwood canyons and oak-madrone woodlands in **Robert Louis Stevenson State Park** to the top of 4,343-foot **Mount St. Helena** (a rigorous 10-mile hike round-trip; carry water). The impoverished Stevenson and his wife, Fanny Osbourne, spent their honeymoon here in

Chill Out

When the sun is beating down, heating up the town, and you're too hot and bothered to tour another winery, jump into Indian Springs' huge, hot spring–fed swimming pool, California's oldest continuously operating pool and one of the best in the Wine Country. It costs $10 per adult and $7 per child on weekdays ($20 and $15 respectively on weekends), but that's not a bad price to pay for a day of R&R in one of Calistoga's most popular resorts. Located at 1712 Lincoln Avenue, near the Calistoga Gliderport, in Calistoga. Open daily; (707)942-4913.

an abandoned Silverado Mine bunkhouse in 1880, a site that inspired Stevenson's *Silverado Squatters*. The author was so taken by Mount St. Helena, the highest point in Napa County, that he used it as his model for Spyglass Hill in *Treasure Island*. The park is just off Highway 29, 8 miles north of Calistoga; (707)942-4575. If you'd rather get the bird's-eye view of the valley without exerting so much energy (and you're willing to bust your budget), climb aboard a glider plane at the **Calistoga Gliderport** for a stunning wine country tour (1546 Lincoln Avenue, Calistoga; (707)942-5000), or for the ultimate flight of fancy, whip out the credit card and go up, up, and away in a hot-air balloon at **Once in a Lifetime Hot-Air Balloon Company** (at the Calistoga Gliderport; (707)942-6541).

CHEAP SLEEPS

The Chablis Lodge
3360 Solano Avenue (off Highway 29), Napa, CA 94558 •
(800)443-3490 or (707)257-1944

Two reasonably priced inns sit side by side on Napa's Solano Avenue, and while both offer similar amenities, the Chablis Lodge edges out the Napa Valley Budget Inn (see below) by a notch or two. The 34-room Chablis looks a little older, but its rooms are larger and more comfortable (and a little more expensive). Each unit has a king- or queen-size bed, phone, TV, wet bar, and a small refrigerator; some have kitchenettes. The small heated swimming pool and spa—a godsend during the sweltering summer months—are surrounded by cement, but the potted flowers and baby-blue-and-white umbrellas add a little zip. Small dogs are welcome. Ask for a room facing away from Highway 29.

Napa Valley Budget Inn
3380 Solano Avenue (off Highway 29), Napa, CA 94558 • (707)257-6111

The runner-up to the Chablis Lodge offers just what it says—rooms at budget rates, about $10 to $15 cheaper per night than those at the Chablis. But you get what you pay for, and in this case the 58 cramped rooms don't provide much beyond the basics—queen-size bed, cable TV, a solitary chair, and a phone. The inn had a former life as a Motel 6, which accounts for the uninspired (i.e., cheap) architecture. The large heated swimming pool is clean but rather dreary looking, with its bare, fenced-in cement patio. Busy Highway 29 runs behind Solano Avenue, so request a room that doesn't get too much traffic noise. The inn does allow small pets.

El Bonita Motel

195 Main Street, St. Helena, CA 94574 •
(800)541-3284 or (707)963-3216

Thanks to an extensive remodeling, El Bonita is indeed *bonita*. Hand-painted grapevines grace many of the room entrances, and inside, the walls are colored a faint pink, with floor-length baby-blue drapes and pink-and-baby-blue floral bedspreads. Each of the 41 rooms has a private bath, color TV, and phone; for a little more money, you can have cable TV, microwave, refrigerator, and even a kitchen and a whirlpool bath. Huge oak trees surround the motel, a heated kidney-shaped swimming pool sits in front, and there's a sauna and an outdoor whirlpool on the premises (massages are available by appointment). The rates vary from month to month (depending on business), but in general, you (and your pet) can get a reasonably priced room Sunday through Thursday year-round. El Bonita fronts Highway 29, so try to get a room as far from the street as possible. St. Helena's shopping district is a short drive (or a 20-minute walk) away.

Hotel St. Helena

1309 Main Street (Highway 29), St. Helena, CA 94574 • (707)963-4388

Those who'd like to stay in the heart of charming St. Helena need look no further. Unfortunately, you may be able to afford only a winter week-day stay, since the rates are twice as much the rest of the year. But even if you don't book a room, take a peek at the amazing lobby, which looks like someone transported all the props from Disneyland's "It's A Small World After All" and deposited them here. Hundreds of elaborately dec-orated dolls and marionettes are draped over the furniture and hung from the ceiling. Fortunately, the excessive doll theme doesn't continue in the rooms, which are decorated in rich tones of burgundy, gold, and mauve, with polished antique furnishings (no smoking allowed). Most of the 18 units have private baths. If you look hard enough beyond the lobby's dollscape, you'll see a small coffee-wine-and-beer bar tucked in the back, where—with the wide-eyed plastic faces staring at you from all angles—you'll never drink alone.

White Sulphur Springs Resort & Spa

3100 White Sulphur Springs Road (off Spring Street), St. Helena, CA 94574 •
(800)772-8837 or (707)963-8588

This 330-acre resort is only a 3-mile winding drive from St. Helena's Main Street, but it's nestled in such a secluded canyon covered with hundreds of beautiful redwood, madrone, and fir trees that you'd swear you were 100 miles from anywhere. Founded in 1852, White Sulphur Springs is the oldest operating resort in California. The proprietors have

Clear Lake

Clear Lake, California's largest freshwater lake, once had more than 30 wineries ringing its shore, but Prohibition put an end to all that in 1919. The land was converted to walnut and Bartlett-pear orchards, and only in the last few decades have the grapes (and the wineries) been making a comeback. This area north of Napa County may one day become as celebrated as Napa and Sonoma, but unlike these trendy stepsisters to the south, there ain't nothin' nouveau about Clear Lake. Country music wafts from pickup trucks, bored (and bared) youths wander the roads (perhaps in search of their shirts), and there's generally not a lot going on until the weekend boaters and fishers arrive. Clear Lake's annual blowout is the Fourth of July festival, when thousands of born-again patriots amass (and timorous locals split) for a three-day, sunburnt orgy of flag-waving, fireworks, and waterskiing.

If you want to dive into the aquatic activities, boats of all shapes and sizes, as well as Jet Skis, Toobies, and Wave-Runners, can be rented at Mike's Watersports (6235 Old Highway 53, Clearlake; (707)994-6267) or from On the Waterfront (60 3rd Street, Lakeport; (707)263-6789). Clear Lake also draws crowds eager to snag some of its largemouth bass, catfish, perch, and crappie. Although the lake has earned the title of "Bass Capital of the West," there aren't any shops renting fishing equipment, so you'll have to tote your own. Or purchase gear at Coast to Coast

successfully maintained its rustic charm and beauty, offering a variety of lodgings—from large, fully equipped creekside cottages to little rooms with shared baths—that suit a world of budgets and tastes. The most affordable rooms are in the Carriage House (where you'll share bathrooms) and the Inn (which offers rooms with a half or full bath). Neither building has air conditioning, but the Carriage House has a kitchen and refrigerator available to resort guests who'd like to prepare their own meals. One of the resort's highlights is the series of hiking trails that wind alongside rippling creeks and waterfalls; another don't-miss attraction is the natural sulphur soaking pool, which maintains a temperature of 85 to 87 degrees year-round. There's also a Jacuzzi and a sauna, along with massages, volcanic mud wraps, and other pricey luxuries. A continental breakfast is included in the room rate, and if you stay here midweek, the rates are reduced by 20 percent. No smoking allowed.

Hardware (1205 S Main Street, Lakeport; (707)263-3050) or K-Mart (2019 S Main Street, Lakeport; (707)263-9305.

With its small, old-fashioned downtown, **Lakeport** is the prettiest town on Clear Lake. Formerly known as Forbestown (after early settler William Forbes), the area is usually very peaceful until people from outlying cities pack up their all-terrain vehicles and caravan out here in the summer for fishing, camping, swimming, waterskiing, and wine-tasting. Clear Lake State Park, on the southwest side of the lake, is one of the area's main draws, with its campground, miles of hiking trails, and beaches (on Soda Bay Road, south of Lakeport; (707)279-4293). Folks also flock to Lakeport every Labor Day weekend for the Lake County Fair, featuring 4-H exhibits, livestock auctions, horse shows, and a carnival (Lake County Fairgrounds, 401 Martin Street, Lakeport; (707)263-6181). Wine lovers stop at Kendall-Jackson Winery, one of the most popular wineries in Lake County, for a taste of the barrel-fermented chardonnay, Johannisberg riesling, sauvignon blanc, and cabernet sauvignon and a picnic in the gazebo (600 Matthews Road, off Highland Springs Road, Lakeport; (707)263-9333).

For more information on Clear Lake and its surrounding towns and wineries, call or drop by the Lake County Visitor Information Center (875 Lakeport Boulevard, Vista Point, Lakeport; (800)LAKESIDE or (707)263-9544).

Napa Valley Railway Inn

6503 Washington Street (at Yount Street), Yountville, CA 94599 •
(707)944-2000

Sitting on the original tracks of the Napa Valley Railroad are three turn-of-the-century cabooses and six railcars that have been converted into one-room suites with private entrances, skylights, and bay windows. The vintage slate-blue and brick-red railcars are actually more interesting on the outside, with some of their original fixtures intact and their "Southern Pacific Lines" and "Great Northern Railway" logos painted on the side. Inside, each car has dated but comfortable furnishings, including a queen-size brass bed, an armchair and love seat that look like '60s remnants, a pair of reading lights, and some tacky artwork (no phones or TVs). But these granny-style interiors probably help keep the rates down, and at least there are private baths and air conditioning. The Railway Inn is conveniently located in the center of tiny Yountville, with many of Napa Valley's most popular wineries and restaurants a short drive away. The inn's west side faces Highway 29, with a small strip of vineyards planted in between, and the opposite side overlooks a parking lot, which is partially shaded by eucalyptus trees and vines of star-jasmine. Rates vary depending on the season, but between November and May you usually can get a room for less than the rate sheet suggests.

Calistoga Inn
1250 Lincoln Avenue (next to the bridge), Calistoga, CA 94515 •
(707)942-4101

The Calistoga Inn is probably best known for the homemade brews it serves on its beautiful, flower-covered patio, but its 18 very reasonably priced rooms merit attention, too. Each has a double bed and pretty white-wicker, floral-print decor and furnishings. Nasturtiums overflow from window boxes, and some rooms overlook Calistoga's main street and the inn's towering trees. There are no phones or TVs, and all baths are shared. The inn is one of the few B&Bs in the Wine Country that doesn't have a two-night minimum on weekends during peak season, although hot summer nights are tough to tolerate here (there's no air conditioning, only fans). The simple grilled fare served on the outdoor patio (weather permitting) is better (and cheaper) than the food on the menu in the inn's handsome restaurant. There's a small beer and wine bar on the first floor.

Calistoga Village Inn & Spa
1880 Lincoln Avenue (north of the gliderport), Calistoga, CA 94515 •
(707)942-0991

Located at the northernmost end of the valley, the Calistoga Village Inn & Spa is a one-story, 41-room sprawling white inn trimmed in slate blue, with baskets of colorful begonias hanging out in front. The rooms are spare but comfortable and spacious, and include a private bath, air conditioning, a queen-size or double bed, and TV. The least expensive ones are in back, facing a parking lot and the rear of the Calistoga water-bottling plant. A natural mineral well supplies the hot water to the inn's swimming pool, wading pool, and the 12-person Jacuzzi, which is set under a handsome natural-wood and glass-block gazebo. The pools aren't always as sparkling-clean as others in the neighborhood, but they're still inviting. You can also get the full gamut of body treatments here—from mud baths to salt scrubs—although as elsewhere in the valley, most cost as much as a night in a cheap sleep.

Golden Haven Hot Springs

1713 Lake Street (off Grant Street at Arch Way), Calistoga, CA 94515 •
(707)942-6793

If only Golden Haven Hot Springs were as colorful as its name, perhaps it would be a more pleasant place to spend the night. This dreary-looking, gray hotel looks even drearier inside, but the prices are low year-round, and if you can't get a room elsewhere, it'll do. The least expensive rooms are carpeted with a mottled brown shag, navy spreads cover the queen-size beds, and when you open the gray plastic drapes, you'll get an eyeful of the oak tree–lined asphalt parking lot. At least there's a full, though aging, bathroom, a color TV, and air conditioning. An unimpressive nat-ural-mineral-water pool and Jacuzzi are housed in an adjacent barnlike metal structure. None of the 26 rooms are reserved for nonsmokers. There's a two-night minimum on weekends, a three-night minimum on holiday weekends, and children under 12 are not allowed on weekends or holidays. If you decide to indulge in one of Golden Haven's spa treat-ments, look for the discount coupons frequently featured in the free Wine Country magazines distributed throughout the valley.

Nance's Hot Springs

1614 Lincoln Avenue (next to the gliderport), Calistoga, CA 94515 •
(707)942-6211

Many Bay Area residents escape the hustle and bustle of city life by hiding out at Nance's, a reasonably priced, comfortable hotel just steps from Calistoga's shops and cafes. The color scheme leaves a bit to be desired (dark-green shag carpeting clashing with turquoise-and-navy bedspreads), but in a second-floor room, with a balcony overlooking the gliderport and tree-covered hills, such issues fade in importance. Each room has a kitchenette, a cushioned, chocolate-brown Naugahyde chair, air condi-tioning, cable TV (with HBO), and phone. What more do you need? Nance's even offers massages, mud baths, and blanket wraps, and all guests have access to the 102-degree indoor mineral pool.

NORTH COAST

Stinson Beach and Point Reyes National Seashore

Bodega Bay and Jenner

Mendocino and Fort Bragg

Eureka and Arcata

Stinson Beach and Point Reyes National Seashore

On those treasured weekends when the fog has lifted and the sun is warming the Northern California coast, bleary-eyed Bay Area residents grab their morning papers and beach chairs, pile into their Miatas and Jeep Cherokees, and scramble to the sands of Stinson Beach—the North Coast's answer to Malibu. Three-mile-long Stinson Beach may not have the warm, calm waters of its too-sexy-for-my-hat southern cousins, but when traffic along the two-lane coastal highway slows to a crawl, passengers have something truly beautiful to look at every inch of the way. Natural wonders abound at every hairpin turn, from the magnificent redwoods of Muir Woods (the tallest living organisms in the world) to the brilliant wildflowers carpeting the rolling hills.

If you're looking for a stellar strip of the coast where you can ditch the beer-guzzling surfer set and the Bart Simpson family scene, keep driving north to Point Reyes National Seashore, where miles of spectacular windswept beaches are practically deserted every day of the year. Point Reyes also offers thousands of acres of lush meadowlands, chaparral ridges, valleys, and forests, none of which have been defaced by a burger emporium, condo complex, or *used-car dealership. And because commercial excess has taken a backseat to land and animal preservation, Point Reyes is crisscrossed with the footprints of tule elk, deer, raccoons, and squirrels, and the playful sea lions, harbor seals, and gray whales still swim near the pristine shore.*

ON THE ROAD

Half the fun of going to Stinson Beach and its neighboring nature areas is the wild, wonderful drive getting there. Stinson Beach is located right off Highway 1 at the base of Mount Tamalpais in Marin County, and although it's only 10 miles from San Francisco as the crow flies, those without feathers must negotiate 20 miles of steep turns before they finally arrive. From the Bay Area, take the Stinson Beach/Highway 1 exit off Highway 101 just north of Sausalito, and follow Highway 1. As the road descends toward the shore, it forks; take the left fork, which is the continuation of Highway 1, leading to the beach. The fork to the right veers toward **Muir Woods National Monument,** a 560-acre fern-filled sanctuary of ancient redwoods dedicated to legendary conservationist John Muir. People flock to Muir Woods (many in tour buses) to walk the miles of well-marked trails—and spectacular trails they are. The 250-foot tall, 800-year-old trees (the Bay Area's only large, intact stand of old-growth redwoods) provide a solid canopy of shade for the ferns, wildflowers, Sonoma chipmunks, moles, bats, birds, black-tailed deer, and Pacific giant salamanders that live here (it's typically a cool, damp environment, so dress appropriately). Although the park can get absurdly crowded on summer weekends, you can usually circumvent the masses by hiking up the Ocean View Trail, returning via Fern Creek Trail. Admission to Muir Woods is free; picnicking is not allowed, but there's a snack bar at the entrance (open from 8am to sunset daily; on Muir Woods Road, off the Panoramic Highway via Highway 1; (415)388-2595).

Past Muir Woods, along Highway 1, is another tempting detour: a small, crescent-shaped cove called **Muir Beach**. Littered with bits of driftwood and numerous tide pools, Muir Beach is a more sedate alternative to the beer-n-bikini crowds at Stinson. If all you want is a sandy, pretty place for some R&R, park the car right here and skip Stinson altogether (but be aware that swimming isn't allowed at Muir Beach because of the strong rip currents). And should you build up a thirst for a cold mug of beer, the very British **Pelican Inn**, with its dart boards and dark

Aw, Shucks

Johnson's Oyster Farm, located in the heart of Point Reyes National Seashore, offers you the golden (if also odoriferous) opportunity to see briny bivalves being harvested. The farm doesn't look like much—a cluster of trailer homes, shacks, and oyster tanks surrounded by huge piles of shells—but that doesn't detract from the taste of right-from-the-water oysters dipped in Johnson's special sauce. Eat 'em on the spot or buy a bag for the road; either way, you're not likely to find California oysters as fresh or as cheap anywhere else. (Closed Monday. Off Sir Francis Drake Highway in Point Reyes National Seashore, about 6 miles west of Inverness; (415)669-1149.)

intimate pub, is just a short walk away (off Highway 1 at the entrance to Muir Beach; (415)383-6000).

A wickedly curvaceous, 6-mile drive to the north takes you to **Stinson Beach**, one of Northern California's most popular sun-and-surf spots. Although overrun with Bay Area refugees on summer weekends, the wide stretch of beige sand offers enough elbow room for everyone to spread out their beach blankets, picnic baskets, and toys. Swimming is permitted, but notices giving detailed instructions on how to escape a raging riptide tend to make folks think twice about venturing too far into the water (then again, so do the toe-numbing temperatures and the threat of sharks). The town of Stinson Beach, sustained purely by the influx of fun-loving beach bums, is only a few blocks long and can be toured entirely on foot in less than 30 minutes. A couple of recommended stops are **Stinson Beach Books**, which has a great selection of children's books and toys (3455 Highway 1, Stinson Beach; (415)868-0700), and the **Parkside Cafe**, Stinson's best (and coincidentally its cheapest) restaurant, which serves breakfast, lunch, and dinner and is perpetually packed; many customers opt to dine alfresco at the adjoining Parkside Snack Bar (43 Arenal Avenue, off Highway 1, Stinson Beach; (415)868-1272).

A short drive north of town on Highway 1 leads to **Bolinas Lagoon**, a placid expanse of salt water that serves as a refuge for numerous shorebirds and harbor seals. Nearby is the **Audubon Canyon Ranch's Bolinas Lagoon Preserve**, a 1,014-acre wildlife sanctuary that supports a major population of great blue herons and great egrets. This is the prime spot along the Pacific Coast to watch the immense, graceful seabirds as they court and mate and rear their young, all accomplished on the tops of towering redwoods. Admission is free, although donations are requested (open from mid-March to mid-July on Saturdays, Sundays, and holidays, 10am to 4pm, and by appointment for groups; 4900 Highway 1, Stinson Beach; (415)868-9244).

At the north end of the lagoon is the unmarked turnoff to the town of **Bolinas**, home to a handful of famous writers and '60s rock stars and the requisite number of former hippies. In an attempt to preserve their town's reclusive mystique, residents regularly take down any directional or identifying highway sign (an act that, ironically, has created more publicity for Bolinas than any sign ever would). Set in a forested knoll between the ocean and the lagoon, the artsy community has a thriving cultural scene, including numerous dance, music, and theatrical performances held at the **Bolinas Community Center** (14 Wharf Road, Bolinas; (415)868-2128). **Smiley's Schooner Saloon** is also a happening spot on weekends, when the live jazz, country, blues, or rock music kicks in (41 Wharf Road, Bolinas; (415)868-1311). For some great, inexpensive road snacks, stop by the **Bolinas Bay Bakery & Cafe**, renowned for its cinnamon buns made with organic flour, as well as croissants, breads, pizzas, and pasta salads (20 Wharf Road, Bolinas; (415)868-0211). Or load up on fresh, organically grown fruits and vegetables at the **Bolinas People's Store** (14 Wharf Road, Bolinas; (415)868-1433).

For those who are tired of driving and want to stretch their legs, three local side trips offer some adventurous exercise. The **Duxberry Reef Nature Reserve** is a rocky outcropping with numerous tide pools

If You Like to Bike

As most ardent Bay Area mountain bikers know, Point Reyes National Seashore has some of the finest mountain-biking trails in the region—narrow, winding dirt paths that lead through densely forested knolls, ending with spectacular Pacific vistas. What? Forgot to bring your $2,000 custom-built graphite Cannondale with GripShifters and Rock Shocks? No problem: for less than $25 a day, you can rent a quality mountain bike at Bear Valley Inn and Rental Shop in the town of Olema. Binoculars are also a popular rental item here, and you'll wish you had a pair when you reach the Sea Lion Overlook. (Closed Wednesday except by appointment; 88 Bear Valley Road in Olema, a block north of the Highway 1 and Sir Francis Drake Boulevard intersection; (415)663-1958.)

harboring a healthy population of starfish, sea anemones, snails, sea urchins, and other creatures. During low tide, you are allowed to admire and touch the marine life as long as you don't remove anything from its home (from downtown Bolinas, head north a few miles; then turn left on Mesa Road, left on Overlook Road, and right on Elm Road). About a mile up the coast is the **Point Reyes Bird Observatory**, established in 1964. Here ornithologists keep an eye on more than 400 species, and visitors may observe the banding of birds' legs (free admission; open daily 7am to 5pm; near the west end of Mesa Road, Point Reyes; (415)868-0655). At the very end of Mesa Road is the **Palomarin Trailhead**, the start of a popular hiking path that leads into the south entrance of Point Reyes National Seashore. The 6-mile round-trip trek—one of Point Reyes' prettiest—passes several small lakes and meadows before it reaches Alamere Falls, a freshwater cascade that rushes down a 40-foot bluff onto Wildcat Beach.

Ten miles north of Bolinas is the main entrance to **Point Reyes National Seashore**, a 71,000-acre playground of forested hills, deep-green pastures, and gorgeous windswept beaches. Before exploring, stop at the big, wooden-barn-style Bear Valley Visitors Center, which happens to sit alongside the **San Andreas Fault Zone** (on Bear Valley Road, off Highway 1; look for the small sign just north of the town of Olema; (415)663-1092). Grab a free Point Reyes trail map and a newsletter listing the several daily park events, and take a look at the center's exhibits, which include a seismograph. The Visitors Center is also the starting point for several spectacular hiking, mountain-biking, and equestrian trails. The popular, flat **Bear Valley Trail** (8.2 miles round trip) begins just a few steps away from the visitors center parking lot and winds through a lush creek canyon rimmed with ferns, flowers, and towering trees. The trail ends at Arch Rock, a natural arch in the seaside cliffs that visitors can walk through at low tide (but be careful not to get stranded on the other side during high tide).

Athletic sorts will want to test their stamina on the 308 stone steps leading down to the **Point Reyes Lighthouse**—one of the West Coast's few surviving lighthouses—where you can see (and hear) sea lions battling for basking space. When the fog burns off (a rare occurrence, unfortunately), the lighthouse and headlands provide a fantastic lookout point for spotting **gray whales** during their annual 5,000-mile round-trip migration from the Arctic Sea to their Baja California breeding grounds; they swim south from December through February and return north in March and April. Visitors have access to the lighthouse steps from 10am to 4:30pm Thursday through Monday (no fee), barring hazardous high winds or rain (for more information, call the lighthouse visitor center at (415)669-1534).

The 10-plus miles of pristine Point Reyes beaches include **Limantour Beach**, excellent for bird-watching and swimming (although the water is always chilly), and **Drake's Beach**, another good swimming spot, thanks to its protected cove (there's also a small cafe on shore). Be forewarned, however, that many Point Reyes beaches are unsafe for swimming due to pounding surf and treacherous riptides and undertows; consult the Bear Valley Visitors Center (see above) for a guide to the safest spots. Those who'd rather stroll than swim should not miss **Kehoe Beach** in spring, when a riotous display of violets, larkspur, California poppies, wild roses, fuchsias, and many other wildflowers blankets the terrain.

Besides incredible scenery, the area boasts some great low-priced restaurants. The **Gray Whale Inn** in downtown Inverness serves a wide array of soups, salads, sandwiches, pastas, pizzas, and gourmet coffee, with outdoor seating on the shaded patio next to Tomales Bay (12781 Sir Francis Drake Boulevard, Inverness; (415)669-1244). The **Bovine Bakery**, with its "udderly divine" sandwiches, pastries, and breads, is an ideal stop for picnic supplies (11315 Main Street/Highway 1, downtown Point Reyes Station; (415)663-9420). For a large selection of inexpensive Mexican-American standards, try **Taqueria La Quinta**; best bets are the tacos, burritos, and tostadas, which come with a choice of fillings (including vegetarian), or the weekend fresh-seafood specials (11285 Main Street/Highway 1, downtown Point Reyes Station; (415)663-8868). On sunny mornings, grab a seat on the **Station House Cafe**'s outside patio

Kayaking on Tomales Bay

If the best things in life are free, then the next-best things must be in the $30 range, which is about how much you'll need to rent a sea kayak from the friendly folks at Tomales Bay Kayaking. The kayaks are very stable and you won't have to contend with any waves on beautiful, placid Tomales Bay, a haven for migrating birds and marine mammals. Rental prices start at about $28 for a half-day ($40 for a double-hulled kayak), and guided day trips, sunset cruises, and romantic full-moon outings are also available. Instruction, clinics, and boat delivery are offered, and all ages and levels are welcome. The launching point is on Highway 1 at the Marshall Boatworks in Marshall, 8 miles north of Point Reyes Station. Open Friday through Sunday, 9:30am to 5:30pm, and by appointment. For more information, call (415)663-1743.

and order the heavenly apple-cinnamon pancakes and tart olallieberry muffins. Not the lowest prices in the area, but worth the splurge (11180 Main Street/Highway 1, downtown Point Reyes Station; (415)663-1515).

CHEAP SLEEPS

Green Gulch Farm Zen Center
1601 Highway 1, Sausalito, CA 94965 • (415)383-3134

When was the last time your bodhisattva spirit ("the spirit of kindness") had a vacation? Green Gulch Farm, a Soto Zen practice center hidden in a verdant valley off Highway 1 near Muir Beach (10 minutes west of the Muir Woods turnoff), offers fantastically priced "guest practice retreats" for those interested in learning the art of Zen meditation. Retreat participants are offered a minimum three-night stay (Sunday through Thursday only), and they're expected to attend *early*-morning meditations (i.e., 5am), and then go to work (usually in the farm's expansive organic gardens) until noon. After that, you're on your own to wander down to Muir Beach, hike through Muir Woods or on nearby trails, attend classes on Buddhism, or do whatever else your heart desires. Rates are an enlightening $30 per person per day ($50 for double occupancy), including, amazingly, three square meals *and* snacks. Nightly lodgings are also available without program participation, but they cost about twice as much.

Steep Ravine Environmental Cabins
Mount Tamalpais State Park • For reservations call Mistix: (800)444-7275

How much would you expect to pay for a night in a rustic, romantic redwood cabin just steps from a small, secluded beach? $200? $300? How about a paltry 30 bucks? Three Andrew Hamiltons buy you and your party a night at one of 10 bare-bones cabins that were once the private getaways of powerful Bay Area politicians and their cronies (they lost their long-term leases in a battle with the state). The cabins are now available to those who are lucky enough to snag a reservation (which are taken only up to eight weeks in advance) and who don't mind bringing their own sleeping bags and pads. Platform beds, running water, wood-burning stoves, and outhouses are provided, but there's no electricity and firewood costs an extra $4. Each cabin sleeps up to five (all for the same $30-a-night rate), but only one car per cabin is allowed. Cabins are located off Highway 1, a mile south of Stinson Beach; look for a paved turnout and a brown metal sign.

Stinson Beach Motel

3416 Highway 1 (PO Box 64), Stinson Beach, CA 94970 • (415)868-1712

A gravel walkway leads through a garden setting to six small rooms in this pleasant motel in the heart of downtown Stinson Beach. The rooms, all with private baths, are individually decorated with aging yet homey furnishings. Prices range from about $60 for a studio to less than $90 for a small apartment that sleeps up to four (a steal given the prime location). Try to reserve room 7, which is located apart from the rest and is therefore more private. And if you're tired of sunbathing at the beach, the motel's garden area offers a shady retreat.

Knob Hill

40 Knob Hill Road (PO Box 1108), Point Reyes Station, CA 94956 •
(415)663-1784

Janet Schlitt built her rustic-looking home in 1990 with an eye toward providing lodgers with a lovely, economical setting for a stay on the North Coast—complete with a dramatic view across the Point Reyes Mesa and Inverness Ridge. Schlitt offers a one-room cottage with queen-size bed and wood-burning stove (unfortunately priced too high for the budget-minded), but the small room adjoining the main house is certainly a bargain. Accessed by its own stairway and entrance, and complete with double bed, private bath, and a door leading to a tiny garden, this cheap sleep rents for $45 to $60 (depending on the season), in an area where such charming accommodations are difficult to find.

Point Reyes Hostel

Point Reyes National Seashore (PO Box 247), Point Reyes Station, CA
94956 • (415)663-8811

Formerly a working ranch house, this popular hostel off Limantour Road in the national seashore area has 45 dormitory-style bunks that are often filled with college students and foreign travelers (there's also a separate room that will accommodate a family). The location is idyllic—isolated deep inside the park and surrounded by numerous hiking trails, including a beautiful 2-mile walk to Limantour Beach. The two common rooms are each warmed by wood stoves, and there's a large, fully equipped kitchen, outdoor barbecue, and patio. If you don't mind sharing sleeping quarters with strangers, this is a $10-per-person deal that can't be beat (children under age 18 only $5 per night if accompanied by a parent). Reservations (and earplugs) are strongly recommended. Reception is open from 7:30am to 9:30am and 4:30pm to 9:30pm daily.

Motel Inverness

12718 Sir Francis Drake Boulevard (PO Box 292), Inverness, CA 94937 •
(415)669-1081

Yes, the rooms are a bit musty and the facade could use a facelift, but the Motel Inverness offers Tomales Bay–front accommodations at great rates. In fact, this is one of the few budget deals in the area—the place usually undercuts its competition by as much as 50 percent. Each of the seven small rooms has a color TV and private bath, and if you actually reach a point where you just can't take any more of nature's wonders, you can play pool or pinball in the huge rec room or lounge in front of the big-screen TV.

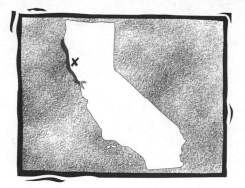

Bodega Bay and Jenner

Alfred Hitchcock probably wouldn't recognize Bodega Bay these days. When the filmmaker directed The Birds here, Bodega Bay was little more than a tiny, white-clapboard seacoast town. Today it's more of a vacation destination than a sleepy little fishing village. But although more than 30 years have passed since Hitchcock yelled "Action" in the streets of Bodega Bay and the neighboring town of Bodega, thousands of his fans still flock here every year to try to identify buildings and landscapes from his classic flick.

The true star attraction, however, has nothing to do with Hollywood—it's Mother Nature. Dramatic ocean vistas are punctuated by towering sea stacks, natural arches, teeming tide pools, and crescent-shaped coves. The birds are also a big crowd-pleaser—not Hitchcock's spooky movie versions, but wild great blue herons, snowy egrets, brown pelicans, and other fine-feathered friends. Strolling the beach, picnicking, hiking, fishing, clam-digging, and whale-watching are favorite local pastimes—and virtually free. Unfortunately, inexpensive accommodations are extremely limited, except for the sleeping bag and tent variety, and even campsites get booked up far in advance during peak season (although some are available first-come, *first-served). If you can't find a place to sleep, don't despair—just head farther north.*

A short drive north of Bodega Bay is the tiny, charming town of Jenner, where the Russian River spills into the sea. Jenner marks the beginning of the most beautiful, cliff-hugging stretch of coastal Highway 1. A few campgrounds dot the beaches and forests on either side of this narrow, scenic road, and a three-hour drive north leads to Mendocino and Fort Bragg, an area much richer in budget accommodations and cafes (see the Mendocino and Fort Bragg chapter). But if sunset is near and the fog is rolling in, don't risk the dizzying hairpin turns just to find a bed; instead, go east from Jenner into the nearby Russian River Valley.

ON THE ROAD

No matter what direction you're coming from, getting to Bodega Bay is a rather long haul, because there are no fast, direct routes. From the San Francisco area, the easiest way is via **Petaluma**. From Highway 101, take the Bodega Bay/Central Petaluma exit and turn left toward the town. After a straight shot though the center of Petaluma, you'll spend about 45 minutes driving through a countryside of rolling emerald-green hills dotted with grazing sheep and whitewashed farmhouses. Eventually the deep-blue Pacific will appear on the horizon.

Just before you reach the ocean, take a quick detour through the town of **Bodega** (not to be confused with the town of Bodega Bay a few miles farther on). On Bodega Road is the hauntingly familiar schoolhouse immortalized in Hitchcock's *The Birds* (it's now a bed and breakfast). The two or three boutiques in Bodega entice a few visitors to park and browse, but most seem content with a little rubbernecking and finger-pointing as they snake through town.

Rolling into Bodega Bay, keep an eye out for the local Chamber of Commerce in the center of town (850 Highway 1, Bodega Bay; (707) 875-3422). Load up on free maps, camping information, guides, and brochures, including the "Bodega Bay Area Map & Guide," which pinpoints all the town's attractions.

Next, take the short drive to the sea at Bodega Head, the small peninsula that shelters the bay (from Highway 1, turn west on Eastshore

Bodega Bay and Jenner

97

Road, then right at the stop sign onto Bay Flat Road and follow it to the end). This is one of the premier whale-watching points along the California coast; the annual migrations of the humpback and California gray run from December through April. Two superb walking trails begin here, too. From the park's west parking lot, a 4-mile round-trip trail leads past the Bodega Marine Preserve and ends at the sand dunes of **Salmon Creek Beach**. An easier, 1½-mile round-trip walk begins in the east parking lot and encircles Bodega Head, branching off for an optional side trip to the tip of the point for a spectacular 360-degree view.

In the afternoon, be sure to spend some time at the docks watching the fishing boats returning and unloading their catches. **Tides Wharf** (835 Highway 1, Bodega Bay; (707)875-3652) has the most active dock scene, including a viewing room near the processing plant that lets you witness the fish's ultimate fate—a swift and merciless gutting by deft hands, followed by a quick burial in ice. Just outside, sea lions linger by the dock hoping for a handout.

Linking Bodega Bay and nearby Jenner are the **Sonoma Coast State Beaches**, 16 miles of pristine sand-and-gravel beaches, tide pools, rocky bluffs, and hiking trails. A few campgrounds are located nearby; call the Salmon Creek Ranger Station, (707)875-3483, for more information, and Mistix, (800)444-7275, for reservations. The southernmost beach is tranquil **Doran Park Beach**, just south of Bodega Bay. This is also one of the safest spots for kids—when the water's rough everywhere else, Doran is still calm enough for swimming, clamming, and crabbing. Bird-watchers should stake out the Doran mud flats, a favorite haunt of egrets, big-billed pelicans, and other seabirds, while tide-pool trekkers ought to

Dig 'n' Dine

How often do you have a legitimate, legal excuse to get down and dirty on a public beach? Well, as long as you're on the hunt for a sack of fresh clams, you can do it year-round at Bodega Bay. The only skill required is digging, the only equipment a shovel and a sturdy bag. The rest is childishly straightforward: find a good spot (hint: try the western side of the bay); wait for low tide; search the sand closest to the water for a small, bubbling siphon hole; then dig like heck with whatever's handy (a narrow clammer's shovel works best). What you'll discover is a long "neck" leading to a horseneck clam, the most abundant bivalve in Bodega Bay. A fishing license is required for anyone over 16 (one-day licenses are available at most sporting-goods stores and bait shops).

Fishy-Suave

If you're the kind of person who spends a weekend fishing only to return home with an empty ice chest and a bad cold, well, here's your chance to catch a mess of big, beautiful rock cod, ling cod, salmon, halibut, or albacore. It's this simple: (1) Get on a fishing boat in Bodega Bay; (2) grab a pre-rigged fishing pole; (3) lower your line in the water when everyone else does; and (4) reel in the fish. All the rest, from taking the fish off the hook to cleaning it, is handled by the friendly deckhands. Then you get to take your haul home and indulge in a feeding frenzy of your own.

On the fish-and-crab combination trips (even more fun than the straight fishing jaunts), you get to keep not only your finned catch but also a few of the enormous Dungeness crabs caught in traps set out the previous day. Both the fishing and fish-crab-combo trips cost approximately $45 to $55 per person (rod-and-reel rental is an additional $7.50), and almost everyone takes home a sack so full of seafood it's nearly too heavy to lift off the boat. For information and reservations, call Bodega Bay Sportfishing Center at (707)875-3344.

visit the north end of **Salmon Creek Beach** (off Bean Avenue, 2 miles north of town), or **Shell Beach**, a small low-tide treasure trove (10 miles north of Bodega Bay, near Jenner).

Dining on a budget in Bodega Bay is mostly reserved for the birds, but it *is* possible to get some inexpensive meals. Top choice is a $5 pint of crab cioppino at the **Lucas Wharf Deli**, located next to the Lucas Wharf Restaurant (595 Highway 1, Bodega Bay; (707)875-3562). It's a wonderfully messy affair, best sopped up with a side of sourdough bread. Second choice is the fresh fish 'n' chips or fish chowder at the **Tides Snack Bar** (835 Highway 1, Bodega Bay; (707)875-3652). Ambience is limited to a row of noisy arcade games, but you can always take your meal onto the dock. Definitely more upscale is the small **Breakers Cafe**, where numerous plants thrive in the sunny dining room (in the Pelican Plaza, 1400 Highway 1, Bodega Bay; (707)875-2513). For breakfast, try the baked polenta with black-bean chili and salsa or the yummy Belgian waffles topped with hot spiced peaches and whipped cream. The cafe's lunch and dinner seafood entrees are budget busters, but the sandwiches, burgers, and house-made soups are within the $5 to $10 range. (By the way, the costlier seafood restaurants in town are not only overpriced, they're overrated—so you're not missing much by sticking to the cheap eats.)

About 16 miles north of Bodega Bay on Highway 1 is **Jenner**, a hamlet built on a bluff rising from the mouth of the Russian River. It's a small jewel of a town, comprised of little more than a gas station, three restaurants, two inns, and a deli, but Jenner is (ironically) well known as Northern California's "secret" spot for getting away from the masses. One of the local highlights is beautiful **Goat Rock Beach**, which is also a breeding ground for harbor seals. "Pupping season" begins in March and lasts till June, and orange-vested volunteers are usually on hand to protect the seals (which give birth on land) from dogs and overzealous tourists. They'll also answer questions about the playful animals and even lend binoculars for a closer look.

A good lunch stop is at the **Sizzling Tandoor**, an Indian restaurant perched high above the placid **Russian River**. The view, particularly from the outside patio, is fantastic, as are the inexpensive lunch specials— huge portions of curries and kabobs served with vegetables, soup, *pulao* rice, and great *naan* bread. Even if you don't have time for a meal, drop by and order some warm *naan* to go (9960 Highway 1, just south of the bridge, Jenner; (707)865-0625).

From Jenner, follow Highway 1 north for a winding, spectacular 12-mile stretch to **Fort Ross State Historic Park**, a beautifully restored redwood fort built by Russian fur traders in 1812 and partially destroyed by the great 1906 earthquake (19005 Highway 1, Jenner; (707)847-3286). About 3 to 4 miles north of the fort on Highway 1 are **Timber Cove**, one of photographer Ansel Adams's favorite places, and the 3,500-acre **Salt Point State Park**, (707)847-3221, which offers 139 camping sites in the redwoods and numerous day-hike trails that zigzag through coastal woodlands, wildflower-filled meadows, and rocky beaches. Within the state park lies the 317-acre **Kruse Rhododendron**

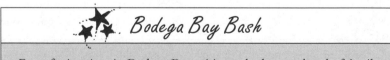

Bodega Bay Bash

For a festive time in Bodega Bay, visit on the last weekend of April, when as many as 25,000 partiers let loose at the Fisherman's Festival, a two-day orgy of lamb and oyster barbecues, Sonoma County wine tastings, craft fairs, pony rides, bathtub races, parades, kite-flying contests, live music, and dancing. The festival highlight is the Blessing of the Fleet, a colorful, jubilant boat parade where clergymen stand on a vessel and bless the fishing fleet as it floats by. For more information, call the Bodega Bay Chamber of Commerce at (707)875-3422.

Something to Spout About

Sure, spotting gray whales from shore is exciting, but nothing compares to getting within *listening* distance of a 40-ton cetacean— so close you can actually hear the blast from the blowhole. Fishing charters offer whale-watching trips from late December through April, typically charging about $15 to $25 per person (it pays to shop around) to take you as close to the whales as legally permitted. Excursions last about three hours (seemingly forever if you get seasick). While nobody can guarantee you'll see or hear a whale, most people get at least a glimpse of these majestic mammals, and the boat trip alone, with its view of the shore from a whale's perspective, is worth the price. Several companies offer morning and afternoon trips departing daily from Bodega Bay. Captain George's 55-foot *Challenger* is a favorite; for reservations and information, call the captain at (707)875-2474.

Preserve, an uncultivated native garden bursting with shocking-pink and purple flowers that grow up to 30 feet tall in the shade of a vast redwood canopy; the peak blooming period varies yearly, but April is usually the best time to see them.

CHEAP SLEEPS

Bodega Harbor Inn
1345 Bodega Avenue, Bodega Bay, CA 94923 • (707)875-3594

A homey old-timer in a town of mostly modern motels, the Bodega Harbor Inn consists of seven clapboard buildings (with a total of 14 guest rooms) set on a large lawn overlooking the harbor. The small, tidy rooms have private baths, cable TV, double beds, and access to a private yard where you can kick back in the lawn chairs. Rates are often at the very top of *Cheap Sleeps'* price range, but they're the best deal in town. If you're willing to shell out a bit more, ask for room 12 or 14 and you'll get a partial ocean view and a small deck. The inn, located off Highway 1 at the north end of Bodega Bay, also rents seven houses and cottages, some located on the property, others scattered throughout the town.

Lazy River Motel

10624 Highway 1, Jenner, CA 95450 • no phone

The Lazy River would be quite a find for the budget traveler if it weren't for the rather vexing aroma inside the rooms—something akin to overly ripe fruit—and the fact that you can't make a reservation (there's no phone, so it's first come, first served). Perched above the Russian River's estuary just south of Jenner, the two weathered buildings house a total of five small guest rooms replete with dark-wood paneling and aging furnishings. Each room has a private bath, and the best ones have a small deck overlooking the estuary—which almost makes up for the funny smell. Not for everyone, but it's the *only* cheap sleep in Jenner.

Mendocino and Fort Bragg

The village of Mendocino has managed to retain more of its gracious, small-town allure than most picturesque coastal getaway spots. Founded in 1852, this classic New England–style fishing village, complete with a white-spired church, is still home to a few fishers and loggers, but writers, artists, therapists, and other urban transplants now outnumber the natives. Springtime is Mendocino's best season, when the streets aren't flooded with tourists and the climbing tea roses and wisteria are in full bloom. The village is so compact you can abandon your car and tour it on foot, visiting the quaint rows of shops that form the heart of Mendocino.

Fort Bragg, Mendocino's working-class cousin 10 miles to the north, was built in 1855 as a military outpost supervising the Pomo Indian Reservation. Now it's primarily a logging and fishing town (as well as the largest city along the Mendocino coast), although gentrification is slowly creeping in with the relentless rise of the tourist trade. If it weren't for Fort Bragg, however, the budget traveler would be hard pressed to find an affordable hotel room within 50 miles. Most cost-conscious vacationers browse the boutiques and galleries of pretty-yet-pricey Mendocino by day, then dine and recline in inexpensive Fort Bragg by night.

ON THE ROAD

Like many towns hugging the Northern California coast, Mendocino's premier attractions are provided gratis (or nearly so) by Mother Nature and the Department of Parks and Recreation. **Mendocino Headlands State Park**, the grassy stretch of land between Mendocino village and the ocean, is one of the town's most popular attractions. The park's flat, 3-mile-long trail winds along the edge of a heather-covered bluff, providing spectacular sunset views and good lookout points for seabirds and California gray whales. A few miles south of Mendocino off Highway 1 is **Van Damme State Park**, (707)937-5804, a 2,072-acre preserve blanketed with ferns and second-growth redwoods. The park has a small beach, a museum, and a campground, but its main attraction is the 15 miles of spectacularly lush trails—ideal for a stroll or a jog—that start at the beach and wind through the tree-covered hills. **Fern Canyon Trail** is the park's best, an easy, incredibly scenic, 2½-mile hiking and bicycling path that crosses over the Little River. You may also hike or drive (most of the way) to Van Damme's peculiar **Pygmy Forest**, an eerie scrub forest of waist-high stunted trees that grew on a limestone deposit (by car, follow Highway 1 south of the park and turn up Little River Airport Road, then head uphill for about 3½ miles).

On the opposite side of Mendocino, about 2 miles north of town off Highway 1, lies the often-photographed, 1,500-acre **Russian Gulch State Park**, (707)937-5804, a paradise for sunbathers, fishers, bird-watchers, and snorkelers. Pick up a trail map at the park's entrance, then walk down the path to **Devil's Punch Bowl**—a 200-foot-long tunnel carved by the sea, with an immense blowhole that's particularly spectacular during a storm. For another good hike (or bike ride), follow the Falls Loop Trail to the Russian Gulch Falls. Farther north on Highway 1, 1½ miles north of the town of Caspar, is **Jug Handle State Reserve's Ecological Staircase Trail**, (707)937-5804. Hike up the series of

Hurray for Mendo-wood

If the house on the corner of Little Lake and Ford Streets in Mendocino looks familiar, perhaps that's because it's the set for the hit TV show "Murder, She Wrote," starring Angela Lansbury. Mendocino's Cape Cod–style architecture and beautiful landscapes have made it to the big screen, too. Did you recognize them in *East of Eden, Summer of '42, Same Time Next Year*, and *Forever Young*?

naturally formed, steplike bluffs—each one about 100 feet higher and 100,000 years older than the one below—and observe how the trees and soil differ dramatically on each "ecological step."

The top beachcombing spot in the area is at **MacKerricher State Park**, (707)937-5804, 3 miles north of Fort Bragg off Highway 1. Here you'll find an 8-mile stretch of sandy beaches speckled with tide pools, as well as numerous sand dunes, miles of hiking trails, and even an underwater park for divers. Within the state park is **Laguna Point**, one of the region's best spots for viewing harbor seals and gray whales.

If you have a passion for plants and pretty scenery, spend a few dollars to take the self-guided tour of the **Mendocino Coast Botanical Gardens**. The nonprofit gardens feature 47 acres of native plants—from azaleas and rhododendrons to dwarf conifers and ferns—as well as a picnic area and a restaurant. You can even purchase some of your favorite flower and plant species at the nursery (18220 Highway 1, 2 miles south of Fort Bragg; (707)964-4352).

Outdoor enthusiasts willing to dole out money for adventure will find plenty of recreation in the Mendocino/Fort Bragg region. **Ricochet Ridge Ranch** offers guided horseback rides (English- and Western-style) along the beach and in the redwoods (24201 Highway 1, Fort Bragg; (707)964-PONY). At **Lost Coast Adventures** you can rent an ocean kayak to explore the shoreline, coastal rivers, or—along with a guide—nearby sea caves (19275 S Harbor Drive, Fort Bragg; (800)961-1143 or (707)961-1143). **North Coast Divers Supply** offers half-day scuba-diving trips that depart from Noyo Harbor in Fort Bragg, anchoring at nearby offshore reefs. And if you want to free-dive for abalone during an open season (typically April through June and August through November), Divers Supply will provide all the equipment, including wet suits (19275 S Harbor Drive, Fort Bragg; (707)961-1143). To rent mountain bikes for exploring nearby Van Damme and Russian Gulch State Parks, or to rent a kayak, canoe, or outrigger for a leisurely paddle up the Big River, go to **Catch A Canoe & Bicycles, Too!** (at Highway 1 and Comptche-Ukiah Road, a half-mile south of Mendocino; (707)937-0273).

Between December and April, the migrating California gray whale and humpback whale make their annual appearances along the North Coast. Although they're visible from the bluffs, you can meet the 40-ton cetaceans face-to-face by boarding one of the whale-watching boats in Fort Bragg; the *Tally Ho II* **charter** offers two-hour tours for about $20 (in the Old Fish House, N Harbor Drive, Fort Bragg; (707)964-2079). Another great way to get out on the ocean is to book a trip on one of the numerous fishing charters that depart from Fort Bragg's Noyo Harbor. For approximately $55 per person, which includes rod, bait, and a

Shopping Strategies

You can spend more time shopping and less time walking if you pick up a free copy of the handy "Guide to Shops & Galleries, Restaurants & Lodgings." The guide provides a map and a brief description of most stores in the area; the Mendocino edition is available at the Ford House Visitor Center at 735 Main Street (next to the public restrooms) in Mendocino; (707)937-5397. For the Fort Bragg edition, go to the Fort Bragg–Mendocino Coast Chamber of Commerce at 332 N Main Street in Fort Bragg; (800)726-2780 or (707)961-6300.

one-day fishing license, **Anchor Charter Boats** will take you on a five-hour salmon or bottom-fishing trip. Equipment, instruction, and fish-cleaning services are provided; (707)964-4550.

You can give your tired dogs a break from beating up and down those coastal trails by booking passage aboard Fort Bragg's popular **Skunk Train** (so named because the odoriferous mix of diesel and gasoline once used to fuel the train allowed you to smell it before you could see it roaring down the tracks). Depending on which day you depart, a steam, diesel, or electric-engine train will take you on a scenic six- to seven-hour round-trip journey through the stupendous redwoods to the city of **Willits** and back again (or you can take the four-hour round-trip excursion to Northspur). Reservations are recommended, especially in summer (100 Laurel Street Depot, Fort Bragg; (707)964-6371).

The North Coast has never been famous for golf or tennis, but if you get the urge to smack a ball across the range or over the net, head for the **Little River Inn Golf and Tennis Club**. Located a few miles south of Mendocino on Highway 1, the club has a regulation nine-hole course, driving range, lighted tennis courts, and a pro shop that are open to the public (7750 Highway 1, Little River; (707)937-5667).

Recreational shoppers should whip out their Gold Cards and head straight for **Mendocino**. The majority of its stores and boutiques are sandwiched between a 4-block stretch of Ukiah and Main Streets. The village is well-known for its classy jewelry shops and stylish clothing boutiques; a few others that shouldn't be missed are **Mendocino Jams & Preserves** (440 Main Street at Woodward Street, Mendocino; (707)937-1037), a town landmark that offers free tastings of marmalades, dessert toppings, mustards, chutneys, and other spreads; the **Gallery Bookshop** (Main Street at Kasten Street, Mendocino; (707)937-2665), which has wonderful selections for kids, cooks, and local-history buffs; and **Good Taste** (Little Lake Street at Lansing Street, Mendocino; (707) 937-0104), a gourmet cheese-and-wine store geared toward picnickers with urban tastes.

Mendocino also has two museums with changing exhibitions that are worth a brief visit: the **Ford House**, one of the area's oldest homes (735 Main Street, between Kasten and Lansing Streets, Mendocino; (707)937-5397), and the **Kelly House** (45007 Albion Street at Lansing Street, Mendocino; (707)937-5791). The highly regarded, nonprofit **Mendocino Art Center**, where scenes for the James Dean flick *East of Eden* were filmed, offers art classes, poetry readings, storytelling sessions, and occasional concerts (45200 Little Lake Street, between Williams and Kasten Streets, Mendocino; (707)937-5818).

After you've explored the village and headlands, walk down to the east end of Ukiah Street and treat your tired body to one of **Sweetwater Garden**'s private or group hot tubs and saunas. Or for some true TLC, blow your budget on a soothing Swedish massage (955 Ukiah Street, Mendocino; (800)300-4140 or (707)937-4140).

And if you've browsed all over Mendocino and still have the shopping bug, head to downtown **Fort Bragg**, which has enough shops and galleries—all within walking distance of one another—to keep you entertained for hours. Another good place for a spree is the **Fort Bragg Depot**, a 14,000-square-foot marketplace with more than 20 shops and restaurants, as well as a historical logging and railroad museum (401 Main Street at Laurel Street, Fort Bragg; (707)964-6261).

Mendocino lodgings may be unaffordable for most budget travelers, but the same is not always true of the dining. The **Mendocino Cafe**, one of the last vestiges of the Mendocino of the '60s, serves a tasty Thai burrito that's a meal in itself: a steamed flour tortilla filled with brown rice, sautéed vegetables, a choice of smoked chicken, pork, or beef, and a healthy dash of the cafe's fresh chile sauce (10451 Lansing Street, next to the firehouse, Mendocino; (707)937-2422). Just up the street, the **Mendocino Bakery & Cafe** has a healthy selection of salads and pasta dishes at bargain prices (10485 Lansing Street, across the street from Savings Bank, Mendocino; (707)937-0836). Also cheap and filling are the scrumptious beef, chicken, fish, turkey, and veggie burgers served with a side of fresh-cut fries at **Mendo Burgers**, on the back patio of the Mendocino Bakery & Cafe (10483 Lansing Street, Mendocino; (707)937-1111).

The place to splurge on a gourmet meal is the nationally renowned **Café Beaujolais**, which serves a fantastic brunch between 9am and 2:30pm on Saturday and Sunday (reservations strongly recommended). Owner/chef Margaret Fox is the talent behind the buttermilk and

Lettuce Rejoice

Long before "pesticide-free" became the mantra of California growers, organic gardening was the modus operandi of Mendocino-area farmers. For years, they've catered to such health- and quality-conscious clients as the famous chefs of Mendocino's Café Beaujolais; although the produce is pricey, you'll pay less for it if you forgo the stores and buy direct from the growers. From May through October, they sell their luscious strawberries, asparagus, melons, and other goodies to the public at the Mendocino Farmers Market on Fridays, from noon to 2pm (Howard Street, between Main and Ukiah Streets), and at the Fort Bragg Farmers Market on Wednesdays from 3:30pm to 5:30pm (Laurel Street, between Franklin and McPherson Streets).

cornmeal waffles, the smoked-salmon-and-cream-cheese omelets, and the pecan-berry pancakes—among other to-die-for dishes—that have helped make her little restaurant famous (961 Ukiah Street, Mendocino; (707) 937-5614).

Fort Bragg also has its share of commendable cheap eats. A couple of good lunch spots are **Schat's Fort Bragg Bakery and Cafe**, where the locals snatch up Schat's signature Sheepherder's Bread (360 N Franklin Street at Laurel Street, Fort Bragg; (707)964-1929); and the **Laurel Deli**, famous for its house-made pies (136 E Laurel Street at McPherson Street, Fort Bragg; (707)964-7812). For lunch or dinner, try **Viraporn's Thai Cafe**, one of Fort Bragg's best restaurants. Viraporn Lobell, a native of Thailand and a former Café Beaujolais chef, has mastered the art of balancing the five traditional Thai flavors (hot, bitter, tart, sweet, and salty) to create wonderful (and wonderfully inexpensive) classics, including satays, shrimp-and-beef salads, and a wide range of curry dishes (500 S Main Street, across from PayLess, Fort Bragg; (707)964-7931). **D'Aurelio & Sons** dishes out classic, old-fashioned pizza for dinner, and the antipasto salad, bulging with fresh vegetables, mozzarella, and feta cheese, serves as a good dinner salad for a party of four (438 S Franklin Street, in the Franklin Street shopping center, behind PayLess, Fort Bragg; (707)964-4227).

After dinner, why not top off the evening with a little nightcap and music in Mendocino? Classical tunes and warm snifters of brandy grace an evening at the elegant bar and lounge in the **Mendocino Hotel and Restaurant** (45080 Main Street, Mendocino; (707)937-0511). When blue jeans and baseball caps are your preference, hang out next door at **Dick's**

Place, which has the cheapest drinks in town and the sort of dark, spit-and-sawdust atmosphere you'd expect from this former logging town's oldest bar (45080 Main Street, Mendocino; (707)937-5643). For a rowdy night of dancing and drinking, head a few miles up the highway to the **Caspar Inn**, where everything from rock and jazz to rhythm and blues is played live every night (open Thursday through Sunday only, Caspar Road, Caspar; (707)964-5565). At the **North Coast Brewing Company**, Fort Bragg's beer connoisseurs gather nightly to savor a pint of their local pride and joy: Scrimshaw Pilsner, a gold-medal winner at the Great American Beer Fest, the Super Bowl of beer tastings (455 N Main Street, just south of the Grey Whale Inn, Fort Bragg; (707)964-BREW).

CHEAP SLEEPS

Fools Rush Inn
7533 Highway 1 (PO Box 387), Little River, CA 95456 • (707)937-5339

There's much more to the Fools Rush Inn than a cute name. This place wins the prize for being the best all-around lodging deal in the Mendocino/Fort Bragg region. Imagine this: Your own private cottage perched high above the Pacific in a secluded grove of redwood, pine, and cypress trees. Through one window you see the distant ocean glimmering, through the other a dense, inviting forest. As the wood-burning fireplace roars to life, you make a pot of coffee in the kitchen, contemplating your options for the day. Will it be a hike along the fern trails of nearby Van Damme State Park, golfing at the adjacent nine-hole course, relaxing at the beach, or making the 2-mile drive into Mendocino to do a little shopping? Yep, life is rough. . . .

Jug Handle Creek Farm
Highway 1, south of Jug Handle Beach (PO Box 17), Caspar, CA 95420 •
(707)964-4630

If you brought along your sleeping bag, you can rent some floor space and a foam mat for $15 to $18 per night at this beautiful century-old farmhouse in Caspar, a tiny town hidden off Highway 1 between Mendocino and Fort Bragg. The farmhouse offers only 20 sleeping spaces, so reservations are recommended; you also may pitch a tent on the 39-acre property or, if you're lucky enough to get a vacancy, rent one of the farm's two small cabins for a reasonable rate. Guests are expected to do one hour of chores for each night they stay—or, instead, pay an additional $5 a night. The basic nightly rate also includes cooking privileges in the huge kitchen—another way to cut costs on meals.

Coast Motel
18661 Highway 1, Fort Bragg, CA 95437 • (707)964-2852

Even if there aren't any cheap sleeps in Mendocino, Fort Bragg's Coast Motel is only 6 miles away. Located off Highway 1 at the southernmost end of town, this 28-room motel has all the standard amenities—color TV, private bath, double bed, desk—plus a few extra perks, such as a heated pool, four acres of woods that children enjoy exploring, and—hold on to your tackle box—a fish-cleaning facility. Many rooms have refrigerators; three have kitchenettes. The motel isn't within walking distance of any restaurants or shops, but it offers more seclusion and serenity than the motels along Fort Bragg's Main Street. And for an extra $5, you can bring your pooch.

Columbi Motel
647 Oak Street, Fort Bragg, CA 95437 • (707)964-5773

Without a doubt, the Columbi is one of the least expensive motels on the North Coast. Yet ironically, this 21-room motel has more amenities than any other in Fort Bragg. Most of the rooms come with cable TV, double or queen-size bed, private bathroom, full-size fridge, stove, sink, small desk, and your own carport. If you're traveling with the family or a large group, reserve one of the two-bedroom units or suites that sleep up to six. The motel is located 5 blocks from Main Street in a quiet residential neighborhood, and it's within steps of a laundry, a taqueria, and the Columbi Market, which is where the motel's guests check in and out.

Fort Bragg Motel
763 N Main Street, Fort Bragg, CA 95437 •
(800)253-9972 or (707)964-4787

The 48-room Fort Bragg Motel is only a 3-block stroll from Glass Beach, and within staggering distance of the North Coast Brewing Company.

Comfort Camping

Like to camp along the coast, but hate the hassle of pitching tents and picking grains of sand out of your food? Here's the solution: Call North Coast Trailer Rentals at (619)648-7509 and ask them to set up one of their self-contained, fully equipped trailers for you and your friends. You select the seaside campground (it must be in the Fort Bragg/Mendocino area); they take care of the rest. There's a three-night minimum, and prices start at about $65 a night—a real deal for beachfront property.

While it earns zero points for character, it scores a perfect 10 for cleanliness. Each of the "soundproof" rooms is equipped with a queen-size bed, lamp, chair, phone, television, and bathroom—all the creature comforts of home.

Ocean Breeze Lodge

212 S Main Street, Fort Bragg, CA 95437 • (707)961-1177

Husband-and-wife owners Linda and Tino Tarantino work hard to keep their gleaming peach-colored lodge in pristine shape. The eight-room Ocean Breeze is located on the main strip of downtown Fort Bragg, so it's plagued by the steady drone of traffic, but if a large, comfy bed, spotless bathroom, TV, and reasonable room rate is enough to keep you content for a night or two, then you won't be disappointed. Linda pours complimentary coffee for guests each morning and is happy to offer sightseeing suggestions.

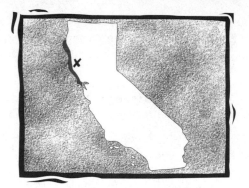

Eureka and Arcata

One can only wonder what city officials in the early 19th century were thinking when they named this town after the popular gold-mining expression "Eureka!" (Greek for "I have found it"). They certainly never found any gold in these parts. Perhaps the Eureka of yesteryear offered more to get excited about, but today the North Coast's largest city has little for the visitor except a slew of cheap (and mostly dingy) motels, fast-food restaurants, gas stations, and a somewhat entertaining Old Town dignified by stately Victorian buildings. Most travelers take advantage of Eureka's budget prices and bunk down here for the night, then head north to Arcata and the Lost Coast for more stimulating explorations.

Arcata is home to Humboldt State University (the northern-most college of the California State University system), and as with most college towns, everyone tends to lean toward the left. Environmentalism, artistry, and good beads and bagels are indispensable elements of the Arcatian philosophy—as is a cordial disposition toward tourists, making this one of the more interesting and visitor-friendly towns along the North Coast.

The heart of Eureka (and the only place worth visiting) is **Old Town**, a 13-block-long stretch of shops, restaurants, and hotels, most of which are housed in painstakingly preserved Victorian structures (a favored architectural style in these parts). Bordered by 1st and 3rd Streets, between C and M Streets, the neighborhood takes only about an hour or two to ramble through, although bookworms might get sidetracked at the **Booklegger,** a marvelous store with thousands of used paperbacks (especially mysteries, westerns, and science fiction), as well as children's books and cookbooks (402 2nd Street, Eureka; (707)445-1344). For a look at one of the country's finest examples of Victorian architecture, visit the multi-gabled-and-turreted **Carson Mansion**, built of redwood in 1886 for lumber baron William Carson, who initiated the construction to keep mill workers occupied during a lull in the lumber business. Although the three-story, money-green mansion is closed to the public (it's now a snooty men's club), you can stand on the sidewalk and click your Kodak at one of the state's most-photographed houses (corner of 2nd and M Streets, Eureka).

History buffs should stroll through the Clarke Memorial Museum, which has one of the top native American displays in the state, showcasing more than 1,200 examples of Hupa, Yurok, and Karok basketry, dance regalia, and stonework (240 E Street at 3rd Street, Eureka; (707)443-1947). A block away, there's more native American artwork, including quality silver jewelry, at the **Indian Art & Gift Shop**, which sells many of its treasures at reasonable prices (241 F Street at 3rd Street, Eureka; (707)445-8451).

Eureka's Old Town is also the place to eat cheaply. At **Ramone's Bakery & Cafe**, you can make a good meal out of the bakery and lunch items—soups, salads, sandwiches, and excellent coffee—for less than $10 (209 E Street, between 2nd and 3rd Streets, Eureka; (707)445-1642). Two other popular Old Town dining spots are the **Lost Coast Brewery & Café**, which does a brisk lunch business serving pints of Downtown Brown Ale and low-priced pub food, including great rock cod tacos for

Worried about getting lost in the Lost Coast? Curious about Eureka's Victorian architectural heritage? Let the loquacious historian Ray Hillman lead the way on one of his reasonably priced guided tours offered from May through September; (800)400-1849.

Down the Hatch

When you take the 75-minute narrated bay cruise aboard the M.V. *Madaket*, you'll not only be riding on the oldest continuously operating vessel in the United States, you'll be ordering drinks from the smallest licensed bar in California. Sip your spirits while you watch the seals play and listen to veteran Captain Leroy Zerlang's witty—well, after you've had a few gin-and-tonics he's witty—and well-rehearsed narrative of Eureka's tempestuous maritime past. The ship departs several times daily from the foot of C Street in Eureka's Old Town; (707)445-1910.

only $1.50 apiece (617 4th Street, between G and H Streets, Eureka; (707)445-4480); and **Tomaso's Tomato Pies,** a two-story pizza parlor that reeks of baked garlic and olive oil: order one of their popular spinach pies and wash it down with an Italian Cremosa—a blend of milk, soda water, whipped cream, and fruity Torani Italian syrup (216 E Street, between 2nd and 3rd Streets, Eureka; (707)445-0100).

At the north end of Eureka is the turnoff to the Samoa Peninsula, home of the **Samoa Cookhouse**—the last surviving cookhouse in the West (in operation for more than a century) and a Humboldt County institution. In fact, visiting the Eureka/Arcata area without a stop here is like visiting the United States without eating a slice of apple pie. Guests are served lumber camp–style in the enormous barnlike building at long tables covered with checkered tablecloths. Few decisions are required—just sit down and the food will come until you say Uncle. Breakfast typically features sausages, biscuits, scrambled eggs, potatoes, and French toast or pancakes. Lunch and dinner include potatoes and the meat-of-the-day, which might be ham, fried or barbecued chicken, pork chops, roast beef, or fish. Mind you, the food isn't great (except for the delicious bread, baked on the premises), but it's plentiful. And just when you think you're about to burst, along comes the fresh-baked pie. After your meal, spend a few minutes waddling through the adjoining logging museum (from Highway 101 in Eureka, take the Samoa/R Street exit, cross the Samoa Bridge, turn left on Samoa Road, then left on Cookhouse Road; (707)442-1659).

Six miles north of Eureka on Highway 101 lies Arcata, about half the size of Eureka but with twice the appeal. **Arcata Plaza** (at 8th and G Streets) marks the center of this seaside community, and a statue of President McKinley stands guard over the numerous shops and cafes housed in the historic buildings. At the plaza's southwest end is its flagship structure, Jacoby's Storehouse, a handsomely restored 1857 pack-train station that now holds shops, offices, and restaurants (791 8th Street at H Street, Arcata; (707)822-2434). Also worth a look are the Tin Can Mailman, a terrific used-book store with 130,000 hard- and soft-cover titles, including a few collector's items (1000 H Street at 10th Street, Arcata; (707)822-1307), and Moonstone Factory Store, heaven-on-earth for outdoor adventurers in need of top-quality clothing and equipment, including parkas, sleeping bags, and backpacks; look for bargains among the clearance items (1563 G Street at 16th Street, Arcata; (707)826-0851).

Once you've toured the downtown, it's time to explore Arcata's numerous parks and preserves. A two-minute drive east on 11th Street will take you to the town's beloved 20-acre **Redwood Park,** an ideal picnic spot with a playground guaranteed to entertain the tots. Adjoining the park is the **Arcata Community Forest,** 600 acres of second-growth redwoods favored by hikers, mountain bikers, and equestrians; before you go, pick up free guides to the forest's mountain-biking and hiking trails at the Chamber of Commerce (1062 G Street at 11th Street, Arcata; (707)822-3619). Across town is the 154-acre **Arcata Marsh and Wildlife Preserve,** a sanctuary for hundreds of egrets, marsh wrens, and other waterfowl (as well as joggers). A free, self-guided walking-tour map is available at the Chamber of Commerce (see above), or join the Audubon Society's free one-hour guided tours (held rain or shine) on Saturday at 8:30am (meet at the south end of I Street, Arcata; (707)826-7031).

To kill some time without killing your budget, investigate Arcata's small-town diversions, such as attending a Humboldt Crabs game; this local semipro baseball team plays in the charming Arcata Ballpark (at the corner of 9th and F Streets, downtown Arcata). Most games are in the evening throughout the summer; the schedule is posted at the Chamber

Beet of a Different Grower

If purple potatoes, cylindra beets, and other fancy foods are on your shopping list, you'll find them at the farmers markets held weekly in Eureka and Arcata. Most of the produce is grown along the local Eel, Mad, and Trinity Rivers, and is sold at bargain prices at Arcata Plaza on Saturdays 9am–1pm, May–November; in Eureka Mall (800 W Harris Avenue, at the south end of town) on Thursdays 10am–1pm, June–October; and in Eureka's Old Town on F Street on Tuesdays 10am–1pm, July–October. For more information, call (707)441-9699.

of Commerce and in shops and restaurants around town. For a wide range of first-run and classic repertory flicks, queue up at the Arcata or the Minor Theatre, both of which charge below-average prices—particularly for matinees (Arcata Theatre: 1036 G Street at 10th Street, Arcata; (707)822-5171; Minor Theatre: 1013 H Street at 10th Street, Arcata; (707)822-5171). You can see (and touch!) 3.66-billion-year-old fossils and view various California flora and fauna at Humboldt State University's **Natural History Museum** (13th and G Streets, downtown Arcata; (707)826-4479). The university also offers art exhibits and theater, dance, and musical performances on campus year-round (14th Street and L.K. Wood Boulevard, Arcata; (707)826-3011).

Like most college towns, Arcata is filled with restaurants and cafes catering to student-size (i.e., small) budgets. The king of the collegiate hangouts is **Los Bagels**. In 1987, when bagel companies all over the country sent their doughy products to NBC's "Today Show," this humble spot won the title for best bagel outside New York City. If you're feeling really adventurous, try the poppy-seed topped with jalapeño jelly and cream cheese, or perhaps "the Slug," a bagel shaped as (what else?) a slug sprinkled with five kinds of seeds (both locations closed on Tuesday; 1061 I Street, between 10th and 11th Streets, Arcata; (707)822-3150; and 403 2nd Street at E Street, in Old Town, Eureka; (707)442-8525). Another local favorite is **TJ's Classic Cafe,** where on weekdays you can order two eggs with pancakes, French toast, or potatoes for only $2.49 between 7am and 10am. The burgers on cornmeal buns and the house-made onion rings are also winners (1057 H Street at

✦✦ Moveable Feats

Arcata is a festival-happy town, and its wackiest event is the World Championship Great Arcata to Ferndale Cross-Country Kinetic Sculpture Race. The three-day event, held every Memorial Day weekend, draws more than 10,000 spectators, who come to watch about 50 crazy competitors try to slog through 38 grueling miles of sand, swamp, and salt water in their custom-made, people-powered amphibious crafts. Contestants start in Arcata Plaza, pass though Eureka, and finish (if they're lucky) in the town of Ferndale. Cheating and bribery are part of the rules, provided they're done with "proper style and panache." The zaniest "sculptures" are showcased in the Kinetic Sculpture Museum at 780 Main Street in Ferndale. For race information, call Hobart Brown at (707)725-3851.

11th Street, Arcata; (707)822-4650). Health nuts will feel right at home at the **Wildflower Cafe & Bakery,** which whips up tofu French toast, tempeh burgers, nut-loaf sandwiches, dairy-free baked goods, and other nutritious fare (1604 G Street at 16th Street, Arcata; (707)822-0360).

When the weather's warm and it's lunchtime, load up on organic picnic treats at **Spoon's Deli** (in the Arcata Co-op, corner of 8th and I Streets, Arcata; (707)822-5947), then take your feast to Redwood Park and eat with the locals. For a good brew with your food, go to the **Humboldt Brewing Company,** where you can wolf down a jumbo burger and chase it with a couple of pints of the award-winning Pale Ale. On weekends, you'll hear some great live country, folk, or blues there, too (856 10th Street at I Street, Arcata; (707)826-BREW).

CHEAP SLEEPS

Bayview Motel
2844 Fairfield Street, Eureka, CA 95501 • (707)442-1673

This is Eureka's top budget motel, and it's so squeaky-clean you could eat off the floor. Each of the 14 rooms has a private bath, remote-control TV, and queen-size bed. Perched on a knoll high above the noisy freeway, the Bayview even has a view of the bay, but you have to look *real hard* past the industrial park to see it. The motel's best views are actually of the lovely, meticulously manicured lawn and garden. To reach the Bayview, exit Highway 101 at Henderson Street.

Downtowner Motel
424 8th Street, Eureka, CA 95501 • (707)443-5061

You can't judge a book by its cover, but you can usually judge a Eureka motel by its exterior. Of the town's 40 or so budget lodgings, only a handful aren't really run-down, and the Downtowner is one of them. The motel's best asset is its location—well off the noisy main strip (between E and F Streets), yet within walking distance of Old Town. It also has great amenities, including a heated pool, sauna, Jacuzzi, and a funky cocktail lounge. The 72 plain-Jane rooms are decorated in brown tones and equipped with queen-size beds, remote-control cable TV, and direct-dial phones. Rates include a continental breakfast.

Fireside Inn
1716 5th Street, Eureka, CA 95501 • (707)443-6312

If Eureka's Downtowner and Bayview Motels are full, try the Fireside Inn, which is certainly more hospitable than its cheap-sleep competitors **117** along Highway 101. Each of the 65 rooms has a refrigerator and cable TV, and some have a microwave oven. Family and kitchen units are also available, and the inn's tiny laundry room is open to guests. Located at the north end of downtown, the motel is a short walk from Old Town shops and restaurants.

Arcata Crew House
1390 I Street, Arcata, CA 95521 • (707)822-9995

You'd never guess from the outside that this stately forest-green Victorian, ensconced within a wall of well-tended shrubbery in a quiet residential neighborhood, is a college dorm. From June 25 to August 25, however, it doubles as a hostel. For a measly $10 a night, you can sleep on one of the 18 beds (some are bunks, some are doubles). If you're traveling with a companion, try to sign up for one of the two rooms reserved for couples for about $20 per night (although they're usually booked far in advance). The reception desk is open 5pm to 11pm.

Fairwinds Motel
1674 G Street, Arcata, CA 95521 • (707)822-4824

Aside from the Arcata Crew House dormitory, the Fairwinds Motel is the only budget accommodation in Arcata. Located 2 blocks from Humboldt State (Highway 101 at 17th Street), this motel has 27 plain but pleasant rooms, all with direct-dial phones, cable TV, and double or queen-size beds. Although the hotel has been around for a few decades and its age-lines are showing, the rooms have been completely remodeled, with new beds and modern furnishings and prints.

CASCADE RANGE

Mount Shasta

Lassen Volcanic National Park

Mount Shasta

Magnificent, snow-capped Mount Shasta soars 14,162 feet into the sky, making it the tallest mountain in California's Cascade Range and the largest volcano in the contiguous 48 states. Shasta is a dormant volcano: not dead, just sleeping until it decides to blow its snowy stack—something it hasn't done since the late 1700s. And while it may seem long overdue for an eruption, fear not; geologists constantly monitor movement within the volcano and claim they will be able to predict an eruption well in advance—early enough for you to pack your bags and safely skedaddle.

Shasta is only the fifth-highest peak in the state, but unlike its taller cousins, which are clustered with other large mountains, this volcano stands alone, a position that seems to intensify its grandeur. "Lonely as God and white as a winter moon" is how author Joaquin Miller described this solitary peak in the 1870s. The mountain dominates the horizon from every angle, and on clear days it's visible from as far away as 150 miles.

Some native Americans who lived in its shadow believed Mount Shasta was the home of the Great Spirit and vowed never to disrespect it by climbing its sacred slopes. Today, men and women from around the world pay tribute to the volcano by *making the spectacular trek to the top. This is not a mountain for novice hikers, however; its many tremendous crevasses have swallowed careless climbers, and the extreme, unpredictable weather changes at high altitudes make expert equipment a must. But with some basic mountain-climbing instruction and a good study of Shasta's various routes, physically fit adventurers can safely reach its stunning summit.*

This region of Northern California is actually known for its "three Shastas": Shasta Dam, the second-largest and -tallest concrete dam in the nation (containing enough concrete to build a 3-foot-wide sidewalk around the world); Shasta Lake, the largest reservoir in California; and the mighty mountain itself. Together they make for an immense recreational playground that draws hikers, rock climbers, fishers, campers, houseboaters, snow skiers, water-skiers, river rafters, bird-watchers, and many other outdoor enthusiasts. Fortunately, this northernmost region of California is so vast it's possible to escape the summer crowds by backpacking into the wilderness, where your only companions will be bald eagles, black bears, Rocky Mountain elk, and the other numerous critters that call the Shasta area home.

ON THE ROAD

As you zip along Interstate 5 heading north, keep an eye out for the monolithic **Shasta Dam**, a great place to pull over for a lengthy pit stop. Granted, the visitors center and viewing area are rather ho-hum, but the free 45-minute tour of the dam is outstanding (tours are held from 9am to 4pm daily; call ahead for winter and holiday hours). The tour kicks off with a speedy elevator ride down into the chilly bowels of the 15-million-ton, 602-foot-high structure (definitely not recommended for claustrophobes). Next comes a brief spiel on what it takes to make the behemoth dam function, followed by a look at the ominous spillway and inner workings of this impressive power plant. All in all, it's one of the best and most entertaining free tours in Northern California (kids love it) and a

A Houseboating Hiatus

Most savvy Northern Californians will agree that renting a houseboat and basking in the sun on Shasta Lake is one of the not-to-be-missed recreational activities of this region. So what are you waiting for? Smooth-talk your beer-guzzling, bass-fishing, book-reading buddies to chip in on a big ol' Shasta Cruiser. Prices range from about $150 to $300 a day, which means if you get five friends together, that's only $30 a night each for prime lakefront property. Houseboats are in high demand during summer, so make reservations (deposits are required) very early. Shasta Lake rental companies include Antlers Marina, (800)238-3924; Bridge Bay Resort, (916)275-3021; Holiday Harbor, (800)776-2628; Lakeshore Marina, (916)238-2303; Lakeview Marina, (916)223-3003; Packers Bay Marina, (800)331-3137; and Shasta Marina, (800)959-3359.

great way to beat the summer heat (from Interstate 5, take the Shasta Dam Boulevard exit and follow the signs; about 50 miles south of Mount Shasta, Shasta Lake; (916)275-4463).

About 10 miles up the highway is another popular attraction: guided tours of the impressive, crystal-studded stalagmites and stalactites in the **Lake Shasta Caverns** (you'll have to fork over $12 per adult and $6 per child over 3 for this two-hour excursion). Getting there is an adventure in itself; after you pull off the highway and check in at the cavern head-quarters, you'll hop aboard a ferry for a 15-minute trip across Shasta Lake, then climb onto a bus for a white-knuckle ride up to the caverns (open daily year-round; from Interstate 5, take the Shasta Caverns Road exit and follow the signs, Shasta Lake; (916)238-2341).

Back on the highway, continuing toward the town of Mount Shasta, you'll see many arms of **Shasta Lake**, which is fed primarily by the Sacramento, Pit, and McCloud Rivers. Plagued by years of drought, the enormous lake—with 370 miles of shoreline—was something of an eye-sore until recent floodings brought it back to normal levels. Although a haven for houseboaters and fishers who arrive by the thousands in summer, most of the lake is accessible only by boat, which limits many budget travelers' options to a free swim (and sunburn) and some picnick-ing. A better bet is to continue north along Interstate 5 to **Castle Crags State Park**, one of California's geologic wonders. The enormous 6,500-foot spires of ancient granite are visible from the highway, but they deserve a much closer look. If you're anxious to really stretch your legs, hike up the park's moderately strenuous 2.7-mile **Summit Dome Trail** to the base of the crags—the view of Mount Shasta alone is worth the trip. Less adventurous souls can stroll along the one-mile Root Creek or Indian Creek trails or picnic among the pines and wildflowers—a refreshing break from the long, hot drive (from Interstate 5, take the Castle Crags State Park exit, about 13 miles south of Mount Shasta; (916)235-2684).

If ever a community owed its existence to a 14,162-foot pile of volcanic rock (albeit a *pretty* pile of rock), it's the friendly town of **Mount Shasta**. The downtown area's shops, motels, and restaurants all cater to the thousands of climbers, skiers, naturalists, and spiritualists who make the long journey here each year. And fortunately for the low-budget traveler, just about every hotel and restaurant offers small-town prices (most rooms start at about $30 a night, and it's not hard to find a meal for less than $7). After securing a hotel room, head right over to the Mount Shasta Visitors Bureau to pick up a free copy of the "Things To See & Do" brochure and the informative "Lodging & Dining Guide," which features a map showing the location of every hotel and restaurant in the area (300 Pine Street at Lake Street, Mount Shasta; (800)926-4865).

For years, Mount Shasta has been hailed by spiritualists as one of the seven "power centers" of the world. Although city council members are loathe to admit it (and you certainly won't see the words *channeling* or *crystal* in any Chamber of Commerce brochure), a large percentage of visitors are spiritual pilgrims who have come from around the world to bask in the majestic mountain's mysterious energy. If you're interested in learning about the mountain's alleged mystical powers, visit the delightfully funky **Golden Bough Bookstore,** where the staff can give you the spiritual lowdown and direct you to tapes, books, and all matter of info

The Bald Eagle Returns

If ever there were a reason to keep your eye on the sky while traveling through the Shasta Cascades, it's to catch a glimpse of the nation's symbol, the bald eagle. Shasta Lake is currently the home of 18 pairs of the endangered birds— the largest nesting population of bald eagles in California. The largest bird of prey in North America, the eagle mates for life, replacing its partner only upon death. The majestic birds return to the same nest every January or February to breed. To spot an adult, look for a white head and tail, dark-brown body, and a 6-to-7½-foot wingspan.

To Summit All Up

If you're eager to climb Mount Shasta but you don't know a crampon from a crayon, call the folks at Shasta Mountain Guides. For $65, they'll give you an all-day lesson in basic mountain-climbing skills, including how to use an ice ax, crampons, and ropes. For more information and reservations, call Shasta Mountain Guides at (916)926-3117.

on the topic (219 N Mount Shasta Boulevard at Lake Street, downtown Mount Shasta; (916)926-3228).

A couple of free attractions in town include the **Sisson Museum**, which showcases changing exhibits on local history, nature, geology, and native American life, and the adjacent **Mount Shasta Fish Hatchery**, the oldest hatchery in the West, where thousands of rainbow and brown trout, including a few biggies, fill the holding ponds. For only a quarter you can get some fish food and incite a fish-feeding frenzy (take Lake Street across the freeway, turn left on Hatchery Road, and head to 3 N Old Stage Road, Mount Shasta; hatchery, (916)926-2215; museum, (916)926-5508).

The highlight of Mount Shasta is, of course, the mountain itself. If you're fit and raring to climb the snow-topped volcano ("It's just like climbing stairs nonstop from 9 to 5," says one veteran climber), make sure you have a well-thought-out plan of action before making the steep ascent. The views from the mountain's peak are unbelievably beautiful, but the steep climb isn't without its perils; crevasses cover the mountain, and avalanches and whiteouts are common at certain times of year. If you're a newcomer, go to the **Mount Shasta Ranger District** office for plenty of climbing literature as well as friendly advice. Fill out the free (but mandatory) hiking permit while you're there, so the rangers will know how long you'll be on the mountain (permits are located in a small booth outside the front door; 204 W Alma Street off N Mount Shasta Boulevard, Mount Shasta; (916)926-4511). You also must sign off on your permit *after* you return from your climb so no one sends a rescue team to search for you.

Next stop is the **Fifth Season** sports store, where you can buy a good map of the mountain and rent crampons, an ice ax, and sturdy, insulated climbing boots; equipment can be reserved in advance. And if you have any questions the rangers couldn't answer, ask the store's experienced and helpful staff (300 N Mount Shasta Boulevard at Lake Street, Mount Shasta; (916)926-3606; mountain report, (916)926-5555). **125**

Rolling on the River

For an experience you'll never forget, blow your budget and splurge on a guided whitewater-rafting day trip down the mighty Klamath River. Daredevils can soar down the narrow, steep chutes appropriately called Hell's Corner and Caldera, while saner souls (including children) can navigate the much-less-perilous forks. Prices range from $70 to $100 (multi-day trips are also available). For more information, call the Turtle River Rafting Company in Mount Shasta at (916)926-3223.

Now you should be ready to load up your gear, drive to the mountain, and psych yourself up for the climb. Most hikers set up a base camp at **Horse Camp** (although the best—and easiest—routes vary with the seasons). They begin their ascent at about 4:30am the next day, and it's a 7-mile journey to the top, which takes at least seven to eight hours of steady climbing. Bring plenty of water, food, warm and waterproof clothing (sudden thunderstorms are not unusual near the peak), glacier goggles, a first-aid kit, and the strongest sunscreen money can buy.

Psst . . . If all this climbing sounds a wee bit intimidating, there is an easier way. For the last 10 years, many folks have made their way up Mount Shasta via a chair lift (though it doesn't reach the peak) and their way down on skis. For about $26 (less on weekdays) you can purchase an all-day lift ticket ($17 for a half-day pass) at **Mount Shasta Ski Park**, which offers mostly intermediate runs with nary a mogul in sight. Ski Park also has a ski and snow-board rental/repair shop, restaurant, snack bar, and ski school. In summer, the resort offers naturalist-led walks, mountain-biking trails accessible by chair lift (bike rentals are available, too), and an indoor recreational climbing wall for people of all ages and abilities (at the end of Ski Park Highway, off Highway 89, 10 miles east of I-5, Mount Shasta; (916)926-8610; snowphone, (916)926-8686). About ¼-mile down the highway is the **Nordic Lodge**, a cross-country-ski center with several miles of groomed tracks (on Ski Park Highway, Mount Shasta; (916)926-8610).

As you would expect in a town that caters to climbers, Mount Shasta's restaurants dish out lots of carbohydrates: pizza, pasta, and pancakes are the big sellers here, as well as bagels, strong coffee, and PowerBars. The best of the budget-dining options is the **Bagel Cafe & Bakery**, which in addition to baking delectable bagels, brews the greatest coffee in the region. Other crowd-pleasers are the fresh vegetarian dishes (try the savory soups), inexpensive chicken and fish dinners, fresh juices, and delicious smoothies (105 E Alma Street off Mount Shasta Boulevard, Mount Shasta; (916)926-1414). For a classic American breakfast, try **Wendie's Italian Restaurant**, where everything is big (the pancakes actually hang off the side of the plate) and cheap. Wendie's also serves its locally famous house-made pies (610 S Mount Shasta Boulevard, Mount Shasta; (916)926-4047).

Carbo-loaders and beef-eaters should stock up on the house-made raviolis and the thick, rare steaks at **Mike and Tony's Italian Restaurant**—don't let the homely decor scare you away (501 N Mount Shasta Boulevard at High Street, Mount Shasta; (916)926-4792). For decent Mexican food at less than $5 a plate, queue up with the locals at **Poncho & Lefkowitz** (a canopied trailer set up in the PayLess parking lot) and order the Pancho Taco or El Supremo Burrito with lots of spicy salsa (at the corner of Lake and Pine Streets, Mount Shasta; no phone). For a good deal on juicy burgers, organic German beer, and five versions of bratwurst, belly up to **Willy's Bavarian Kitchen** and take a seat outdoors to watch the hustle and bustle of Mount Shasta Boulevard (107 Chestnut Street, Mount Shasta; (916)926-3636).

CHEAP SLEEPS

Alpenrose Cottage Hostel
204 E Hinckley Street, Mount Shasta, CA 96067 • (916)926-6724

If you enjoy meeting new people and don't mind sharing a room with strangers, head over to Betty Brown's beautiful Alpenrose Cottage, where you can literally bunk down for a bargain $13 a night (half price for kids under 18). Betty, one of the most easygoing hostel owners you'll ever meet, lives in half the house, leaving the other half open to you (and your roommates). You're welcome to come and go as you like (the door's always open) and to whip up a meal in the fully equipped kitchen. In exchange, you may be asked to help out with an occasional chore or two and you're expected to clean up after yourself—it's that simple. Alpenrose has 12 bunk beds, although on cool summer nights some folks prefer to slumber under the stars on the large deck overlooking a moonlit Mount Shasta. Betty also reserves one room for couples for $26 a night—the best deal in town.

Evergreen Lodge
1312 S Mount Shasta Boulevard, Mount Shasta, CA 96067 •
(916)926-2143

Eenie, meenie, miney, mo. . . . . The number of budget motels lining the streets of Mount Shasta is overwhelming, and while most of them look alike from the outside, they're not all created equal inside. The Evergreen Lodge is one of the better cheap choices. For $30 you can get an air-conditioned room with private bath, cable TV, and telephone. A room with a kitchenette (great for families) is available for an additional $10. There's a tiny pool and hot tub on the premises, though you probably won't even want to dip your big toe into the murky waters.

Mountain Air Lodge
1121 S Mount Shasta Boulevard, Mount Shasta, CA 96067 •
(916)926-3411

Set back from the main road in a pleasant pine-shaded area, this 36-room lodge, offering comfort and plenty of conveniences, is often booked far in advance on weekends. The large, contemporary rooms are equipped with private bath, cable TV, air conditioning, and telephone, and two units have a kitchen. There's also a pool table, Ping-Pong table, and—the pièce de résistance—a huge 8x14-foot Jacuzzi that's ideal for soaking your tired dogs after a hard day's hike. For more savings, ask about the weekday ski packages that give a 20 percent discount on room rates and lift tickets.

Shasta Lodge Motel
724 N Mount Shasta Boulevard, Mount Shasta, CA 96067 •
(916)926-2815

The Shasta Lodge Motel offers all the standard amenities—private bath, cable TV, telephone, and air conditioning—although everything is a little frayed around the edges, and things tend to shake a bit when the Southern Pacific comes rolling through (then again, the entire *town* shakes a bit when the Southern Pacific passes through). But at $33 a night, who's complaining? The 20-room motel is also just steps away from the downtown shops and restaurants.

Stoney Brook Inn
309 W Colombero Street, McCloud, CA 96057-1860 • (916)964-2300

For the best cheap sleep in the area, head for the tiny, quiet burg of McCloud, about 10 miles east of I-5 on Highway 89. There you'll find the charming Stoney Brook Inn, one of the few budget bed and breakfasts in Northern California. The 18 rooms range in price from around $35 for a room with shared bath to just beyond the *Cheap Sleeps* limit for their top-of-the-line accommodations. Rates include a vegetarian breakfast. Within the inn is Simply Vegetarian!, a vegan (meatless and dairyless) restaurant serving house-made soups, organic salads, and a variety of entrees. After filling up on the healthy fare, kick back with a good book on the pine-shaded wraparound porch, soak in the hot tub, or steam away your worries in the sauna. With a group? Sign up for the traditional ceremonial sweat lodge, led by a medicine man from the Karuk tribe.

Lassen Volcanic National Park

Surprisingly, many Californians have never even heard of Lassen Volcanic National Park, much less been there. In fact, it's one of the least crowded national parks in the country, forever destined to play second fiddle to its towering neighbor, Mount Shasta. This, of course, is reason enough to go, since the park's 108,000 acres (including 50 beautiful wilderness lakes) are practically deserted, even on weekends.

The heart of the park is 10,457-foot Lassen Peak, the largest plug-dome volcano in the world (the last fiery eruption was in 1915, when it shot debris 7 miles high into the stratosphere). The volcano also marks the southernmost end of the Cascade Range, which extends to Canada. A visitor's map calls the park "a compact laboratory of volcanic phenomena"—an apt description of this pretty but peculiar place. In addition to wildflower-laced hiking trails and lush forests typical of many national parks, parts of Lassen are covered with steaming thermal vents, boiling mud pots, stinky sulfur springs, and towering lava pinnacles—constant reminders that Mount Lassen is still active. For decades Lassen held the title of the most recently active volcano in the continental United States; it lost that distinction in 1980, when Washington's Mount St. Helens blew her top.

ON THE ROAD

Lassen Park's premier attractions in summer and fall are sightseeing, hiking, backpacking, and camping (sorry, no mountain bikes allowed). The $5-per-car entrance fee, valid for a week, gets you a copy of the "Lassen Park Guide," a handy little newsletter listing activities, hikes, and points of interest. Free naturalist programs are offered daily in the summer, highlighting everything from flora and fauna to geologic history and volcanic processes. If you have only a day here, spend it huffing up the mountain on the **Lassen Peak Hike**, a spectacular 2½-mile zigzag to the top. Most hikers can make the steep trek in four to five hours—just don't forget to bring water, sunscreen, and a windbreaker. Another great—and much easier—trail is the 3-mile Bumpass Hell hike. Poor ol' Mr. Bumpass lost a leg on this one, but that was long before park rangers built wooden catwalks to safely guide visitors past the pyrite pools, steam vents, seething mud pots, and noisy fumaroles that line the trail.

Mount Lassen attracts a hardier breed of tourists in winter, when the park's main thoroughfare is closed and the chief modes of transportation are snowshoes and cross-country skis. Smaller roads are plowed only from the north and south park-entrance points up to the ranger stations, and on sunny weekends parking lots are filled with families enjoying every kind of snow toy imaginable.

Lassen offers just one restaurant, the **Summer Chalet Cafe**, which prepares inexpensive, basic breakfasts, and sandwiches and burgers for lunch (open daily from May to October; at the park's south entrance; (916)595-3376). Consider bringing your own food; you can replenish your supplies at **Manzanita Lake Camper Store**, (916)335-7557, at the

If the Snowshoe Fits . . .

On Saturday afternoons from January through March, a loquacious naturalist will take anyone who shows up at the Lassen Chalet by 1:30pm on a free, two-hour eco-adventure across the snowy dales of Lassen Volcanic National Park. Here are the rules: You must be at least eight years old, warmly dressed, and decked out in boots. Snowshoes are provided free (although a $1 donation for shoe upkeep is requested) on a first-come, first-served basis. Pack a picnic lunch. The chalet is at the park's south entrance, 5 miles north of the Highway 36/89 junction. For more details, call park headquarters at (916)595-4444, extension 5133.

north end of the park, or at **Lassen Mineral Lodge**, (916)595-4422, on the south side, though both offer slim pickings at fat prices.

For additional information, call park headquarters at (916)595-4444.

CHEAP SLEEPS

Hat Creek Resort
On Highway 89 (PO Box 15), Old Station, CA 96071 • (916)335-7121

Owner Harold Devincenzi spends his winter preparing Hat Creek Resort for the summer onslaught, when hunters and fishers—most of whom have made reservations two years in advance—arrive in droves to occupy his 10 picture-perfect housekeeping cabins and 7 motel rooms. What's the attraction? The location. The area around Lassen Volcanic National Park provides some of the best fishing in the world, and fabled Hat Creek runs right through the resort. The cabins, open year-round, come with kitchens where you can cook your catch. Park your RV for less than $20 a night. Uncle Runt's Place, a small saloon and diner, is just down the highway. The resort is located 11 miles northeast of the park's south entrance.

Rim Rock Ranch
13275 Highway 89, Old Station, CA 96071 • (916)335-7114

If having your own rustic cabin for only $36 a day sounds too good to be true, well, that all depends on how you define rustic. Most of Rim Rock's housekeeping cabins were built in the '30s and '40s and don't appear to have been through too many renovations since. But you sure can't beat the price, particularly when it includes a kitchen, utensils, dishes, and a full bath. If the 10 cabins are booked, ask about the 2 budget-priced motel rooms. The ranch has its own small grocery store, which stocks fishing and hunting gear. Uncle Runt's Place, a small short-order diner and saloon, is across the street. The ranch is located 14 miles northeast of the park's north entrance.

Lassen Mineral Lodge
On Highway 36 (PO Box 160), Mineral, CA 96063 • (916)595-4422

Popular with skiers, hunters, and fishers, Lassen Mineral Lodge offers 20 motel-style accommodations on the doorstep of Lassen National Park. It's set back in the pines 9 miles south of the park's south entrance, so you don't hear the highway noise, but the main lodge is usually bustling with guests. A general store, gift shop, ski shop, and old-fashioned saloon and restaurant are connected to the lodge by a wraparound verandah; there's also a pool and a tennis court.

Mill Creek Resort

1 Highway 172, Mill Creek, CA 96061 • (916)595-4449

If it's peace and solitude you're after, Mill Creek, 3 miles south of Highway 36, is the place. The Resort makes you feel as though you've stepped back in time to a quieter, gentler, and infinitely more affordable era (somewhere around 1925). A quaint general store and coffee shop serve as the resort's center; the nine housekeeping cabins, available daily or weekly, are clean and homey. Seclusion is one of the main charms of the place, but it's also close to cross-country-ski trails and Mount Lassen. Pets are welcome, too.

A Toy for All Seasons

Come summer or winter, the friendly proprietors of Lassen Mineral Lodge sell just about every outdoor toy you'd ever want to play with in Lassen Park. Fishing and hunting supplies (this is serious deer country) are sold, and they have the *only* cross-country-ski rentals in the area. You also can get plenty of free advice on where to go and what to do in this neck of the woods. For additional information, see "Lassen Mineral Lodge" under "Cheap Sleeps" (on Hwy 36 in Mineral, (916)595-4422).

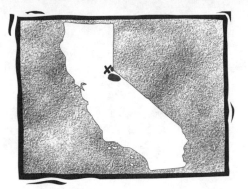

SIERRA NEVADA

North Lake Tahoe

South Lake Tahoe

Yosemite National Park

Mammoth Lakes

North Lake Tahoe

Frontiersman Kit Carson was guiding General John Frémont's expedition across the Sierra Nevada in 1844 when he stumbled on an immense, deep-blue body of water, a lake so vast the native Washoe Indians were calling it tahoe ("big lake"). Carson was the first white man to discover Tahoe, North America's largest alpine lake and the eighth-deepest in the world (its deepest point is at 1,645 feet). If completely drained, Tahoe would cover the entire state of California with 14 inches of water.

The California/Nevada border runs straight through the heart of the lake, leaving its west side in California and the east side in Nevada. Despite this east/west state division, the lake is more commonly referred to in terms of its north and south shores. The South Shore area is the most populous and urban, where you'll hear the jingle-jangle of all those slot machines. If you'd rather keep your budget bankroll intact, steer clear of the one-armed bandits and head for the North Shore. There you'll find fewer casinos (and tourists) and more outdoor recreation, including most of Tahoe's best alpine and cross-country ski resorts.

Despite all the great skiing, Tahoe is actually most crowded in summer, when thousands flock here to cool off at the supposedly public shoreline (what constitutes public versus private waterfront is *still a matter of heated debate between home owners and county supervisors). Warm-weather activities abound: every water sport imaginable as well as snowmobiling, bicycling, hiking, rock climbing, hot-air ballooning, ice skating, horseback riding . . . you name it. Unfortunately, the area pays dearly for its myriad attractions, in the form of tremendous traffic jams, water and air pollution, and a plethora of fast-food joints and condos erected before tough building restrictions were imposed. Yet despite these glaring scars, Lake Tahoe remains one of the premier outdoor playgrounds of the West, dazzling visitors with its soaring Sierra peaks and twinkling alpine waters.*

ON THE ROAD

For a grand introduction to the area, take a leisurely 72-mile drive around the lake itself. Highways 50, 89, and 28 hug the shore, providing gorgeous views from the car. Several stellar sights merit pulling over for a closer look, so be prepared to stop and haul out the camera (or camcorder) along the way. Topping the not-to-be-missed list are **Emerald Bay** (off Highway 89 on the West Shore), one of the most photographed sights in the world; **Cave Rock**, the 200-foot, drive-through tunnel along Highway 50 on the East Shore; and **Sand Harbor State Park** (off Highway 28 on the East Shore), one of the lake's prettiest—and least visited—beaches. Allow about three hours to loop around the lake, or longer if you're traveling on a summer weekend, holiday, or when the road is dusted with snow.

Once you've circled the lake, make a quick stop in **Tahoe City** at the Tahoe North Visitors & Convention Bureau and sort through the mountain of brochures and coupons for good deals on local attractions. If you plan to hike or ride bikes, load up on the free trail maps, too. This is also the place to visit or call if you're having trouble finding a hotel room or campsite (a common problem during peak seasons) or need information on ski packages (950 N Lake Boulevard, above McDonald's, Tahoe City; (800)824-6348 or (916)583-3494).

Summer also brings a phenomenal array of lakeside activities, many of which don't cost a dime. **Day hikers** should head for the Visitor Center on the West Shore (on Highway 89, just north of Fallen Leaf

☕ Traipsing Through Truckee

For some folks, a vacation isn't really a vacation without a good, long shopping spree. If you live to shop, take the 15-minute drive north from Tahoe City (via Highway 89) to the historic railroad-lumber town of Truckee. Here you'll find dozens of alluring specialty shops and cafes housed in century-old facades along Commercial Row (during the Christmas season, when snow blankets the wooden boardwalks and bright little white lights twinkle in the windows, it all looks like a picture from a fairy tale).

A couple of other popular shops in town are Sierra Mountaineer, which carries everything you'll ever need for exploring the Sierra on foot or on skis (Bridge Street at Jibboom Street, downtown Truckee; (916)587-2025) and the Bookshelf at Hooligan Rocks, one of Northern California's best bookstores (11310 Donner Pass Road, at the west end of the Safeway shopping center, Truckee; (800)959-5083 or (916)582-0515). After a long day of browsing, give your feet (and wallet) a break at the budget-priced Squeeze In, which offers 57 palate-pleasin' varieties of hefty omelets and 22 versions of a triple-decker sandwich (10060 Donner Pass Road, downtown Truckee; (916)587-9814).

Road and 3 miles north of South Lake Tahoe; (916)573-2674). It's the starting point for several well-marked trails, ranging from an easy half-mile stroll to a 10-mile, leg-burning trek. Serious mountain bikers shouldn't miss huffing up and down the famous 24-mile **Flume Trail**, with its fantastic views of the lake; the trailhead begins at Nevada State Park on the lake's eastern shore. Casual and asphalt-only pedalers can vie with in-line skaters, joggers, and strollers for room on North Tahoe's 15-mile-long, paved trail, beginning at **Sugar Pine Point State Park** on the West Shore and stretching north along the lake to **Dollar Point** on the North Shore. There's also a 3½-mile paved trail that parallels the **Truckee River** and passes through Tahoe City; the trail starts at the turnoff to Alpine Meadows ski resort on Highway 89. For the truly lazy (or crazy) rider, **Northstar-at-Tahoe** and **Squaw Valley** ski resorts offer miles of pedal-free trails accessible by chair lift or cable car—simply let the lifts tote you and your bike up the slopes, then spend the day cruising (or careening like a deranged daredevil) down the mountains. Expect to pay about $19 at Northstar and $12 at Squaw for an all-day lift ticket.

If you didn't manage to pack all your recreational toys, **Porter's Ski**

Granted, there's nothing cheap these days about downhill skiing, but a few deals exist, especially if you ski midweek, purchase a multiday pass, or buy a hotel/ski-pass package. Most Tahoe resorts offer super-saver ski packages or discounts each season, so it pays to call your favorite destination and ask about the specials. Here's a roundup of North Lake Tahoe's major downhill ski areas:

Alpine Meadows • A favorite with locals, Alpine's runs are on a par with Squaw Valley's best, but without snow boarders (they're banned from the slopes) and the holier-than-thou attitude of the Squaw staff. (Off Highway 89; (800)441-4423 or (916)583-4232.)

Boreal • Although small and easy, Boreal is a good beginner's resort. It's also the only place in the Tahoe area that offers night skiing (open until 9pm) and, thanks to extensive snowmaking equipment, is usually one of the first ski areas open for business. (Off Interstate 80; (916)426-3666.)

Diamond Peak • Located in Incline Village on the Nevada side of Tahoe's North Shore, this small, family-oriented ski resort *guarantees* good skiing—if you don't like the conditions, you can turn in your ticket within the first hour for a voucher that's good for another day. (From Highway 28, exit on Country Club Drive, turn right on Ski Way, and head to Diamond Peak; (702)831-3249.)

Donner Ski Ranch • Just up the road from Sugar Bowl is Donner, where the best feature is the price of the ski passes—you'll pay about half of what neighboring ski areas charge for an all-day ticket. Despite its small size, this unpretentious resort has a lot to offer skiers of all levels: tree skiing, groomed trails, and a few steeps and jumps, not to mention convenient parking and a cozy, rustic lodge. (Take the Soda Springs exit off Interstate 80; (916)426-3635.)

Granlibakken • Tiny and mainly for tots, this is a great place to teach kids the fundamentals. Later, when you'll surely need a libation, you won't have far to go to find the Tahoe City night spots. (Off Highway 89 at the junction of Highway 28; (800)543-3221 or (916)583-4242.)

Northstar-at-Tahoe • Northstar is consistently rated one of the best family ski resorts in the nation, thanks to its numerous amenities. It also has the dubious honor of being called Flatstar by locals because of its frequently groomed trails. This is a completely self-contained resort (you'll find everything from lodgings to stores to a gas station here), so you can park your car and leave it there for the duration of your stay. (Off Highway 267; (800)GO-NORTH or (916)562-1010.)

Ski Homewood • This underrated midsize resort has a little of everything for skiers of all levels—along with one of the best views of Lake Tahoe. Midweek specials often knock down the price of a ticket by as much as 50 percent (call ahead for quotes), easily the best ski discount in town. (Off Highway 89; (916)525-2992.)

Squaw Valley USA • Site of the 1960 Winter Olympic Games, Squaw is a resort that people either love (because it has everything a skier could hope for) or hate (because staff members *know* it has everything and say so with their nose-to-the-sky attitudes). Squaw offers some of the country's most challenging terrain, intensive ski-school programs, top-of-the-line chair lifts, and advanced snowmaking. Unfortunately, it tends to attract the most obnoxious snow-boarders and the most egotistical skiers in North America. (Off Highway 89; (800)545-4350 or (916)583-6985.)

Sugar Bowl • Here's another good all-around midsize ski resort, with about 60 runs. Sugar Bowl's top attraction is accessibility—it's the closest resort from the valley off Interstate 80, about 30 minutes before Squaw Valley (and several bucks less a pass, thank you). Whether it's worth the drive from the North Shore, however, is questionable. (Take the Soda Springs exit off Interstate 80; (916)426-3651.)

Tahoe Donner Ski Area • If you're a beginner or a beginner/intermediate skier and are staying on the North Shore, Tahoe Donner is a viable option, offering short lift lines, few (or no) parking hassles, and relatively low prices. (From Interstate 80, take the Donner State Park exit, turn left on Donner Pass Road, then left on Northwoods Boulevard and follow the signs; (916)587-9444.)

& Sport in Tahoe City has the best prices in town for outdoor rental equipment—everything from bikes to skates to rackets, as well as a full line of skis and snow boards (501 N Lake Boulevard, Tahoe City; (916)583-2314). For a dose of aerobics or heavy breathing on the Stairmaster, make a beeline for the **North Tahoe Beach Center**. Pay $7, and you can jump up and down till you drop. This is also the spot for a good hot soak in a 26-foot-long outdoor Jacuzzi (7860 N Lake Boulevard, across from Safeway, Kings Beach; (916)546-2566).

Still feeling the urge to try your luck at blackjack or spinning the big wheel? Well, **Nevada** is only a short drive away, and the casinos will be delighted to see you. Although the North Shore's casinos are more sub-dued and less glitzy than the South Shore's high-rolling highrises, the dealers are still adept at taking your money. If you're a greenhorn, this is a good place to learn the ABCs of the games, especially during off-hours. **North Shore casinos** include the Tahoe Biltmore Hotel, (702)831-0660; Cal-Neva Lodge and Casino, (702)832-4000; Hyatt Regency Lake Tahoe, (702)831-1111; and Crystal Bay Club Casino, (702)831-0512.

North Lake Tahoe also offers a few nocturnal alternatives to the dice and the slots. You can dance any night of the week at **Pierce Street Annex**, which caters to a thirtysomething crowd but attracts swingers of all ages (850 N Lake Boulevard, behind Safeway, Tahoe City; (916) 583-5800). **Humpty's**, on the other hand, resembles (and smells like) a college-town hangout, though this is where you'll find the area's top

---

Hang Ten

Looking for a cheap thrill? Well, for a mere $7 ($10 for kids, who need more supervision) you can climb straight up a wall at Squaw Valley for a full hour (although few folks have the stamina to last that long). Located at the base of Squaw Valley's cable car route, the Headwall is an artificial 30-foot-high cliff dotted with a series of small finger- and toeholds, each more difficult to grasp than the last. Before you begin the challenging ascent, you're hooked up to a harness, which makes it impossible to fall but possible to climb wherever and whenever you choose. For a few more dollars you can rent climbing shoes, though sneakers work almost as well. Headwall Cafe and Climbing is open to people of all ages and abilities, including toddlers, who actually outshine the adults with their nimble moves. Open daily year-round. (Located off Highway 89 in Squaw Valley; for more details call (916)583-ROPE.)

Nordic Ski Notes

Tahoe's top cross-country ski center is Royal Gorge, the largest of its kind in the United States, with 200 miles of trails for skiers of all levels, 9,172 acres of skiable terrain, an average annual snowfall of more than 650 inches, 10 warming huts (for defrosting those frozen fingers and toes), and 2 lodges. (To get there, take the Soda Springs exit off Interstate 80; (916)426-3871.) More experienced Nordic skiers should head over to Eagle Mountain (one of the area's best-kept secrets), which offers 47 miles of challenging trails with fantastic Sierra vistas. (From Interstate 80, exit at Yuba Gap, turn right, and follow the signs; (800)391-2254 or (916)389-2254.)

dance bands and the cheapest drinks; the 4-to-9pm happy hour, when drinks are only two bucks, is one of the best deals in town (877 N Lake Boulevard, across from Safeway, Tahoe City; (916)583-4867). During ski season, the lounge of the **River Ranch Lodge** has a raging après-ski scene, with ski bums from all over kicking back and chowing down on cheap hors d'oeuvres (on Highway 89, at the entrance to Alpine Meadows, about 10 miles north of Tahoe City; (916)583-4264).

North Lake Tahoe offers surprisingly cheap, tasty, and even healthy food—if you know where to go. **Coyote's Mexican Grill** prides itself on hearty portions prepared without lard or preservatives, and most dishes are less than five bucks, with many vegetarian choices available (521 N Lake Boulevard, Tahoe City; (916)583-6653). **Fire Sign Cafe** owner/ chef Bob Young smokes his own salmon and whips up superb salmon omelets. His made-from-scratch coffee cake and blackberry-buckwheat pancakes draw crowds, too, so be prepared to stand in line (1785 W Lake Boulevard, Tahoe City; (916)583-0871). For great Italian food at budget prices, stand in line with the locals again for dinner at **Za's**, where patient, Chianti-loaded patrons are rewarded with creations like savory smoked-chicken fettuccine with fresh artichoke hearts in a garlic-cream sauce—for less than $10 (395 N Lake Boulevard, Tahoe City; (916)583-1812). After dinner, stroll down the street to the **Bridgetender Tavern and Grill** for a beer—choose from about 20 on tap—and a chilled Jagermeister chaser (30 W Lake Boulevard at Fanny Bridge, Tahoe City; (916)583-3342).

CHEAP SLEEPS

Family Tree Restaurant & Motel
551 N Lake Boulevard (PO Box 6689), Tahoe City, CA 96145 •
(916)583-0287

Perhaps it's just a ploy to get you to eat here, but if you want a room at this motel you must register with the cashier in the restaurant, and then walk through the dining room (or all the way around the outside of the restaurant) to reach your digs. But when less than $50 a night buys a big, comfy room with a TV and queen-size bed (or two doubles), it's well worth the detour. Plus, Family Tree is planted right in the heart of Tahoe City. And of course, your breakfast table is just steps away. There are only 10 rooms, so reserve early.

Rodeway Inn
645 N Lake Boulevard (PO Box 29), Tahoe City, CA 96145 •
(800)624-8590 or (916)583-3711

Although a room at the Rodeway is typically priced just out of *Cheap Sleeps* range, the inn's ski packages are definitely priced right. How right? How about a room (Sunday through Thursday only) and an all-day lift ticket to Alpine Meadows or Squaw Valley for less than $60 per person? Add a whirlpool, cable TV, in-room coffee, and a prime location in downtown Tahoe City, and you've got a deal that's hard to beat.

Tamarack Lodge
2311 N Lake Boulevard (PO Box 859), Tahoe City, CA 96145 •
(916)583-3350

How often do you have the chance to sleep in the same little cabin that once housed Clark Gable and Gary Cooper? Not very, which is one of the reasons the rustic, secluded Tamarack Lodge should be your first-choice accommodation in Lake Tahoe. It's located a mile east of Tahoe City on busy N Lake Boulevard, yet the 21 wood-paneled rooms and cabins are well hidden behind a grove of pines. Rates range from about $35 for one of the converted old "poker rooms" to $80 for a two-bedroom, two-bath cabin with kitchen and living room (a real deal for two couples).

North Lake Lodge
8716 N Lake Boulevard (PO Box 955), Kings Beach, CA 96143 •
(916)546-2731

Although it's far from the action in Tahoe City, the North Lake Lodge is ideal for gamblers (the casinos are less than a mile away) and skiers who prefer the slopes of nearby Northstar. The 21 units range in price from about $40 for a bungalow to $60 for a small cabin to more than $100 for a cabin that sleeps up to six. A few of the rustic buildings, some dating back to the 1920s, have lake views; some units also have a kitchenette or a refrigerator and microwave. The lodge offers a hot tub and picnic area, and there's a public beach nearby. Pets are welcome, too.

Northwood Pines Motel
8489 Trout Street (PO Box 717), Kings Beach, CA 95719 •
(916)546-9829

If you need an inexpensive room and are willing to lower your standards a few notches, head to Kings Beach and turn left on Bear Street, where you'll find about half a dozen rather run-down motels scattered through the neighborhood. The best of these (which isn't saying much) is the Northwood Pines, a spartan, nine-room lodging that charges as little as $37 a night. It ain't the Ritz, but if all you need is a bed, it'll do in a pinch.

 *High-Altitude Hostels*

If you don't mind toting around a sleeping bag, it's possible to get accommodations within walking distance of Squaw Valley, Donner, and Sugar Bowl ski resorts for less than the price of a lift ticket. Donner Spitz Hütte, an isolated, Swiss-style, 68-bed lodge just steps from Donner Ski Ranch, provides a bunk and a hearty breakfast for about $23 a day and a huge family-style dinner for an additional $12—a budget ski bum's dream. During the summer months, Spitz Hütte doubles as an international climbing center, where climbers from around the world stay and study the sport. The hostel is located at 19195 Donner Pass Road, at the top of Donner Pass, in Norden. Reservations are recommended; call (916)426-9108 for more information.

You'll also have to book a bunk far in advance if you want to stay at the popular Squaw Valley Hostel, a privately run enterprise near the Squaw ski resort. There are 100 beds packed into 9 rooms, which cost about $20 a night on weekdays, $25 on weekends, and even less in the off season. Located at 1900 Squaw Valley Road, off Highway 89 in Squaw Valley; for more details call (800)544-4723 or (916)583-7771.

ACCESS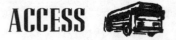

By car, the main artery to North Lake Tahoe is Interstate 80, which is open year-round, though chains are often required during winter, so don't leave home without 'em. It's a 196-mile, four-hour haul from San Francisco, which many people break up with a pit stop in Sacramento or Auburn. Once you reach the town of Truckee, look for the Highway 89 South turnoff, which leads to North Lake Tahoe (on weekends this stretch can get unbelievably congested, so be prepared). For a quicker route to the casinos, take the Highway 267 exit off Interstate 80, which winds through downtown Truckee, past Northstar-at-Tahoe ski resort, and into the town of Kings Beach.

Although driving here can be more convenient, it *is* possible to get to Tahoe by public transportation. Greyhound, (800)231-2222, runs several buses a day from San Francisco and Sacramento (and some smaller cities) to Truckee. Amtrak, (800)USA-RAIL, offers a train a day between Oakland and Truckee. Once you're in Truckee, TART (Tahoe Area Regional Transit) shuttles will take you and your mountain bike or skis along the north half of the lake for a buck (drivers don't give change) from 6:30am to 6:30pm, seven days a week. For TART schedule information, call (800)736-6365 or (916)581-6365. If you'd rather fly, see "Access" in the South Lake Tahoe chapter.

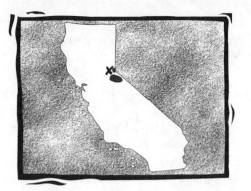

South Lake Tahoe

T hree premier attractions separate sassy South Lake Tahoe from its sportier northern counterpart: glitzy casinos with celebrity entertainers, several sandy beaches, and the massive Heavenly Ski Resort, the only American ski area that straddles two states. If 24-hour gambling parties or schussing down the slopes of Heavenly is your idea of paradise, then you're in for a treat.

Most of the weekend warriors who flock here on Friday after-noons book their favorite budget lodgings weeks—if not months—in advance. Follow their lead and plan early. For long-term stays, it's often more economical to go in on a condo rental with a group of friends. Then again, many of the casinos offer bargain sleep-and-eat packages (especially during the week) that are the best bets you'll ever make in Tahoe. As long as you don't succumb (too often) to the slot machines, you can pig out at the casino-subsidized restaurants, pass out in the casino-subsidized lodgings, and then hightail it back to the lake without blowing your budget.

ON THE ROAD

As soon as you roll into town, stop at the **South Lake Tahoe Chamber of Commerce**, where you'll find an entire room filled with free maps,

Paddle Pleasures

Care to get a better look at that mysterious stone teahouse in the heart of Emerald Bay? The folks at Kayak Tahoe, located at Camp Richardson on Tahoe's South Shore, can set you up in one of their stable sea kayaks (single, $12 per hour; tandem, $24 per hour) and point you in the right direction—then you're on your own to paddle wherever you please. Guided tours and lessons are also available (1900 Jamison Beach Road, off Highway 89 at Camp Richardson, 2½ miles north of the Highway 50 junction, South Lake Tahoe; (916)544-2011.)

brochures, coupons, and guidebooks to the South Lake region. And if you risked traveling to Tahoe without a hotel reservation, ask the staff to help you find a room in your price range (3066 S Lake Tahoe Boulevard, South Lake Tahoe; (916)541-5255). You could also contact the casinos for an update on their package deals—sometimes their rates beat out the best budget motels; call Harrah's, (800)648-3773; Caesars Tahoe, (800)648-3353; and Harvey's, (800)427-8397.

In the summer, droves of tourists and locals arrive by bike, car, or boat at **The Beacon** restaurant and bar to scope out the beach, babe, and bar scene—easily the best on the lake. Sit on the Beacon's huge outdoor deck overlooking the beach and order their famous Rum Runner cocktail, a potent blend of rums and juices guaranteed to put a smile on your face (1900 Jamison Beach Road, off Highway 89 at Camp Richardson, 2½ miles north of the Highway 50 junction, South Lake Tahoe; (916)541-0630). Other popular public beaches include **Nevada Beach**, which has spectacular views of Lake Tahoe and the Sierra Nevada (on Elk Point Road, 1 mile east of Stateline, Nevada), and **El Dorado Beach**— not as pretty, but much closer to town (off Lakeview Avenue, across from Pizza Hut, downtown South Lake Tahoe). In the winter, skiing is the big sport, and **Heavenly** is the big crowd-pleasin' resort. And no matter what time of year, the scenic three-hour drive around the azure lake provides views of Tahoe you won't soon forget (see the North Lake Tahoe chapter for more information).

The South Lake's number one nighttime entertainment is—you guessed it—the casino. The three top guns are **Harrah's**, **Caesars Tahoe**, and **Harvey's**, which are squeezed next to each other on Highway 50 in Nevada and burn enough bulbs to light a small city. Even if you can't take a chance yourself, stroll through to watch the high rollers throw away more bucks than you make in a month or to gawk at those "just-*one-*

148

more-try" players at the flashy money machines. If you want to try your luck, a mere $10 can keep you entertained for quite a while on the nickel slots. Or spend the night kicking up your heels on the dance floor at Nero's 2000 Nightclub in Caesars (55 Highway 50, Stateline, Nevada; (702)588-3515) or at Turtle's Sports Bar and Dance Emporium in the Embassy Suite (4130 Lake Tahoe Boulevard, South Lake Tahoe; (916)544-5400).

For more than a century, **Walley's Hot Springs Resort** in Nevada has been *the* place for South Lake residents to unwind after a hard day of

---

Stellar South Shore Slopes

When the winter months roll around, the tension is almost palpable in South Lake Tahoe as snow-starved locals pray for an early dump. At the first snowstorm, the town springs to life with skiers who make the pilgrimage from Sacramento and the Bay Area to test their prowess on the slopes. Although the South Shore has half as many resorts as the North Shore, they're some of the best: Heavenly, Kirkwood, and Sierra-at-Tahoe. Furthermore, all these resorts run free shuttles from downtown South Lake Tahoe— one heck of a deal that the North Shore resorts have yet to match.

Heavenly Ski Resort • South Lake Tahoe's pride and joy has something for skiers of all levels. And Heavenly is so immense it extends all the way into Nevada; those in the know park on the Nevada side to avoid the crowds or catch a ride on the free shuttles. Don't look for bargain prices here; Heavenly's all-day lift ticket is one of the costliest in Tahoe. (Off Highway 50; (800)2-HEAVEN or (702)586-7000.)

Kirkwood • When ski conditions just don't get any better, Tahoe locals make the journey over the passes to where the snow is the deepest and the skiing is the sweetest. Kirkwood also offers some tempting ski/lodging packages. (Off Highway 88 via Highway 89; (209)258-6000.)

Sierra-at-Tahoe • Formerly named Sierra Ski Ranch, Tahoe's third-largest ski area is a good all-around resort, offering a slightly better price than most comparable places in Tahoe. It's not worth the drive from the North Shore, but it's a good alternative to Heavenly if you want a change of venue near the South Shore. (Off Highway 50; (916)659-7453.)

Ski for Free

Perhaps the best things in life *are* free. The South Shore's choicest cross-country ski tracks are at Sorensen's Resort in Hope Valley, and, yep, they're open to the public at no charge. You'll find more than 60 miles of trails winding through the Toiyabe National Forest—plenty of room for mastering that telemark turn and escaping the Tahoe crowds. Rentals, lessons, tours, and trail maps are available at the Hope Valley Cross-Country Ski Center, located within Sorensen's Resort. From Highway 50 in Myers (the town just before South Lake Tahoe), take Highway 89 South over the Luther Pass to the Highway 88/89 intersection, turn left, and continue a half-mile to Sorensen's. For more details, contact the Ski Center at (916)694-2266 or Sorensen's at (800)423-9949 or (916)694-2203.

skiing or mountain biking, even though it's about an hour-long drive from town. For $12, you can jump into their six open-air pools (each is set at a different temperature) and watch ducks and geese at the nearby wildlife area. If a good soak doesn't get all the kinks out, indulge in a rubdown at the resort's massage center (no children under 12 allowed in the resort; 2001 Foothill Boulevard, 2 miles north of the east end of Kingsbury Grade, near Genoa, Nevada; (702)782-8155).

South Lake Tahoe boasts dozens of **cheap eats**. For breakfast, just about everyone in town heads to Ernie's Coffee Shop, the "Cheers" of Tahoe's greasy diners, where service doesn't get any friendlier (1146 Emerald Bay Road/Highway 89, South Lake Tahoe; (916)541-2161). South Lake's premier vegetarian hangout is Sprouts, which dishes up such standard fleshless favorites as tempeh burgers and veggie sandwiches, and whips up some mighty fine fruit smoothies (3123 Harrison Avenue, at S Lake Tahoe Boulevard, South Lake Tahoe; (916)541-6969). On a cold winter's day, nothing beats a large, steaming plate of fettuccine at Heidi's Family Restaurant, which is also famous among skiers for its huge, carbo-loading breakfasts (3485 S Lake Tahoe Boulevard, South Lake Tahoe; (916)544-8113). For dinner, try Cantina Los Tres Hombres, another local favorite, mostly because it's cheap (nearly everything on the menu is less than $10) and filling and there always seems to be a daily drink special (765 Emerald Bay Road, just north of the "Y"—the Highway 50/Highway 89 junction, South Lake Tahoe; (916)544-1233). And of course, there are those stuff-your-face,

> ### Steamboat Skiing
>
> Tahoe's brilliant-blue lake is so deep it never freezes, so it's navigable even in the dead of winter. Capitalizing on that fact, the *Tahoe Queen*, an authentic Mississippi stern-wheeler regularly used for scenic lunch and dinner cruises, doubles as a ferry for South Shore skiers who want to explore the North Shore's resorts. Skiers hop aboard at the base of Ski Run Boulevard in South Lake. The 25-mile ride takes about two hours, disembarking at the West Shore's tiny town of Homewood, where a waiting shuttle transports riders to Squaw Valley ski resort. Passengers return to South Lake the same way they came; however, on the trip back the bar is open, the band is playing, and the boat is rockin'. Round-trip fare is only $18, and for an additional $9 skiers can fill up on a big breakfast on the morning ferry. Reservations required; call (916)541-3364.

all-you-can-eat **bargain buffets** advertised at restaurants in and around the gambling centers, so, if you're *really* hungry, head over to Nevada for a bellyful.

CHEAP SLEEPS

Chamonix Inn
913 Friday Avenue, South Lake Tahoe, CA 96150 •
(800)447-5353 or (916)544-5274

Chamonix Inn, located near the California–Nevada border, is a haven for skiers and gamblers. The inn offers direct shuttle service to surrounding ski resorts and casinos, and there's a coffee shop (for that quick breakfast before hitting the slopes) and a pool and hot tub (for that long soak afterward). The 32 rooms are basic yet clean, with firm beds, direct-dial phones, and TVs with HBO. Great ski packages are available, too.

Emerald Motel
515 Emerald Bay Road/Highway 89, South Lake Tahoe, CA 96150 •
(916)544-5515

It's hardly the gem its name would suggest, but the Emerald does offer rooms at a jewel of a price. The motel is located on the west end of town, far from the glitzy casinos, so if your goal is to keep your distance from the gambling scene, this may be the place. Most of the nine rooms offer a queen-size bed, a kitchen with microwave oven and coffee maker, telephone, and cable TV. A few good, reasonably priced restaurants, including Cantina Los Tres Hombres, are within walking distance.

Lamplighter Motel
4143 Cedar Avenue, South Lake Tahoe, CA 96150 • (916)544-2936

Surrounded by dozens of cheesy hotels and motels catering to low rollers, the Lamplighter is set apart by its meticulously maintained facade. On the inside, the Mr. Clean theme continues, with 28 ultra-tidy (we're talking dust-free) and comfortable rooms. The rates include such standard amenities as direct-dial phone, remote TV, and in-room brewed coffee. There's also a Jacuzzi, the casinos are a mere 50 yards away, and ski packages are available.

Manzanita Motel
532 Emerald Bay Road/Highway 89, South Lake Tahoe, CA 96150 • (916)541-6400

Located across the highway from the Emerald Motel, the Manzanita has the same amenities as its neighbor—TV, refrigerator, microwave oven— at approximately the same price, yet it has almost twice as many rooms, thus doubling your chances of finding a vacancy during peak season. The shrewd traveler might even be able to haggle the price down a few dollars, using the Emerald's rates as a bargaining chip.

ACCESS

The drive from San Francisco to South Lake Tahoe takes about four hours—about the same time it takes to get to North Lake Tahoe, except you have to navigate a few dozen miles of graded S-turns (*treacherous* S-turns during snowstorms). From San Francisco, take Interstate 80 to Sacramento and follow the signs to Highway 50, which leads to South Lake. Watch out for deer bounding onto the highway, and during winter, carry chains.

Thanks to the many casinos in South Lake, catching a bus from Sacramento or San Francisco is simple and cheap; call Greyhound at (800)231-2222 for schedule and price information. Once you're in South Lake, the STAGE (South Tahoe Area Ground Express) will shuttle you around town 24 hours a day, year-round; (916)542-6077. South Lake's ski resorts run their own free shuttles daily in winter, and most casinos provide free shuttle service from nearby hotels year-round.

Flying to Lake Tahoe is also an option, albeit an expensive one. Reno Air, (800)736-6247, and TW Express, (800)221-2000, service the South Lake Tahoe Airport, (916)542-6180, but your best budget bet is to fly into Reno-Tahoe International Airport in Nevada, (702)328-6400, and then spend about $15 more for a ride on the Casino Express shuttle bus, (800)446-6128, into South Lake Tahoe.

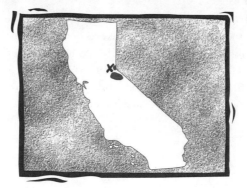

Yosemite National Park

What was once the beloved home of the Ahwahneechee, Miwok, and Paiute Indians is now a spectacular international playground for four million annual visitors. Designated a national park in 1890, thanks in part to Sierra Club founder John Muir, the 1,200-square-mile Yosemite National Park is only slightly smaller than the state of Rhode Island. During peak season, however, it seems more like a 1,200-square-foot park. Crowds more typical of Disney World clog the 7-square-mile valley for a glimpse of some of nature's most incredible creations, including El Capitán, the largest piece of exposed granite on earth, and Yosemite Falls, the highest waterfall in North America and the fifth highest in the world.

To avoid most of the crowds, visit in spring or early fall, when the wildflowers are plentiful and the weather is usually mild. You can virtually escape civilization by setting up a tent in Tuolumne Meadows, where numerous trails wind through the densely forested and sparsely populated high country. This grande dame of national parks is most dazzling, and least crowded, in winter, the time of year Ansel Adams shot those world-renowned photographs of the snow-laced valley. Unfortunately, most of the hiking trails will be inaccessible at this time of year and the drive may be treacherous;

snow and ice limit access to the park, and many of the eastern passes are closed. Those who do brave the elements, however, will be rewarded a truly unforgettable winter vista.

ON THE ROAD

No matter what the time of year, visitors to Yosemite National Park must pay the friendly rangers a $5-per-car entrance fee. In return, you receive a seven-day pass, a detailed park map, and the "Yosemite Guide," a handy 16-page tabloid featuring the park's rules, rates, attractions, exhibits, and—most important—freebies. Gratis events include guided wildlife walks (many birds, mule deer, mountain lions, coyotes, and American black bears make their homes here), rock-climbing talks and tours, and photography and painting classes. Schedules change monthly, so those interested should check the guide and structure their visit accordingly.

One of the best ways to sightsee on the valley floor is by bike. Curry Village, (209)372-8319, and Yosemite Lodge, (209)372-1208, have bike stands that rent one-speed cruisers daily for about $5 an hour or $16 a day, including a helmet. More than 8 miles of paved bicycle paths wind through the eastern end of the valley, but bicycles (including mountain bikes) are not allowed on hiking trails.

Day hikers in the valley have a wide variety of those trails to choose from, some boring, some mind-blowing, all well-charted on the visitor's map. The best easy hike is the **Mirror Lake/Meadow Trail**, a 2-mile round-trip walk (5 miles if you circle the lake) that provides a magnificent view of Half Dome. More strenuous is the popular hike to **Upper Yosemite Falls**, a 7.2-mile round-trip trek with a spectacular overview

Hired Hands

If you've always wanted to backpack in Yosemite but don't have the equipment or experience, here's your chance. Call Southern Yosemite Mountain Guides at (209)658-TREK and ask for a free brochure of their guided and catered backpacking adventures, which range from leisurely weekend family outings to challenging two-week treks. Guided mountain-bike tours, fly-fishing excursions, and rock-climbing clinics are also available (and are surprisingly affordable).

155

Yosemite by the Book

For just a few dollars, you can get the ultimate tour of Yosemite National Park. Just pick up a copy of the *Yosemite Road Guide* or the *Yosemite Valley Tour* cassette tape at the Yosemite Valley Visitors Center. It's almost as good as having Ranger Rick in the backseat of your car.

of the 2,425-foot drop. (Note: Don't wander off the trail, or you may join the unlucky souls who have tumbled off the cliffs to their deaths.) The granddaddy of all Yosemite day hikes is the very steep ascent to the top of **Half Dome**, a 17-mile, round-trip, 10- to 12-hour-long thigh-burner that requires Schwarzenegger-like gusto and the nerve to hang onto climbing cables anchored in granite—clearly not a jaunt for every-one. When the snowstorm season hits, most hiking trails are closed, and many people haul out their snowshoes or cross-country skis for valley excursions, or snap on their alpine skis and schuss down the groomed beginner/intermediate hills of **Badger Pass Ski Area** (on Glacier Point Road, 6 miles east of Highway 41; (209)372-1330).

If you'd rather keep your feet firmly planted on lower ground, tour the **Yosemite Valley Visitors Center**, which houses some mildly interesting galleries and museums. The center's **Indian Cultural Museum** holds live demonstrations of the native Miwok and Paiute methods of basket weaving, jewelry making, and other crafts. Nearby are a reconstructed Miwok-Paiute Village, a self-guided nature trail, and an art gallery showcasing the master photographer whose name is almost synonymous with this place: Ansel Adams.

While the sightseeing in Yosemite is unparalleled, the dining is not. Bring as much of your own food as possible, because most of the park's restaurants offer mediocre (or worse) cafeteria-style food (the only excep-tion is the lofty Ahwahnee Restaurant, but you'll have to fork over a bundle to eat there). In **Yosemite Village**, the Village Grill serves a full breakfast for less than $5, and Degnan's Deli sells jumbo-size sandwiches for about $4. Pricier options include The Loft, located above the deli, with a more upscale menu that leans towards Southwestern fare, along with your standard burger and salad. Most people, however, stand in line at the numerous snack stands or stock up at the park's six grocery stores.

Unless bumper-to-bumper traffic is your idea of a vacation in the woods, skip the actual Yosemite Valley during the summer weekends and join the rebel minority who know there's more than one way to view the

Yosemite by the Numbers

General Park Information:	(209)372-0200 (recorded)
Road and Weather Conditions:	(209)372-0200 (recorded)
Lodging Reservations:	(209)252-4848
Campground Information:	(209)372-0265 or
	(209)372-0200 (recorded)
Campground Reservations (Mistix):	(800)365-2267
Wilderness (Backpacking) Permits:	(209)372-0310

area. **Glacier Point**, at the end of Glacier Point Road, has what many consider one of the best vistas on the continent—a bird's-eye view of the entire valley and a panoramic expanse of the **High Sierra**. The view is particularly striking at sunset and under a full moon.

At the southern entrance to the park, 35 miles south of the valley, lies the **Mariposa Grove**, home to some of the planet's largest and most ancient living things. The most popular attraction is the 2,700-year-old **Grizzly Giant**, the world's oldest sequoia. Pick up a self-guided trail map in the box at the grove trailhead or attend one of the free ranger-led walks, offered regularly; check the "Yosemite Guide" for current schedules.

Due north of Yosemite Valley is the famous **Tioga Road** (Highway 120), the highest automobile pass in California, which crests at 9,945 feet (closed in winter). The ideal time to tour the 60-mile-long east-west stretch is in early summer, when the meadows are dotted with wildflowers and you can occasionally spot some wildlife lingering near the lakes and exposed granite slopes. Numerous turnouts offer prime photo opportunities, and roadside picnic areas are located at Lembert Dome and Tenaya Lake. This is also the route to **Tuolumne Meadows**, a popular camping area (half the campsites are first-come, first-served and half require reservations) and the base for backpackers heading into Yosemite's beautiful high country (wilderness permits are required and they're free, but only a limited number are distributed).

CHEAP SLEEPS

Reservations for all Yosemite National Park accommodations may be—and usually are—made up to a year in advance, so try to plan your trip as early as possible. Rates are subject to change daily for all lodgings; the fees listed here are averages. For more information on Yosemite lodgings and to make reservations, call

Saddle Trips for City Slickers

A two-hour horseback ride will set you back $30, but the thrill (and ease) of riding a horse into Yosemite's beautiful backcountry just might make it worth the splurge. Select a stable in Yosemite Valley, Wawona, or Tuolumne Meadows, then call (209)372-8348 to make a reservation.

(209)252-4848. Most Yosemite campsites may be booked up to eight weeks in advance; for camping reservations, call Mistix at (800)365-2267.

Housekeeping Camp
Yosemite Village, west of Curry Village • (209)252-4848

The emphasis here is on "camp," which is more or less what you'll be doing if you're lucky enough to get a reservation for one of the 282 identical concrete-and-canvas structures (two walls and the roof are made of cloth). The good news is that regardless of whether you're a party of one or four (the maximum allowed), the price is the same: $39 a night. The bad news is that the units are cramped, uncomfortable, and serve as sacred feeding ground for the voracious alpine mosquito (bring repellent). Each unit is equipped with one double bed and two fold-down cots (attached at one end to the wall), and outside are a picnic table, shelves, and an outlet for a hot plate and other appliances. Shared bathroom, shower, and laundry facilities and a grocery store are nearby. Open from mid-April to early October, weather permitting.

Curry Village
Yosemite Valley, southeast of Yosemite Village • (209)252-4848

The cheapest sleeps in Curry Village are the 427 canvas tent cabins (about $37 a night) that sleep up to five people. Bathroom facilities are shared and, to avoid tempting the always-hungry bears, no food or cooking is allowed. The 80 small wood cabins sleep up to five people and are costlier, but some have private bathrooms. Unfortunately, both the tent cabins and the wood cabins have sagging, uncomfortable beds, and only the wood cabins are heated. These lodgings are actually just a step up from camping, but if you adopt the right "roughing it" attitude, they can be a lot of fun. Open year-round.

Yosemite Lodge
Yosemite Valley, west of Yosemite Village • (209)252-4848

If camping or sleeping in a canvas tent cabin sounds more like something out of Dante's *Inferno* than a stay in paradise, your only inexpensive alternative in the park is the 495-room Yosemite Lodge, which has standard motel-style rooms and a smattering of small wood cabins (private bath optional for both). On summer weekends, the area around the lodge is a zoo, with parades of tour buses roaring through. Fortunately, a short walk in any direction gets you away from the masses. Lodge reservations are definitely needed far in advance. Open year-round.

Tuolumne Meadows Lodge/White Wolf Lodge
Off Tioga Road, north of Yosemite Valley • (209)252-4848

Tuolumne Meadows Lodge and White Wolf Lodge are the park's only inexpensive accommodations located outside of Yosemite Valley. They offer the same type of lodgings as their cousins in the valley—small wood cabins and canvas tent cabins—yet they're far from the madding crowds. White Wolf has 24 tent cabins (shared bath only) and 4 wood cabins (private bath optional) that are always booked a full year in advance. Tuolumne Meadows Lodge has 69 tent cabins (shared bath only). Open from mid-April to early October, weather permitting.

Off-Season Savings

From late October through late March (excluding holidays), you can save up to 30 percent on room rates and quadruple your chances of getting a preferred reservation date. Bring lots of warm clothing; Yosemite is usually covered with more than a foot of snow in winter.

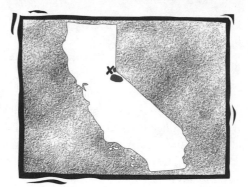

Mammoth Lakes

At the base of 11,053-foot Mammoth Mountain are nearly a dozen alpine lakes and the sprawling town of Mammoth Lakes—a mishmash of inns, motels, and restaurants built primarily to serve patrons of the popular Mammoth Mountain Ski Area. Ever since resort founder Dave McCoy mortgaged his motorcycle for $85 in 1938 to buy his first ski lift, folks have been coming here in droves (particularly from Southern California) to carve turns and navigate the moguls at one of the best downhill areas in the United States. In addition to skiing, this section of the eastern Sierra Nevada has been famous for decades for its fantastic fishing holes. In fact, here the trout is king, and several fishing derbies celebrate its royal status. This natural kingdom is no longer the exclusive domain of fishers and skiers, however. Word has gotten out about Mammoth's charms, attracting every kind of outdoor enthusiast and adventurer to this spectacular region in the heart of the High Sierra.

ON THE ROAD

Whether you've migrated to the Mammoth area to ski, fish, play, or simply rest your weary bones, stop by the **Mammoth Lakes Visitors**

Melting Pots

Dozens of natural hot springs dot the Mammoth area, although most of the remote ones are kept secret by tourist-weary locals who probably wouldn't make you feel very welcome even if you discovered one. The more accessible springs, however, definitely welcome visitors, including the free Hot Creek Geologic Site, where the narrow creek feeds into a series of artificial pools— some only big enough for two, others family-size. These pools are equipped with cold-water pipes that usually keep the water temperature toasty yet not unbearably hot. Although the Forest Service discourages soaking in the pools because of sporadic spurts of scalding water—yes, there *is* a small risk of getting your buns poached—most people are more concerned about whether or not to show off their birthday suit (swimsuits are optional). Open daily from sunrise to sunset; take the Hot Creek Hatchery Road exit off Highway 395 (at the north end of Mammoth Lakes Airport) and follow the signs. Call the Mammoth Lakes Visitors Bureau for more details at (800)367-6572 or (619)934-2712.

Bureau. You'll find wall-to-wall maps, coupons, brochures, and day planners, as well as copies of the forest service's excellent (and free) "Winter Recreation Map" and "Summer Recreation Map," which show the area's best routes for hiking, biking, sledding, snowmobiling, and cross-country skiing. The friendly bureau staff will even help you find an affordable place to stay in Mammoth (in the Village Shopping Center, on Main Street, Mammoth Lakes; (800)367-6572 or (619)934-2712). If you need to rent ski gear or practically any other athletic and outdoor equipment, visit the bustling **Kittredge Sports** shop (on Main Street, next to the Chevron gas station, Mammoth Lakes; (619)934-7566).

Once you've unpacked your bags, it's time to lace up your hiking boots and explore. A top attraction is **Devils Postpile National Monument**, one of the world's premier examples of basalt columns. The tall, slender rock columns were formed nearly 100,000 years ago when lava from the erupting Mammoth Mountain cooled and fractured into multisided forms; they've become such a popular attraction that between June 15 and September 15, rangers close the access road to daytime traffic and require visitors without a special permit to travel by shuttle. Shuttles pick up riders every 15 minutes at the Mammoth Mountain Ski Area parking lot (on Minaret Road, off Highway 203 West) and drop them off at a riverside trail for the less-than-half-mile walk to the monument (shuttle fee is about $7 round-trip; the road is closed in winter; (619)934-2505). After you've seen the Postpile, follow the trail for another 2 miles to the beautiful **Rainbow Falls**, where the San Joaquin River plunges 101 feet over an ancient lava flow into a deep pool, often creating rainbows in the mist. If you follow the trail to Red's Meadow, you'll be at one of the entrance points to the 228,500-acre **Ansel Adams Wilderness**, a popular backpacking destination highlighted by the jagged **Minarets**, a series of steep, narrow volcanic ridges just south of massive Mount Ritter.

True to its name, the Mammoth Lakes area boasts 10 lakes (none of which, oddly enough, are named Mammoth). The largest and one of the most striking is **Lake Mary**, and even though it's set high in the mountains, it's easy to get to: head west on Main Street, which turns into Lake Mary Road; drive past Twin Lakes; and continue on till you see it. Numerous hiking trails at Lake Mary lead to nearby smaller, less crowded lakes, including **Horseshoe Lake**, a great place for swimming (the water is slightly warmer than in neighboring lakes). Trout fishers frequently try their luck at Lake Mary, although most anglers prefer to cast their lines in **Convict Lake**, where you can rent a boat and stock up at the Convict Lake Resort's tackle shop (from Highway 395 a few miles south of town, take the Convict Lake Road exit, just south of Mammoth Lakes Airport; (619)934-3800). Another hot spot for snagging some meaty trout is **Hot Creek**, the most popular catch-and-release fishery in California (on average, each trout is caught and released five to six times a month). Only a few miles of the creek are accessible to the public; the rest is private property (on Hot Creek Hatchery Road, just off Highway 395 at the north end of Mammoth Lakes Airport; (800)367-6572 or (619)934-2712).

Another hugely popular sport at Mammoth—**mountain biking**—holds sway during the summer, when the entire Mammoth Mountain Ski Area is transformed into one of the top bike parks in the country, and a national mountain-bike championship race takes place (on Minaret Road, off Highway 203 West, Mammoth Lakes; (800)367-6572 or (619)934-0606). Twenty dollars ($10 for kids) will buy you an all-day pass to 60 miles of single-track trails and a gondola that will zip you and your bike up to the top of the mountain. From there it's downhill all the way (be sure to wear a helmet), with trails ranging in difficulty from the mellow "Paper Route" ride to the infamous "Kamikaze" wheel-spinner. If you don't want to pay to ride a bike, there are dozens of great trails where mountain bikes are permitted.

With winter comes an onslaught of downhill skiers, who journey here to schuss the slopes of **Mammoth Mountain Ski Area**; (800)832-7320. With 3,500 skiable acres, 150 runs, 30 chair lifts, and a 70 percent chance of sunny skies, Mammoth is lauded as one of the nation's top downhill resorts. Unfortunately, it can also be one of the country's most *crowded* ski areas, particularly on weekends, when more than 10,000 Los Angelenos make the lengthy commute. (Tip: About 90 percent of the skiers arrive on Friday night and leave Sunday afternoon, so come on a weekday.) A Mammoth lift ticket costs at least $40 for an adult, but you can shave about 10 bucks off the price by purchasing a half-day pass, and a multiple-day ticket will reap even greater savings. Discounts are available for children, teens, and senior citizens.

Mammoth Lakes also has mile upon mile of perfectly groomed **cross-country** ski trails, winding through gorgeous stretches of national forest and immense meadows. Nordic skiers of all levels favor the **Tamarack Cross-Country Ski Center** at Tamarack Lodge on Twin Lakes, which offers 25 miles of groomed trails, extensive backcountry trails, lessons, rentals, and tours (on Lake Mary Road, 2½ miles southwest of town, Mammoth Lakes; (619)934-2442).

Fortunately for budget diners, Mammoth Lakes offers a larger selection of cheap eats than most small cities in Northern California. For morning carbo-loading, dig into the huge omelets and other egg dishes at the **Breakfast Club**, which also makes its own muffins and pastries and stays open until 1pm (Old Mammoth Road at Main Street, Mammoth Lakes; (619)934-6944). Any local will tell you that **Anything Goes Cafe** makes the region's best scones, cinnamon rolls, and sandwiches (in Sherwin Plaza, 645 Old Mammoth Road, Mammoth Lakes; (619)934-2424).

After a hard day of playing in the mountains, slip into a seat at **Slocum's** for the number-one dining deal in town. During happy hour (4 to 6pm daily), Slocum's (known to locals as "The Office") serves platters of pesto ravioli, escargot, smoked salmon, fried calamari, and steamed

Mammoth Lakes

MAS Transit: Leave the Driving to Them

If you've ever seen the several-mile-long traffic jams converging on Mammoth Mountain Ski Area's parking lot, then you know why veteran Mammoth skiers always park their wheels in town and take the shuttle to the resort. These shuttles are not only convenient, they're free. And no matter where you're staying, a Mammoth Area Shuttle (MAS) stop is most likely nearby. The ubiquitous buses run from 7am to 5:30pm daily during ski season, and swing by their stops every 15 minutes to shuttle skiers to one of the resort's three entrances. For more information, call (619)934-0687.

🎵 A Kick in the Brass

Granted, life is often one big outdoor party in Mammoth Lakes, but when the annual Mammoth Lakes Jazz Jubilee swings into gear in July, hold on to your Tevas—nearly everyone in this toe-tapping town starts kicking up their heels when a dozen world-class bands start tootin' their horns. This three-day jazz extravaganza usually happens the first weekend after the Fourth of July, and opening day is free (after that it's about $25 per day). A much more sedate but definitely worthwhile musical event is the annual Sierra Summer Festival Concert, a tribute to everything from chamber to classical that begins in late July and winds down in early August. For more information about either event, call the Mammoth Lakes Visitors Bureau at (800)367-6572 or (619)934-2712.

clams for less than $4 and mugs of Anchor Steam beer on tap for only $1.75 (321 Main Street, across the street from Kittredge Sports, Mammoth Lakes; (619)934-7647). For the town's top tamales, tortillas, and fajitas, go to **Roberto's Café** (271 Old Mammoth Road at Sierra Nevada Road, Mammoth Lakes; (619)934-3667); for pizza, visit **Giovanni's Pizza**, voted the best in Mammoth. Try their gourmet clam and garlic version (in the Minaret Village Mall, Old Mammoth Road, Mammoth Lakes; (619)934-7563). You can indulge in budget entertainment while noshing on big burgers, steaks, and ribs at **Grumpy's Saloon & Eatery**, which boasts pool tables, shuffleboards, video games, volleyball tournaments, and seven big-screen TVs (37 Old Mammoth Road at Tavern Road, Mammoth Lakes; (619)934-8587). Folks who've sworn off red meat will like the **Good Life Cafe**, which offers a cholesterol-free menu featuring pita sandwiches, Mexican food prepared without beef, veggie burgers, and the like (in the Mammoth Mall, Old Mammoth Road at Tavern Road, Mammoth Lakes; (619)934-1734).

CHEAP SLEEPS

Davison Street Guest House
19 Davison Street, Mammoth Lakes, CA 93546 • (619)544-9093

For as little as $15 a night in summer, you can slumber on a bunk bed at this classy, five-bedroom A-frame lodge, which once served as a private residence. Although the Guest House is cramped and you have to share the bathrooms and kitchen with other visitors, it is clean, cute, comfortable, warm, and—a plus for sun worshipers—there's a large deck in back. In the winter, its location near the slopes makes this a skiers' paradise. Inexpensive private rooms (without baths) are also available. Rates increase slightly in winter.

Kitzbuhel Lodge
On Berner Street (PO Box 433), Mammoth Lakes, CA 93546 •
(619)934-2352

You can spend a week here for the price of one night at a Mammoth Lakes condo if you're willing to part with some privacy. Each of the Kitzbuhel Lodge's 16 rooms is lined with bunk beds (100 beds total), and though the lodge caters primarily to large groups and clubs, individuals are also welcome for about $10 a night in summer and $20 in winter. These are bargain prices, especially since guests may use the kitchen, Jacuzzi, and ski-storage and -waxing room. There's even cable TV in the lounge.

Mammoth Budget Inn
54 Sierra Boulevard, Mammoth Lakes, CA 93546 • (619)934-8892

This hotel won't win any beauty contests, but the proprietor does a commendable job of providing the basic creature comforts—queen-size bed, coffee maker, telephone, TV, heater, and private bath with tub—at reasonable rates. Located just off Main Street, the 40-room inn is within walking distance of several restaurants and ski-shuttle stops.

Ullr Lodge
5920 Minaret Road (PO Box 53), Mammoth Lakes, CA 93546 •
(619)934-2454

Let's face it: The Ullr (pronounced YOU-ler) Lodge's 19 spartan, garish rooms look best with the lights off (everything—from the carpets to the bedcovers—reeks of cheapness), but the prices make it worth considering. You can choose from the dorm rooms (about $12 a night in summer and $16 in winter), a room with shared bath (from $20 to $50), or a room with private bath and TV (in the $40 to $60 range). There's also a community kitchen, sauna, lounge with fireplace, and easy access to a ski-shuttle stop. (Note: Internet users can get a very up-to-date Mammoth Lakes weather report by e-mailing the proprietor at denmanning @delphi.com.)

GOLD COUNTRY

Sacramento

North Gold Country

South Gold Country

Sacramento

Sacramento has long been regarded as San Francisco's second-class stepsister, but with its increasing number of skyscrapers, trendy restaurants, and swanky hotels (not to mention the NBA's Sacramento Kings), California's capital city is no longer the sleepy little valley town folks used to whiz through on their way to Lake Tahoe. Located 90 miles northeast of the Bay Area, the city is best known for its dual status as the seat of state government and the epicenter of California's biggest industry· agriculture (locals affectionately call it the Big Tomato and Sacratomato). But disregard any disparaging words you may have heard about this agricultural hot spot: there are no cows (or even cowboy hats) within city limits, and most of the city slickers do not pick tomatoes for a living.

This former Gold Rush boomtown sprang up where the American and Sacramento Rivers meet—an area now known as Old Sac. In 1839 Swiss immigrant John Sutter traversed both rivers, built his famous fort, and established New Helvetia, his "New Switzerland" colony. But his hopes that the thriving colony would evolve into his own vast empire were dashed when gold was discovered near Sutter's sawmill in 1848. Sutter's colonists deserted New Helvetia to search for the precious nuggets, and as word of the gold discovery spread, thousands more wound their way to the hills above Sacramento to seek their fortune. Sutter himself never prospered from the Gold Rush and died a bitter, penniless man.

Today, Sacramento is home to more than a million people, many of whom play politics with the capitol crowd or practice law. They dote on their spectacular Victorian homes and fine Craftsman-style bungalows, and are justly proud of the tree-lined streets and thick carpets of grass that surround their homes and parks.

In the scorching summer months, when thermometers often soar into the three-digit range, many folks beat the heat by diving into swimming pools, chugging around the delta in a houseboat with a fishing pole in hand, or floating down the American River. Once the sun sets, however, things cool off dramatically, and Sacramentans often enjoy their evening meals alfresco. Winters are punctuated by the famous tule fog—so thick it blocks the sun for weeks at a time—and cooler temperatures than in San Francisco. And as all ski buffs know, locals always get the jump on their Bay Area neighbors racing to the snowy slopes of Lake Tahoe, thanks to the city's proximity to the Sierra Nevada.

ON THE ROAD

To best appreciate the Big Tomato, start your tour of the town in **Old Sacramento**, the historic district. Perched along the Sacramento River, the 4-block-long stretch is filled with dozens of restaurants, gift shops, and saloons, worth a once-over on your way toward the **California State Railroad Museum**. This grand monument to the glory days of locomotion and the Big Four is the largest museum of its kind in the nation and a must-see for locomotive lovers of all ages (111 I Street at 2nd Street, Sacramento; (916)448-4466). The granddaddy of Old Sac attractions is the **Sacramento Dixieland Jubilee,** the world's largest Dixieland jazz festival, which attracts thousands of toe-tappers and bands from around the world each Memorial Day weekend; (916)372-5277.

Transit Tips

In Sacramento, the phrase "within walking distance" is often right up there with "the check's in the mail," so if you don't have wheels, you'd better have a bus schedule. Fortunately, Sacramento Regional Transit is a reasonably reliable bus system that will take you just about anywhere you want to go. Transit maps sell for a buck at 1013 K Street at 10th Street, or, better yet, call (916)321-BUSS and ask the operator to outline the best route for you. One-way fares are $1.25, and an all-day pass (available from any bus driver) costs $3.

One mile south of Old Sac is the **California Towe Ford Museum of Automotive History**, a giant warehouse containing the largest antique Ford collection in the country; nearly every model ever manufactured by the Ford Motor Company is parked here (2200 Front Street, Sacramento; (916)442-6802). Nearby is the **Crocker Art Museum**, home of the largest art collection in the region, including contemporary California art by such talents as Wayne Thiebaud and Robert Arneson. The museum is housed in one of the city's most elaborate Victorian structures (216 O Street, between 2nd and 3rd Streets, Sacramento; (916)264-5423).

A few blocks northeast of the Crocker Art Museum is the awe-inspiring **state capitol building**, restored in the 1970s to its original magnificence with $67.8 million in taxpayers' dollars (so come see what you paid for). You may wander around the building on your own, but you really shouldn't miss the free tours given daily every hour between 9am and 4pm, which include an overview of the legislative process and, if you're lucky, a chance to see the political hotshots in action. Tickets are

Braking Away

The American River Parkway, a 5,000-acre nature preserve that runs along the river from Discovery Park to Folsom Lake, is a great spot for two-wheeling. On sunny Sunday afternoons, even the locals spend a few hours pedaling their bikes along the mostly flat 22-mile-long bike trail that parallels the river. You can rent a bike for about $15 a day at City Bicycle Works (2419 K Street at 24th Street in downtown Sacramento; (916)447-2453).

★★ *Those Lion Eyes*

Have you mingled with the monkeys or marveled at the mighty roar of a lion lately? Well, here's your chance. Take a gander at these amazing critters and their friends at the Sacramento Zoo, which boasts more than 150 species of exotic animals housed in 15 acres of elaborate zoological gardens. Afterwards, picnic at the duck pond across the street, and if you have tots in tow (and some energy left), take them to Humpty Dumpty's Fairytale Town, a giant kid-pleasin' playground full of slides, swings, and tunnels graced by fairy-tale characters (in William Land Park, corner of Land Park Drive and Sutterville Road, Sacramento; (916)264-5885).

handed out a half hour before the tour on a first-come, first-served basis in the basement of room B-27 in the capitol (10th Street, between L and N Streets, Sacramento; (916)324-0333). After you've marveled at the capitol's interior, spend some time feeding the brazen squirrels scampering around the beautifully landscaped 40-acre **Capitol Park**. Stop by the poignant Vietnam Veterans' Memorial in the park's northeast corner. Etched into panels of India black granite are the names of 5,615 Californians who died in the war. For a step back in time, take a stroll through pioneer **John Sutter's fort**, built in 1839 (27th and L Streets, Sacramento; (916)445-4422).

Thanks to a recent influx of Generation X-ers, a cadre of cheap cafes, coffee shops, and breweries now proliferates in the downtown area. East of the capitol you'll find the original (ergo the coolest) coffee hangout, **Java City** (1800 Capitol Avenue at 18th Street, Sacramento; (916)444-5282), and **Greta's Cafe**, a trendy haunt serving fresh-baked pastries, more than a dozen salads, and great sandwiches at $4 and under (1831 Capitol Avenue at 19th Street, Sacramento; (916)442-7382). One block east of Greta's is the **Rubicon Brewing Company**, which pours some of Sacramento's best brews, including the award-winning India Pale Ale (2004 Capitol Avenue at 20th Street, Sacramento; (916)448-7032). For breakfast, try the **Cornerstone Restaurant**, where a four-egg omelet with home-fries, toast, and fruit is less than five bucks (2330 J Street at 24th Street, Sacramento; (916)441-0948). **Taco Loco Taqueria**, serving outstanding Mexican food (try the charbroiled black-tip shark taco), is a local favorite (2326 J Street at 24th Street, Sacramento; (916)447-0711; and 1122 11th Street at L Street, Sacramento; (916)447-TACO). And for anti-health nuts, there's **Willie's Burgers**, a valley version of Tommy's

Burgers in LA, complete with paper-towel dispensers mounted on the walls (napkins just won't do) to sop up the mess from your artery-clogging double-chili-cheeseburger-with-bacon-and-extra-onions—*whew!* (2415 16th Street, between Broadway and X Street, Sacramento; (916)444-2006).

For great shopping and people-watching downtown, visit the **Tower triangle**, home of the original Tower Records, opened in 1941 (Broadway and 16th Street, Sacramento; (916)444-6688); Tower Books, (916)444-6688, which attracts as many browsers as buyers; Tower Pipes and Cigars, (916)443-8466, a heady-scented shop where a dexterous Cuban hand-rolls fresh cigars in the window; the Tower Theater, (916)443-1982, one of Sacramento's last bastions of foreign, art, and cult flicks; and the Tower Cafe, (916)441-0222, where on balmy summer nights, locals lounge on the patio with their tall glasses of premium brewskis.

Once the America Live! complex opened its doors in the slick Downtown Plaza shopping center, the nightlife in Sacramento cranked up more than a few notches. The mega-nightclub boasts two floors of entertainment, offering something for every night owl under one roof, including country music at **Gatlin's Music City**, big-screen TV at **America's Sports Bar**, hip-hop dance music at **Gator's**, and much more (Downtown Plaza, across from Weinstocks, between J and L Streets and 6th and 7th Streets, Sacramento; (916)447-5483). A more subdued crowd throws darts, sips English ales on tap, and munches quality pub grub at the **Fox and Goose**, where live music ranging from jazz to bluegrass and folk can be heard every night except Sunday (1001 R Street at 10th Street, Sacramento; (916)443-8825). If it's cheap beer, free popcorn, loud jukebox music, and heavy scamming you're after, the legendary **Pine Cove** is the place, serving 75-cent glasses of premium Pabst Blue Ribbon—this ain't no sippin' beer—guaranteed to bring on a buzz (502 29th Street at E Street, Sacramento; (916)446-3624).

Those of you cruising through the city during the last two weeks of August should set aside a hot day or night to visit the **California State**

Chill Out

In the sweltering summer, American River Raft Rentals, (916)635-6400, is your ticket to fun in the sun with all the equipment and information you'll need for a leisurely paddle down Sacramento's docile stretch of the American River. Don't forget the sunscreen.

Fair, Sacramento's grandest party. While the carnival rides and games are predictably head-spinning and zany, even snobby locals who abhor the annual event admit the livestock exhibits alone are worth the admission price. Other fair highlights include daily horse races, nightly rodeos, and live concerts in the beer garden (Cal Expo, off I-80 Business Loop, Sacramento; (916)263-3000).

CHEAP SLEEPS

Americana Lodge
818 15th Street, Sacramento, CA 95814 • (916)444-3980

Budget lodgers might feel compelled to kneel and shout "hallelujah" on the steps of the Americana Lodge—the best cheap sleep in Sacramento. A mere $35 will buy you a night in a newly remodeled, sparkling-clean room with air conditioning (a godsend during Sacramento's hellaciously hot summers), TV (with HBO, no less), direct-dial phones, and a swimming pool. The 41-room Americana is also in a great location—just blocks from the state capitol, the Governor's Mansion, and the Sacramento Convention Center—and there's even plenty of free parking.

Capitol Park Hotel
1125 9th Street, Sacramento, CA 95814 • (916)441-5361

Although the Capitol Park Hotel primarily houses elderly folk on a long-term basis, the friendly proprietor keeps about 15 rooms available for overnighters of any age. Even though there is no parking lot (a public parking garage is down the street), this is one of the best deals in town. For less than $30 you get a slightly worn yet comfy room with air conditioning, cable TV, and large windows. But the best part is the location—just steps away from the state capitol; only a room at the pricey Hyatt Regency could get you closer.

Capitol Travel Inn
817 W Capitol Avenue, Sacramento, CA 95691 • (916)371-6983

If you have wheels and don't mind the short drive into West Sacramento (where there are no tourist—or even resident—attractions), this 38-room inn might be worth your while. A room costs about $30 a night, which pays for a large color TV, a direct-dial phone, air conditioning, and a free place to park the car. Note: The inn *isn't* within walking distance of Sacramento's star attractions, so some sort of transport is essential for sightseeing.

Mansion View Lodge
711 16th Street, Sacramento, CA 95814 • (916)443-6631

Only a handful of cheap hotels in downtown Sacramento will make you feel safe. This is one of them. Located opposite the Governor's Mansion, the Mansion View Lodge has 41 no-nonsense rooms with telephones, TVs, firm beds, and tacky pink doors. In the morning, warm up with a free cup of coffee, grab a free map of Sacramento's downtown attractions, and hit the road.

Sacramento Hostel
900 H Street, Sacramento, CA 95814 • (916)447-8687

First, the NBA's Sacramento Kings bounced into town, then an official AYH-affiliated youth hostel opened its doors—Sacramento, you've hit the big time at last! In 1995, at a cost of more than $2 million, the Llewellyn Williams Mansion, a 12,000-square-foot Victorian beauty, was transformed into one of the finest youth hostels in the country. It offers 60 bunk beds as well as bedrooms for families, and takes all comers at $12 a head (family rates are available). Located just behind city hall in the heart of downtown, the hostel is within walking distance of Sacramento's major sights, including the capitol and Old Sac.

ACCESS

In Italy all roads lead to Rome, and in California all highways lead to Sacramento. If you're coming by car, Highways 99, 16, 50, and 160 and Interstates 80 and 5 lead to the capitol—in fact, it's hard *not* to pass through Sacramento. Barring rush-hour traffic jams, it's about a 90-minute drive from San Francisco, and approximately seven or eight hours from Los Angeles. Amtrak, stationed at 4th and I Streets, has several trains serving the city daily; call (800)USA-RAIL for reservations and schedules. Sacramento is the hub for Greyhound buses traveling throughout the state (715 L Street at 7th Street; (800)231-2222). The Sacramento Metropolitan Airport, 12 miles north of town off Interstate 5, has daily flights to most major cities, including San Francisco and LA; (916)929-5411. For shuttle service to and from the airport, call Aero Shuttle at (916)956-3333.

North Gold Country

By 1849, word had spread throughout the United States, Europe, and other corners of the globe that gold miners were becoming millionaires overnight in California. In just one year, more than 80,000 eager souls stampeded their way across water and land to reach the hilly terrain now known as the Gold Country and the Mother Lode. Many of the "49ers" had to fight for their claims to the land, claims that left the average miner with little more than dirt and grime in his pocket. Crime and starvation were rampant, and when the exhausted miners put away their picks and pans for the night, most sought comfort in drinking, gambling, and prostitutes. It was a wild and heady time that brought riches to relatively few, but that changed the Golden State forever.

You can follow in the miners' footsteps (geographically, at least) by cruising along the aptly numbered Highway 49, the zigzagging, 321-mile road that links many of the mining towns. You'll find some of the most authentically preserved towns in the northern Gold Country, including Grass Valley, where more than a billion dollars in gold was extracted, and Nevada City, former home of one of the region's more famous gold miners, President Herbert Hoover.

ON THE ROAD

Unlike the southern Gold Country, which has towns and attractions extending southward for more than a hundred miles, the places worth visiting in the northern Gold Country are all within a 13-mile radius (something to consider if you prefer walking to driving). Although **Auburn** is the largest town in the area and has been the seat of Placer County since 1850, nowadays it serves mainly as a pit stop for vacationers headed for Lake Tahoe. Its few noteworthy sights, including the many shops and restaurants of Old Town and the impressively domed **Placer County Courthouse**, are best seen out the car window as you head toward the far more congenial towns of Grass Valley and Nevada City.

Only 4 miles apart, **Grass Valley** and its smaller, cuter cousin, **Nevada City**, share many Gold Rush–town characteristics: historic landmarks, a restored "old town," Victorian-era architecture, hardrock-mining museums, and hard-to-find parking. Unfortunately, neither town offers an abundance of inexpensive lodgings—this is fancy B&B country—so vacation here in the off season and make reservations far in advance; otherwise, be prepared to shell out a little more hotel money than you bargained for.

Grass Valley, once known for rich quartz mines and Gold Rush entertainers like Lola Montez and Lotta Crabtree, has a historic and slightly scruffy downtown that's a pleasure to explore. Stop first at the Chamber of Commerce for a free walking-tour map of the town and two terrific brochures listing more than two dozen scenic walking, hiking, and mountain-biking trails (248 Mill Street, Grass Valley; (800)655-4667 or (916)273-4667). Don't miss the 10-ton Pelton Waterwheel (at 30 feet in diameter, it's the world's largest) on display at the exemplary **North Star Mining Museum**, housed in what was once the powerhouse for the North Star Mine (closed in winter; south end of Mill Street, Grass Valley; (916)273-4255). Just outside town is the 800-acre **Empire Mine State Historic Park**, the oldest, largest, and richest gold mine in California; its underground passages once extended for 367 miles and descended 11,007 feet into the ground (10791 E Empire Street, Grass Valley; (916)273-8522).

Thanks to the hordes of miners who emigrated here from the depressed tin mines of Cornwall, England, today's hungry visitors can feast inexpensively on a genuine bit of British legacy: the Cornish pasty, a traditional butter-crust beef-and-vegetable pie. Purchase these pies (vegetarian versions also available) at **Mrs. Dubblebee's Pasties** (251-C S Auburn Street, next to the Veterans' Memorial Building, downtown

This Brew's for You

What's a town without a microbrewery? At the Nevada City Brewing Company, located at 75 Bost Avenue in Nevada City, you can sample some of the Gold Country's finest microbrewed beer. Free tours and tastings are offered Fridays 3–5pm and Saturday 1–5pm, May through December, and Fridays 3–5pm, January through April (group tours also are available by appointment; call (916)265-2446).

Grass Valley; (916)272-7700). For less traditional fare (such as breakfast burritos and veggie burgers) try **Tofanelli's**, a coffeehouse that's also one of Grass Valley's cultural meeting places (302 W Main Street, next to the Holbrooke Hotel, Grass Valley; (916)272-1468). Freshly made Mexican fare, including the house specialty, chiles rellenos, is served at **Peppers**— a little hard to find but worth the effort (151 Mill Street, near Neal Street, downtown Grass Valley; (916)272-7780).

Nevada City, established in 1849 when miners found gold in Deer Creek, occupies one of the most picturesque sites in the Sierra foothills. When the sugar maples blaze in autumn, the town resembles a small New England village, making it hard to believe this was once the third-largest city in California. Pick up a free walking-tour map at the Chamber of Commerce (132 Main Street at Coyote Street, Nevada City; (916)265-2692) and put on your walking shoes. Town highlights include the **National Hotel**, the state's oldest continuously operating hotel, where the cozy Gold Rush–era bar is ideal for a cocktail or two (211 Broad Street at Pine Street, Nevada City; (916)265-4551), and the **Firehouse No. 1 Museum**, where the Gold Rush memorabilia includes relics from the infamous and ill-fated Donner Party (214 Main Street at Commercial Street, Nevada City; (916)265-5468).

Sixteen miles north of Nevada City, up the steep and winding N Bloomfield Road, is the 3,000-acre **Malakoff Diggins State Historic Park**, where you'll find the world's largest hydraulic gold mine, as well as a monument to the devastating results of hydraulic mining. Nearly half a mountain was washed away, leaving behind a 600-foot-deep canyon of exposed, minaret-shaped, rust-colored rock—an eerily beautiful sight to some, but an eyesore to most. The mining didn't stop until a court order was issued in 1884, by which time the runoff had turned the San Francisco Bay a murky brown. Overlooking the park is the semirestored mining town of **North Bloomfield**, where a visitors center displays—

what else?—hydraulic-mining memorabilia (23579 N Bloomfield Road, Nevada City; (916)265-2740).

Nevada City offers surprisingly good, affordable food. Load up with house-made deli items at **Gourmet Food to Go** (110 York Street, Nevada City; (916)265-0558) and take them to nearby Pioneer Park, a popular picnic spot. For a sit-down meal, **Country Rose Cafe** has excellent lunch specials, such as the salmon-cucumber sandwich on squaw bread. On sunny days, ask for a seat in the walled garden patio (300 Commercial Street at Pine Street, Nevada City; (916)265-6248). The locals' favorite for dinner is **Cowboy Pizza**, a garlic-lover's paradise— the place *reeks* of the stinking rose—that's all gussied up in cowpoke kitsch. Sink your teeth into the Greek vegetarian pizza (artichoke hearts, feta, black olives, fresh tomatoes, garlic, and oregano) and wash it down with a pint or two of one of California's premier microbrews (315 Spring Street, near the Miners Foundry Cultural Center, Nevada City; (916)265-2334).

If you plan to stay in the area for more than a day or two, devote half a day to the scenic little mountain town of **Downieville**. Located an hour's drive up Highway 49 at the junction of the Yuba and Downie Rivers, the town hasn't changed much since the 1850s, with venerable buildings lining boardwalks along crooked Main Street and trim homes cut into the canyon walls above. Downieville's population hovers around 300 now, though during its heyday more than 5,000 prospectors panned the streams and worked the mines. Sights to see include the **Downieville Museum** (no phone), housed in a former Gold Rush–era Chinese store, and the **Sierra County Courthouse**, (916)289-3215, where you can admire gold dug out of the rich Ruby Mine. For a sweet snack, stop at the **Downieville Bakery**, (916)289-0108, or just pick up some cheap treats there for the scenic drive home.

🚌 *Try a Shuttler Approach*

If you've ever visited downtown Nevada City or Grass Valley on a weekend, you know how hard it is to find a parking spot (and to think you came here to get away from it all). This time, why not leave the car at the hotel and let Gold Country Stage's shuttles do all the driving? A measly $2 buys you an all-day pass good for both towns as well as rides to major attractions in outlying areas. Call (916)477-0103 for a free map and riders' guide.

CHEAP SLEEPS

Coach & Four Motel
628 S Auburn Street, Grass Valley, CA 95945 • (916)273-8009

If all you're looking for is a clean room with a comfortable bed and the standard amenities—phone, TV, air conditioning, refrigerator, and private bath—the Coach & Four might fit the bill. The aging 17-room motel offers a complimentary continental breakfast and is within walking distance of Grass Valley's Old Town (okay, so perhaps it's a *long* walk), and it's right next to a shuttle stop that will take you to Nevada City for a buck. Your pooch is welcome here, too.

Gold Country Inn
11972 Sutton Way, Grass Valley, CA 95945 •
(800)247-6590 or (916)273-1393

If neither the Coach & Four nor the Holiday Lodge (see below) has panned out, this 84-room Best Western on the outskirts of town may have a room in your price range. The inn offers several price breaks, including a 10 percent AAA discount, a 10 percent senior discount, and a children-under-12-sleep-free deal. Other perks include an outdoor spa, pool, and free in-room coffee.

Holiday Lodge
1221 E Main Street, Grass Valley, CA 95945 •
(800)742-7125 or (916)273-4406

Located just outside downtown Grass Valley, this 36-room pet-friendly motel is a short drive from the Old Towns of both Grass Valley and Nevada City. It's slightly more upscale than the Coach & Four, offering all the same perks—TV, air conditioning, phone, and private bath—with a few bonuses, such as a sauna and swimming pool. A nine-hole golf course beckons from across the street, and for you gold diggers who want to splurge, there's the Holiday Lodge Goldpanning Vacation package, where an "expert guide leads the way through the wilds of the Sierra to the most promising gold-panning location." And we've got some real estate in Florida. . . .

Miner's Inn
760 Zion Street, Nevada City, CA 95959 • (916)265-2253

If you can get a room at the Miner's Inn you've struck it rich. Nevada City's premier cheap sleep offers 20 recently remodeled cabinlike motel rooms surrounded by a small, shady park. The plain-Jane digs are clean, comfy, and equipped with air conditioning, color TV, and phones (non-smoking units are available). And it's a pleasant one-mile stroll down S Pine Street to Nevada City's historic downtown. A nearby restaurant and lounge round out the amenities.

Northern Queen Inn

400 Railroad Avenue, Nevada City, CA 95959 • (916)265-5824

More upscale and expensive than the Miner's Inn, this is still a good deal for the dollar if you're traveling in the "low season" and want a spacious room with queen-size bed (a second bed is only a few bucks more). The attractive, modern, 86-room inn, in a wooded setting at the edge of town, offers all the standard perks: cable TV, in-room coffee, private baths, small refrigerators, and a heated pool and spa. There's a restaurant and bar on the premises, and Nevada City's historic district is just a short walk away. The inn fills quickly, so reserve far in advance.

South Gold Country

The rolling hills of the southern Gold Country are honeycombed with mysterious caverns and abandoned mines, including the deepest gold mines on the continent. Most of the Gold Rush towns were abandoned by the 1870s, although some have survived by mining for tourist dollars instead. As a result, it's not always easy to steer clear of the tourist trappings. Most journey to this area for the fishing, camping, hiking, rafting, and mountain biking—and some come to pan for gold. Yep, there still are some precious nuggets in those hills and mountain streams, and you can even hire a prospector to show you how and where to try your luck. But bear in mind that all that glitters is not gold (there's plenty of fool's gold in these parts), and your chances of hitting the jackpot are probably much better in Reno.

ON THE ROAD

This tour of the southern half of the Gold Country kicks off, aptly, where it all began: **Coloma**, where carpenter James Marshall discovered gold at John Sutter's mill in 1849. A working replica of the famous sawmill, a small museum, and other gold-related exhibits are on display at Marshall Gold Discovery State Historic Park, a 280-acre expanse of shaded lawns and picnic tables that extends through three-quarters of the town (on

When Chicken McNuggets Won't Do

For a true taste of the Gold Country, hire a prospecting company to teach you the art of panning. Prices range from $10 for a half-hour excursion to $600 for a six-day gold-digger's-delight helicopter trip. Learn how to pan, sluice, and snipe (that is, find gold in crevices) just like the 49ers did nearly 150 years ago. And, yes, you get to pocket whatever gold nuggets (or, more likely, gold dust) you find. Panning outfits include Gold Country Prospecting in Placerville, (916)622-2484, Jensen's Pick & Shovel Ranch in Angels Camp, (209)736-0287, Roaring Camp Mining Company in Pine Grove, (209)296-4100, and Gold Prospecting Expeditions in Jamestown, (209)984-4653.

Highway 49, Coloma; (916)622-3470). Coloma is silly with tourists and rafters on summer weekends, so plan your visit during the week, when you can picnic in peace and float down the American River without fear of colliding into wayward rafts.

An 8-mile drive south on Highway 49 leads to Placerville, doomed by its crossroads location at Highway 50 to serve mainly as a pit stop for Tahoe-bound travelers. One of the first camps settled by miners who branched out from Coloma, Placerville was originally dubbed Dry Diggins because of a lack of water. The moniker became Hangtown after a series of grisly lynchings in the mid-1800s (which, for some perverse reason, the town still takes a kind of pride in); eventually, pressure from "respectable" townsfolk resulted in its current name. Home to an uninspiring array of gas stations, budget chain hotels, and 24-hour coffee shops, Placerville doesn't have much to offer visitors except some Old Town gift shops and its famous "Hangtown fry"—a concoction of bacon, eggs, and oysters popular with early miners—which nowadays is dished out at the **Bell Tower Cafe** (423 Main Street, in Old Town, Placerville; (916)626-3483). If spelunking sets your heart aflutter, a mile north of downtown in Bedford Park is the **Gold Bug Mine**, a city-owned hard-rock gold mine. Tours of the mine lead you deep into the lighted shafts (on Bedford Avenue, 1 mile north of town, Placerville; (916)642-5238). **El Dorado County Museum**, adjacent to the county fairgrounds, showcases such Gold Rush–era relics as Pony Express paraphernalia, an original Studebaker wheelbarrow, and a restored Concord stagecoach (100 Placerville Drive, Placerville; (916)621-5865).

Three miles south of Placerville on Highway 49 sits the small town of El Dorado, whose denizens tolerate but in no way cultivate tourism. In fact, most travelers pass right on through—except for those who know about **Poor Red's**. It may not look like much from the outside (or the inside, for that matter), but this bar and restaurant is known throughout the Gold Country for serving great barbecued chicken, steak, and pork ribs at unbeatable prices. Furthermore, it has an international claim to fame as birthplace of the Golden Cadillac cocktail. So many Golden Cadillacs have been poured here that Red's is now the largest user of Galliano liqueur in North America, as a gilded plaque from Italy, on prominent display, proudly attests (6221 Pleasant Valley Road, downtown El Dorado; (916)622-2901).

To the south on Highway 49 are the blink-and-you'll-miss-'em towns of Nashville, site of the first stamp mill in the Mother Lode (now occupied by a trailer park); Plymouth, host of the popular Amador County Fair and Rodeo during the first weekend of August; and Drytown, named for its lack of gold but known (ironically) by 49ers for the 27-or-so saloons that used to profit here. A few miles past Drytown is Amador City, the smallest incorporated city in California. Lined with false-fronted antique and specialty shops, this block-long nonmetropolis is a good place to stop, stretch your legs, and window-shop.

You'll find a better array of shops, however, about 2 miles south in **Sutter Creek**. This self-proclaimed "nicest little town in the Mother Lode" boasts some beautiful buildings from the 1800s, including the landmark Knight's Foundry, the last water-powered foundry and machine shop in the nation; self-guided tours are offered daily (81 Eureka Street off Main Street, Sutter Creek; (209)267-1449). Also of interest: the multicultural artwork and handmade willow furniture at the Cobweb

Just One Bite, Snow White

Every autumn droves of people—about a half-million each year—come to a small ridge just east of Placerville dubbed Apple Hill Orchards. What's the attraction? Why, apples, of course. Baked, fried, buttered, canned, candied, and caramelized apples, to name just a few variations. Dozens of apple vendors sell their special apple concoctions, and on weekends the atmosphere is positively festive, with everyone basking in the alpine sunshine while feasting on such treats as hot apple pie à la mode. In September and October (peak apple-harvest season), it's definitely worth a stop. From Highway 50, take the Carson Road exit and follow the signs. For more details, call the Apple Hill Information Center at (916)622-7740.

Collection (83 Main Street, Sutter Creek; (209)267-0690); contemporary and American arts at Fine Eye Gallery (71 Main Street, Sutter Creek; (209)267-0571); and the regional prints, watercolors, and stone carvings at Sutter Creek Gallery (35 Main Street, Sutter Creek; (209)267-0228).

A 4-mile drive to the south, just past the enormous Georgia Pacific lumber mill, is Jackson, the seat of Amador County and the last place in California to outlaw prostitution. Two sights Gold Rush buffs shouldn't miss are the **Amador County Museum** (225 Church Street, Jackson; (209)223-6386), if only for the scale models of the local hard-rock mines, and Kennedy Tailing Wheels Park, site of the Kennedy and the Argonaut, the Mother Lode's deepest mines. Though the mines have been closed for decades, their headframes and some huge tailing wheels remain to give an idea of how waste from the mines was conveyed over the hills to a settling pond (from Main Street, turn up onto Jackson Gate Road, Jackson; no phone). If all this touring has given you a 49er-size appetite, indulge in a messy Moo-Burger and shake at **Mel and Faye's Diner**, a local landmark since 1956. It's a meal guaranteed to stick with you for the rest of the day (205 Highway 49 at Main Street, bottom of the hill, Jackson; (209)223-0853).

For a great side trip from Jackson, take a spin through the town of Volcano, so wonderfully authentic that it borders on decrepit (it doesn't get more Gold Rush than this, folks). After the winding drive down Ram's Horn Grade, cool off in the funky, friendly bar at the **St. George Hotel** (16104 Pine Grove/Volcano Road, Volcano; (209)296-4458). Or in early spring, picnic amid the nearly half-million daffodils (in 100 different varieties) in bloom along Daffodil Hill, a 4-acre ranch just above town (3 miles north of Volcano on Ram's Horn Grade, follow the signs; no phone). An outdoor amphitheater, hidden behind stone facades along Main Street, is the site of popular summer theatricals performed by the Volcano Theatre Company (1 block north of the St. George Hotel, Volcano; (209)296-2525). And at nearby **Indian Grinding Rock State Historic Park**, you'll find an enormous limestone outcropping—the largest of its kind in America—dotted with thousands of holes created by native Miwoks from years of grinding their acorn meal on the rock. The park also has an Indian artifacts museum (off Pine Grove/Volcano Road, 1½ miles north of Highway 88, Pine Grove; (209)296-7488).

Back on Highway 49, a few miles south of Jackson, is the "Historic 49" turnoff to **Mokelumne Hill**, once so rich with gold that claims were limited in size to 16 square feet. Although there's little going on these days in this sleepy block-long town, it's still a pleasant 15-minute drive through Mokelumne's green pastures, along its historic but miniscule Main Street, and back onto the highway.

Grape Expectations

Between the towns of Placerville and Murphys lie several first-rate wineries producing everything from rich, spicy zinfandels to full-bodied chardonnays and fruity rieslings. Most are small, family-owned establishments offering free public tours, tastings, and picnic sites. Here's a north-to-south roundup of some of the area's best: Placerville's Boeger Winery, (916)622-8094, offers a tasting room in its early 19th-century building plus picnic tables in the shade, and Sierra Vista Winery, (916)622-7221, features picnic areas with great views of the Crystal Range. In Camino, Madrona Vineyards, (916)644-5948, is perched at a 3,000-foot elevation, and in Somerset, Granite Springs Winery, (916)620-6395, boasts a barn-style building, a separate tasting room, and a pondside picnic area.

Nestled in the Shenandoah Valley are Amador Foothill Winery, (209)245-6307, where you can sample wines in a state-of-the-art complex; Charles Spinetta Winery and Gallery (209)245-3384), which has a nature gallery in its beautiful tastings room and a picnic ground overlooking a pond; Montevina Wines, (209)245-6942, with an impressive tasting area and arbor-covered patio; Shenandoah Vineyards, (209)245-4455, which offers tasting in an old cellar, along with an art gallery and grand views; and tiny Story Winery, (209)245-6208, where the tasting room overlooks the scenic Consumnes River. The town of Murphys offers the small tasting room of Black Sheep Vintners, (209)728-2157, and the beautiful setting of Stevenot Winery, (209)728-3436. And at Chatom Vineyards, (209)736-6500, located in an attractive building in the town of Douglas Flat, visitors may picnic on the patio.

Cruise right on through the overcommercialized and truly uninspiring town of San Andreas, and you'll eventually pull into Angels Camp, made famous by Mark Twain's short story "The Celebrated Jumping Frog of Calaveras County." Every year, on the third Saturday in May, thousands of frog fans flock to the Calaveras County Fair to witness the **Jumping Frog Jubilee**, one of the premier frog-jumping contests in the world. The festival takes place at the Frogtown Fairgrounds 2 miles south of town, (209)736-2561, and features a rodeo, carnival rides, live music, and—for those of you who forgot to bring one—frogs for rent. *Ribbit.*

A winding 9-mile drive east of Angels Camp along Highway 4 leads to picturesque Murphys, a former trading post set up by brothers Dan and

John Murphy in cooperation with local Indians (John married the chief's daughter). Though you won't find cheap sleeps here, it's still worth the detour off Highway 49 just to stroll down Murphys' tree-lined Main Street or, better yet, to sample a pint of Murphys Brewing Company's outstanding Murphys Red, served on tap at the **Murphys Historic Hotel and Lodge** (457 Main Street, Murphys; (209)728-3444).

Eighteen miles northeast on Highway 4 is **Calaveras Big Trees State Park**, a popular summer retreat that offers camping, swimming, hiking, and fishing among towering sequoias; (209)795-2334. Many of the numerous caverns in the area (discovered by prospectors) can be toured, including Mercer Caverns, (209)728-2101, which has crystalline stalactites and stalagmites in a series of descending chambers; Moaning Cavern, (209)736-2708, where a 100-foot stairway spirals down into a chamber so huge it could house the Statue of Liberty; and California Caverns, (209)736-2708, the West's first commercially developed cave and the largest single cave system in Northern California (it has yet to be fully explored).

The next major stop to the south is Columbia, where some mighty fortunate 49ers unearthed a staggering $87 million in gold over a 20-year period. This former boisterous mining town also came within two votes of beating out Sacramento in the race to be named state capital. Once the gold-mining business dwindled, however, Columbia's population of 15,000 nearly vanished. You can view the city's well-preserved facades and mining artifacts in **Columbia State Historic Park**, a true Gold Country treasure. This is the Mother Lode's best-preserved park, so if you haven't had your fill of Gold Rush nostalgia, follow the free, short,

Where Skiers Grin and Bear It

If you're touring the Gold Country in winter, don't forget your downhill or cross-country skis, because right off Highway 4 is the eighth-largest ski area in the state—the Bear Valley Ski Company. Downhillers can schuss down more than 60 trails (serviced by 11 lifts that can accommodate 12,000 skiers per hour), while cross-country fans can explore one of the largest trail systems in the country. Bear Valley also has a full line of rental equipment (including snow boards), great ski-school packages, and special weekday discounts that often cut the cost of a ticket in half (call ahead for price quotes). Located off Highway 4, about 50 miles east of the Highway 49 intersection in Angels Camp; (209)753-2301.

self-guided tour. For more history on the area, pick up a walking-tour booklet at the visitors center for $1 or sign up for a guided tour of a mine. For a more leisurely view of the park, hop aboard one of the horse-drawn stagecoaches. And to learn how to pan for gold, ask about the Matelot Gulch Mining Company's free lessons or call park information at (209)532-0150.

When the traffic starts to crawl along Highway 49, you're probably closing in on **Sonora**, which in 49er days continuously competed with Columbia for the title of wealthiest city in the southern Mother Lode. Today, Sonora is the Gold Country's largest and most crowded town. Search for a parking space along Washington Street (no easy feat on weekends), feed the meter, and take a peek at the Tuolumne County Museum, located in the century-old jail (158 W Bradford Street, Sonora; (209)532-1317). A couple of excellent inexpensive restaurants along Washington Street include Good Heavens: A Food Concern, which has outstanding daily lunch specials, house-made desserts, and terrific freshly made jams (49 N Washington Street, downtown Sonora; (209)532-3663), and the Diamond Back Grill, where you can dip into a bowl of black-eyed-pea-and-ham soup for $2.50, or, for less than $10, splurge on such daily specials as grilled venison or salmon (110 S Washington Street, downtown Sonora; (209)532-6661). Just north of town is the Egg Cellar, a popular breakfast house that specializes in *big* country-style omelets—at least 20 versions at last count (22265 Parrotts Ferry Road, ¼ mile south of Columbia State Park, Columbia; (209)532-5988).

A couple of miles southwest of Sonora on Highway 49 is **Jamestown**. For decades this 2-block-long town has been Hollywood's favorite western movie set: scenes from famous flicks like *Butch Cassidy and the Sundance Kid* were shot here, and vintage railway cars and steam locomotives used in such TV classics as "Little House on the Prairie,"

Rapid Transit

Whitewater rafting is big business in the Mother Lode, particularly during summer, when thousands of rafters converge on the weekend to brave the American River's brutal Class IV rapids. Although a full-day trip down the river will cost you a cool $90 or more on weekends, O.A.R.S. (Outdoor Adventure River Specialists), California's leading river outfitter, offers half-day trips for only $49 during the week, as well as one-to-three-day trips down the less-congested Merced, Tuolumne, and Stanislaus Rivers. For more information, call (800)346-6277.

"Bonanza," and "High Noon" are on display at the **Railtown 1897 State Historic Park** (on 5th Avenue at Reservoir Road, near the center of town, Jamestown; (209)984-3953). You can view the vehicles at the roundhouse daily, or, if it's a weekend and you're traveling with young kids, take them for a ride on the rails. For cheap eats, try the Smoke Cafe, serving good gringo-style Mexican and southwestern fare for about $10 a plate (18191 Main Street, Jamestown; (209)984-3733), and Jim Town Frosty, your basic low-budget burger hut that serves above-average shakes, fries, and stuffed jalapeños (north end of Main Street at Humbug Street and Highway 49, Jamestown; (209)984-3444).

CHEAP SLEEPS

Cary House Hotel
300 Main Street, Placerville, CA 95667 • (916)622-4271

For about the same price you'd pay at one of Placerville's many budget chains, you can get a clean, comfy Gold Rush–era room with private bath at Cary House. Although the 34 rooms have that eau-de-Grandma's-house smell, the price is right and the Old Town location can't be beat (for Placerville, that is).

Old Well Motel
15947 Highway 49 (PO Box 187), Drytown, CA 95699 • (209)245-6167

Drytown is so small that if all 11 rooms at this roadside motel were filled, the town's population would probably double. But it's still a great place to stay, primarily because of the price and its prime location in the heart of the Mother Lode. The rooms are a bit cramped and there's not much to feast your eyes on, but should you get hungry and restless, a small cafe on the premises serves breakfast, lunch, and dinner, and a nearby creek will help lull you to sleep.

Jackson Holiday Lodge
850 N Highway 49 (PO Box 1147), Jackson, CA 95642 • (209)223-0486

Although they won't give you much of a feel for Gold Rush times, the 36 modern rooms at the Holiday Lodge are comfortable and tidy. The price includes a continental breakfast served in the lobby, local calls, remote cable TV, and use of the heated pool in summer. Considering the location and amenities, Holiday Lodge is probably the best deal for your dollar in the Mother Lode.

Gold Country Inn Motel
720 S Main Street (PO Box 188), Angels Camp, CA 95222 •
(800)851-4944 or (209)736-4611

If you can get past the garish facade—gold was never a color meant for buildings—you'll find 40 clean, modern rooms equipped with color TVs, direct-dial phones, air conditioning, and queen-size beds. The motel makes a good base for visiting some of the Gold Country's best attractions—caverns, state parks, museums—and the rates won't make a huge dent in your wallet.

Ebbetts Pass Lodge
1173 Highway 4 (PO Box 2591), Arnold, CA 95223 • (209)795-1563

Although it's definitely off the Gold Country circuit, Ebbetts Pass Lodge has its strong points. The 15 rooms include a color TV (with HBO), kitchenette, queen-size bed, and barbecue area. The lodge is set high among cool, sweet-smelling pines directly down the highway from Calaveras Big Trees State Park, Moaning and Mercer Caverns, and Bear Valley Resort, among other attractions. If you don't mind the extra drive to get here, and could care less about sleeping in a historic mining town, this place might be for you.

Columbia Gem Motel
22131 Parrotts Ferry Road (PO Box 874), Columbia, CA 95310 •
(209)532-4508

Small, weathered, and just a little on the dilapidated side, the 12 rooms and cabins of the secluded "Gem" are a great bargain if you don't mind a spot of rust or mildew here and there. Located a mile from Columbia State Park, the Columbia's freestanding cabins (be sure to request the cabins, not the rooms) come with cable TV, air conditioning, in-room coffee, and, best of all, little furnished front porches that overlook the pines.

Gunn House Hotel
286 S Washington Street, Sonora, CA 95370 • (209)532-3421

The first two-story adobe structure in Sonora, built by Dr. Lewis C. Gunn in 1850, is now the best low-priced hotel in town (though rates lift it out of the cheap sleep category during the high season). Each of the 20 rooms is filled with period antiques to create a Victorian atmosphere, yet none of the modern comforts—TV, air conditioning, private bath—have been left out. A swimming pool and patio, shaded balconies, and Italian restaurant with a cocktail lounge are also on the property. Room rates include continental breakfast.

Rail Fence Motel

19950 Highway 108, Sonora, CA 95370 • (209)532-9191

Although bland and uninspiring compared to the Gunn House, this motel just east of Sonora on Highway 108 offers eight small, tidy rooms with TVs, private baths, and air conditioning for about $35 per night. There's also a small pool and patio on the 11-acre property, and dogs are welcome if you make arrangements in advance.

Gables Cedar Creek Inn

22564 Twain Harte Drive, Twain Harte, CA 95383 • (209)586-3008

You may have to dig a little deeper into your pocket (particularly during the high season) to pay for a room, but if you're looking for a romantic, secluded Gold Country getaway that won't cost a bundle, bunk down here. Located a half-mile from the tiny town of Twain Harte, the Gables is literally hidden among hundreds of pines and cedars, surrounded by flowers in spring, and blanketed with colorful leaves in fall. The seven units range from a creekside loft with wood-burning fireplace (the most popular room) to a surprisingly affordable four-bedroom house that faces the Twain Harte golf course. All units come with attractive country furnishings, kitchen area, cable TV, telephone, and bathroom with shower.

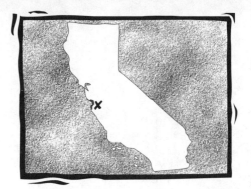

CENTRAL COAST

Santa Cruz

Pacific Grove

Monterey

Carmel-by-the-Sea

Big Sur

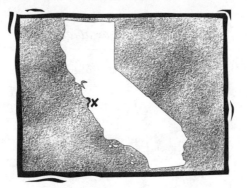

Santa Cruz

Santa Cruz is a chimerical place, skittering from diamond-bright beach to swampy slough to moody redwood grove to cafe society to rustic farm in just about the time it takes to say "Surf's up!" The city rings the north end of Monterey Bay and is bisected by the San Lorenzo River, which spills into the sea. Santa Cruz (Spanish for "holy cross") was founded by the ubiquitous Father Junípero Serra when he built the Mission of the Holy Cross here in 1791 (the mission was destroyed in the mid-19th century by earthquakes). Despite its holy beginnings, Santa Cruz is now a devil-may-care, saltwater-taffy seaside resort, embodied by both the wet suit–clad surfer set and the roller-coaster world of the famous Boardwalk, where the roar of revelers mingles with the plaintive bark of sea lions. But peer a little closer and you'll see the city's intellectual side, bolstered by the presence of a University of California campus and the town's well-known (and occasionally controversial) ultraliberal politics.

ON THE ROAD

Santa Cruz attracts more than three million visitors each year, and most of them flock to the ½-mile-long, nearly 100-year-old **Santa Cruz Beach Boardwalk**, the last remaining beachfront amusement park on the West

Do the Locomotion

Locomotive lovers, kids, and fans of Mother Nature should hop aboard the historic narrow-gauge Roaring Camp Train for a 6-mile round-trip excursion up the steepest grades in North America. The steam-powered train winds through stately redwood groves to the summit of Bear Mountain. Another, called the Big Trees Railroad, offers an 18-mile round-trip ride through mountain tunnels and along ridges with spectacular views of the San Lorenzo River before stopping at the Santa Cruz Beach Boardwalk. Both trains are located on Graham Hill Road, off Highway 17, in Felton; (408)335-4400.

Coast. Take a spin on the famous Giant Dipper, one of the best and oldest wooden roller coasters in the country (with a great view at the top), then grab a seat on one of the intricately hand-carved horses on the 1911 Looff Carousel (both rides are listed on the National Register of Historic Places). Of course, the Boardwalk also caters to the hard-core thrill-seekers who yearn for those state-of-the-art, whirl-and-twirl rides that do their best to make you lose your lunch. Buy a day pass for less than $20 and stand in line for rides like the Riptide and the Bermuda Triangle, and you won't be disappointed. If you're here with the crowds on a Friday night in summer, don't miss the Boardwalk's free concerts, featuring the likes of the Shirelles, Chubby Checker, and Sha Na Na (400 Beach Street, Santa Cruz; (408)423-5590).

Beaches are Santa Cruz's other crowning glory. At the western edge of the city, on the north end of West Cliff Drive, is **Natural Bridges State Beach**, named after the surrounding water-sculpted, bridgelike rock formations. The beach is popular with surfers, wind surfers, tide-pool trekkers, and sunbathers, as well as fans of the Monarch butterflies that roost in the nearby eucalyptus grove from late October through February. On the south end of West Cliff Drive is **Lighthouse Field State Beach**, the birthplace of American surfing. This beach has several benches for sitting and gazing, a jogging and bicycling path, and a park with picnic tables, showers, and even plastic-bag dispensers for cleaning up after your dog (one of the few public places in town where canines are allowed). The nearby brick lighthouse is now home to the **Santa Cruz Surfing Museum** (the first of its kind in the world), which is chock-full of hang-ten memorabilia. Admission is free (at Lighthouse Point, Santa Cruz; (408)429-3429).

Between the lighthouse and the Boardwalk is that famous strip of the sea known as **Steamers Lane**, the summa cum laude of California surfing spots (savvy surfers say *this*—not Southern California—is the place to catch the best breaks in the state). Watch the dudes ride the gnarly waves, then head over to the marvelous (but often crowded) white-sand **Santa Cruz Beach** fronting the Boardwalk. The breakers are tamer here, making this a favorite spot for sunbathing, swimming, picnicking, and sailing. In the center of the action is the 85-year-old **Municipal Wharf**, where you can drive your car out to the shops, fish markets, and seafood restaurants. Within the wharf's sea of pricey establishments is the **Riva Fish House**, a surprisingly inexpensive restaurant with good food and a superb view (Building 31, Municipal Wharf, Santa Cruz; (408)429-1223).

The **Pacific Garden Mall** (aka Pacific Avenue) is Santa Cruz's main shopping district, and until the Loma Prieta earthquake hit in 1989, it was a charming amalgam of Victorian houses, street musicians, bag ladies and gentlemen, inexpensive restaurants, bookstores, antique shops, and New Age head shops. It's slowly recuperating from the apocalypse (the earthquake's epicenter was only 10 miles away), but there's still plenty to gawk at. As you make your way down the mall, look for the **Octagon Building**, an ornate, eight-sided Victorian brick edifice built in 1882 that has survived numerous quakes (705 Front Street, Santa Cruz; (408)429-1964). The building once served as the city's Hall of Records, and now it's part of the **McPherson Center for Art and History**, where museums showcase 10,000 years of the area's past as well as contemporary art of the Pacific Rim. Next door is the excellent **Visitor Information Center** (701 Front Street, Santa Cruz; (800)833-3494).

The Pacific Avenue area is a good place to get some cheap eats, too. Try **Zoccoli's Deli** for a bowl of their locally famous vegetarian

Boardwalk Bargains

Save a bundle at the Boardwalk by visiting on "1907 Nights." Every summer, after 5pm on Monday and Tuesday, the Santa Cruz Beach Boardwalk celebrates the year it opened by reducing its prices to 50 cents a ride (it's normally $1.50 to $3.00), and two bits also buys a hot dog, soft drink, cotton candy, or a red candy apple. At the end of summer, the Boardwalk also hosts "1907 Week," when you can get the same evening deals on Monday through Friday the week before Labor Day; (408)423-5590.

⭐⭐ I Love My Wife, But Oh You Squid!

Where else but in Santa Cruz would you find a month-long salute to the squid? From August 1 through Labor Day, India Joze Restaurant hosts its annual International Calamari Festival, featuring savory squid tastings, squid drawing competitions, squid cooking classes, and several other events celebrating the 10-armed cephalopod. Call (408)427-3554 for squid specifics.

minestrone or a sandwich and salad (1534 Pacific Avenue, Santa Cruz; (408)423-1711). The nearby **Bookshop Santa Cruz** has an inventory worthy of any university town, with a particularly good children's section, an adjacent coffeehouse, and plenty of places to sit, sip, and read a bit of your prospective purchase (1520 Pacific Avenue, Santa Cruz; (408)423-0900). Across the street is the ever-present but fast-moving line of people waiting to buy a freshly baked bagel (14 varieties to choose from) at **Noah's Bagels** (1411 Pacific Avenue, Santa Cruz; (408)454-9555). For great organically grown produce and other picnic-basket goodies, shop at the **Farmer's Market**, held Wednesdays from 2:30pm to 6:30pm on Lincoln Street, between Pacific Avenue and Cedar Street. One block west is the popular **India Joze Restaurant**, serving creative and healthy East Indian food with a California twist. Some dishes are cheap, others quite expensive, but the Nasi Goreng lunch of fried rice, chicken, calamari, and fresh vegetables served with a peanut-coconut milk sauce is a bargain (1001 Center Street at Cedar Street, Santa Cruz; (408)427-3554).

For some serious hiking and mountain biking, drive about 23 miles north to the 18,000-acre **Big Basin Redwoods State Park**, California's first state park and its second-largest redwood preserve. Eighty miles of trails wind past 300-foot-high redwoods and waterfalls, and there's even access to Waddell Beach (21600 Big Basin Way, off Highway 236; 9 miles north of Boulder Creek; (408)338-6132).

Just east of Santa Cruz sits **Capitola-by-the-Sea**, a tiny, very popular resort town nestled around a small bay. The whole downtown is only a few blocks long, but the quaint, jumbled mix of restaurants, gift shops, and beachwear boutiques and the city's intimate scale are reminiscent of resort towns of yesteryear. Capitola's broad, sandy beach attracts lots of sun worshipers, primarily because it's sheltered from the wind; it's also bordered by a charming promenade. At the west end of town is the bustling 867-foot-long **Capitola Pier**—*the* place to hang out, admire the view of the town, and on weekends, listen to live music. Many anglers come here to try their luck at reeling in the big one (you don't need a license to fish from a pier in California).

Capitola offers great inexpensive places to eat, such as the **Coyote Gourmet Taqueria**, which has an extensive selection of inexpensive tapas, soft tacos (the shark tacos are a local favorite), and burritos (201 Esplanade, Capitola; (408)479-4695). Several blocks north of the beach is **Gayle's Bakery and Rosticceria**, home of the best breads and pastries in town (Gayle's husband and co-owner, Jo Ortiz, is the author of *The Village Baker*, a cookbook on classic regional breads from Europe and America). Gayle's also dishes out a wonderful array of soups, salads, pastas, casseroles, and meats hot off the rotisserie for lunch and dinner (504 Bay Avenue, Capitola; (408)462-1200). Another good bet is the legendary **Dharma's Natural Foods** restaurant, which whips up wonderful vegetarian food for breakfast, lunch, and dinner, and may be the only place on the coast where you can order a vegetarian Dharma Dog with chili (4250 Capitola Road, Capitola; (408)462-1717).

CHEAP SLEEPS

Pigeon Point Hostel
210 Pigeon Point Road, Pescadero, CA 94060 • (408)879-0633

The Pigeon Point hostel is located at the base of one of the tallest lighthouses on the Pacific coast, halfway between San Francisco and Santa

Seaside Sex Show

You're not the only one having fun in the sun: drive 22 miles north of Santa Cruz, and you'll come upon Año Nuevo State Reserve, a unique and fascinating breeding ground for northern elephant seals. A close encounter with a 2½-ton male elephant seal waving his humongous schnoz is an unforgettable event. Even more memorable is the sight of two males fighting and snorting (they can be heard for miles) over a harem of a few dozen females. The mating season starts in December and continues through March. Reservations are required for the 2½-hour naturalist-led tours (held rain or shine from December 15 through March 31). Tickets are quite cheap, but they sell out fast, so plan about two months ahead; (800)444-7275.

Cruz. The beautiful windswept grounds are landscaped with native plants, and the 270-degree view of the ocean can't be matched anywhere in the region. The hostel's four houses were residences for the Coast Guard lighthouse staff until high-tech lighthouse electronics gave them the boot. But the Coast Guard's loss is your gain. Separate men's and women's bunk rooms and two rooms for couples (which cost an extra $10 per night) accommodate a total of 52. The facilities are clean and comfortable, and the price can't be beat—the most expensive nightly rate is $14 for a nonmember adult; the lowest is $5.50 for a hostel member's child. Be sure to spend some time in the hostel's legendary hot tub overlooking the ocean, well worth the $3-per-half-hour fee (guests only). Reservations are strongly recommended, although some bunk beds are held for walk-ins starting at 4:30pm. The reception desk is open from 7:30 to 9:30am and 4:30 to 9:30pm daily.

New Davenport Bed & Breakfast Inn
31 Davenport Avenue, Davenport, CA 95017 • (408)425-1818

The rooms at this cheery inn, 9 miles up the coast from Santa Cruz, are decorated with a mixture of antiques, ethnic treasures, and local arts and crafts. Eight of the guest rooms are located on the second floor of the New Davenport Cash Store Restaurant, and four more are in an adjacent historic house. Each room has a private bath, telephone, radio, and a vase of fresh flowers. The units above the store share a large balcony with a great ocean view. Guests are treated to a complimentary drink at the bar and a continental breakfast. The inn's moderately priced restaurant serves some of the best food in the area for breakfast, lunch, and dinner.

Big Basin Redwoods State Park Tent Cabins
21600 Big Basin Way, Boulder Creek, CA 95006 • (800)874-8368

Big Basin has one of the area's best bargains: 36 highly sought-after tent cabins nestled next to a creek in a grove of redwood and huckleberry trees. You can rent one of these cabins (which sleep up to four comfortably) for only $38 a night, and four friends may camp out on the ground in front at no extra cost. Each cabin has wood floors and walls, a canvas roof, and screened doors and windows, and is equipped with a wood-burning fireplace and two double beds. A picnic table, storage cabinet, and grill are set up outside the door. There's no electricity in these units, so bring a propane lantern along with your sleeping bag, or rent one ($6 per day) along with bed linens ($10 for the duration of your stay) at the Big Basin Gift Store. Bathroom facilities (with coin-operated hot showers) and a laundry are in nearby buildings. Although Big Basin is 23 miles north of Santa Cruz, many people make the trek here, and the cabins fill up fast. Reservations are required year-round and are taken by phone only (try to call at least eight weeks ahead). Last-minute cancellations are common, so if at first you don't succeed, keep trying.

Harbor Inn
645 7th Avenue, Santa Cruz, CA 95062 • (408)479-9731

Tucked away on the eastern end of town, only 2 blocks from Twin Lakes State Beach, is the homey, funky Harbor Inn. It's managed by a friendly staff, and the inn's 19 guest rooms have open-beam ceilings, queen-size beds, cable TV, microwaves, hot plates, fridges, and phones. The decor is 1940s antique. The least expensive rooms (some have shared baths) range from about $30 a night in the winter to $65 on a summer weekend. The two-room suites each have two double beds, and although these units cost more, they're priced right for this part of the California coast.

Motel Continental
414 Ocean Street (near Broadway), Santa Cruz, CA 95060 • (408)429-1221

The Continental is typical of the pre-1960 motels just north of the Boardwalk: small, clean rooms with thin walls, comfortable beds, and cheap decor. The 37-room motel sits on a street littered with fast-food chains and small businesses, but it's only about a 15-minute walk to the beach. In exchange for the dull surroundings, you get bargain rates year-round. Besides, this is one of the few motels in Santa Cruz that lets you bring your pooch.

Pacific Inn
330 Ocean Street, Santa Cruz, CA 95060 • (408)425-3722

The relatively new Pacific Inn is a cut above most of the other motels north of the Boardwalk. The 36 beige-and-green rooms are pleasant and comfortable, furnished with a queen-size bed, couch, dresser, and table, along with cable TV, refrigerator, and a coffee maker; some even have hot tubs. You can unwind in one of the hotel Jacuzzis (there's an indoor and an outdoor tub) or take a dip in the pool, which is sheltered from the wind. The beach and Boardwalk are only 4 blocks away.

Ramada Limited
130 W Cliff Drive, Santa Cruz, CA 95060 • (408)423-7737

Perched on a hill just across the street from the beach and the wharf, the Ramada offers 30 simple rooms at bargain rates in the off season. Each well-kept unit has a king- or queen-size bed, a table and chairs, credenza, and cable TV (including the Movie Channel). Some of the higher-priced units have ocean views. The hotel also has a pool and hot tub, and a continental breakfast is part of the deal.

Santa Cruz Hostel at the Carmelita Cottages
321 Main Street (P.O. Box 1241), Santa Cruz, CA 95061 •
(408)423-8304

The popular Santa Cruz hostel has moved into new digs, and they're something special. The hostel's rooms are now spread out among six attractive Victorian cottages that were donated to the establishment and recently renovated. Each sleeps 8 to 13 people in bunk beds and has a shared bathroom with showers. The units are comfortably but not lavishly furnished, and are only 2 blocks from the beach and Boardwalk. The place is a steal at only $15 per person per night, or $12 per night if you're a hostel member (an annual membership, which costs $25, is worth considering, since in summer the place is open to members only). Reservations are accepted only by mail (at least two weeks prior to your desired arrival), and half of the beds are held for walk-ins starting at 5pm. The reception desk is open from 8 to 10am and 5 to 10pm daily.

Sunset Inn
2424 Mission Street, Santa Cruz, CA 95060 • (408)423-3471

Although it doesn't look like much on the outside, the Sunset Inn is quite a find. Sure, Mission Street is a major artery on the western edge of Santa Cruz, and the neighborhood is commercial, but the 28 rooms are finer than the modest prices suggest: tidy, relatively spacious, with modern furnishings (some even have sofas) and cable TV. The friendly owner allows pets, too. Nearby are the popular Natural Bridges State Beach and Avanti, a small, inexpensive Italian trattoria run by a personable staff (1711 Mission Street; (408)427-0135).

Rio Sands Motel
116 Aptos Beach Drive, Aptos, CA 95003 • (408)688-3207

The recently renovated Rio Sands, one of the few cheap sleeps in the area with easy beach access, features a pool, hot tub, and a garden setting, and is tucked away all on its own next to the Rio Del Mar Beach on the eastern end of Aptos. The 50 rooms have king- or queen-size beds, private baths, phones, and cable TV; some also have kitchenettes. A continental breakfast is included, and you can cook up your lunch or dinner in the barbecue pits by the pool. Note: Off-season rates are reasonable, but prices increase dramatically in summer.

Pacific Grove

Established more than a century ago as a retreat for pious Methodists, this beautiful Victorian seacoast village retains its decorous old-town character, though it's loosened its collar a bit since the early days. Less tourist-oriented than Carmel, less commercial than Monterey, P. G. (as locals call it) is a place to settle down in, buy a home, and raise 2.5 obedient children. There's no graffiti, no raucous revelers, and not an unleashed dog in sight. The area exudes peace and tranquility—a city of gorgeous beaches, impressive architecture, and even reasonably priced accommodations just a jog from the sea.

ON THE ROAD

Introduce yourself to the town by strolling the 4 miles of trails that meander between the white-sand beaches and rocky, tide pool–dotted coves at **Lover's Point Beach** (off Ocean View Boulevard on the east side of Point Pinos) and **Asilomar State Beach** (off Sunset Drive on the west side of Point Pinos). You can sit and enjoy the view from the landmark Lover's Point (which, by the way, was named for lovers of Jesus Christ, not the more carnal kind).

At the tip of Point Pinos (Spanish for "Point of the Pines") stands the Cape Cod–style **Point Pinos Lighthouse**, the oldest continuously operating lighthouse on the West Coast, built in February 1855. This

Private Parts

If you want to cruise in your car through the privately owned Pebble Beach and 17-Mile Drive enclave of mansions and manicured golf courses, it will cost you about $6.50, but it's almost worth it just to contemplate the lifestyles of the very rich. You'll see everything from a spectacular Byzantine castle with private beach (the Crocker Mansion near the Carmel gate) to several tastefully bland California Nouvelle country-club structures. The sea and forest setting is as beautiful and perfectly maintained as you would expect in this gated community. In addition to such often-photographed landmarks as the gnarled Lone Cypress clinging to its rocky precipice, there are miles of hiking and equestrian trails winding through groves of native pines and wildflowers that provide glorious views of Monterey Bay. Self-guided nature tours are outlined in a variety of brochures, available for free at the gate entrances and at the Inn at Spanish Bay (on the 17-Mile Drive, near the Pacific Grove gate, (408)647-7500) and the Lodge at Pebble Beach (near the Carmel gate, (408)624-3811).

There are five entrance gates to this province for the very rich. The most famous stretch is along the coast between Pacific Grove and Carmel. Visitors may enter the 17-Mile Drive for free on foot or bike, although cyclists are required to use the Pacific Grove gate—and must dust off the wheels of their bikes, of course.

National Historic Landmark is open to the public on Thursdays and weekends, from 1pm to 4pm, and admission is free (Asilomar Boulevard at Lighthouse Avenue, Pacific Grove; (408)648-3116).

Pacific Grove bills itself as "Butterfly Town, U.S.A." in honor of the thousands of Monarchs that migrate here from late October to mid-March. Two popular places to view the butterflies are the **Monarch Grove Sanctuary** (at Lighthouse Avenue and Ridge Road, Pacific Grove) and **George Washington Park** (at Sinex Avenue and Alder Street, Pacific Grove). To learn more about the Monarchs, visit the charmingly informal and kid-friendly **Pacific Grove Museum of Natural History**, which has a video and display on the butterfly's life cycle, as well as exhibits of other insects, local birds, mammals, and reptiles; admission is free (at the intersection of Forest and Central Avenues, Pacific Grove; (408)648-3116).

For good books (particularly local guidebooks) and coffee, amble over to the nearby **Bookworks** (667 Lighthouse Avenue, Pacific Grove;

(408)372-2242), which also has an extensive array of magazines and newspapers. You can nibble on snacks here, too, but if all your hiking, biking, and browsing has given you a big appetite, Pacific Grove has plenty of good, inexpensive restaurants. Grab a seat at **Tillie Gort's Cafe** for tasty, predominantly vegetarian food (111 Central Avenue, Pacific Grove; (408)373-0335). For pizza, the locals prefer **Allegro Gourmet Pizzeria**, which also tosses together a great caesar salad (1184 Forest Avenue, Pacific Grove; (408)373-5656). **Peppers Mexicali Cafe** specializes in Mexican seafood dishes (170 Forest Avenue, Pacific Grove; (408)373-6892), and the **Fishwife Restaurant** is another popular spot for impeccably fresh fish and friendly service (1996½ Sunset Drive at Asilomar Boulevard, Pacific Grove; (408)375-7107).

CHEAP SLEEPS

Asilomar Conference Center
800 Asilomar Boulevard, Pacific Grove, CA 93950 • (408)372-8016

Located on 105 choice acres next to a wide, gorgeous beach, the state-owned Asilomar is a peaceful, nonprofit retreat frequently used for conferences, although many of its 315 units are rented to visitors, too. In the rustic but pleasant Historic Buildings (less expensive than the newer, larger Deluxe Buildings), you can rent a room for two for about $65 a night (all rates include a full breakfast). Or bring the family and friends and share the low cost of an apartment-style Guest Inn Cottage that sleeps up to seven. Architect Julia Morgan, of Hearst Castle fame, master-planned the center's layout and designed some of the original buildings. Designated a National Historic Landmark, the resort has a large heated swimming pool and its beach is popular with surfers.

The Beachcomber
1996 Sunset Drive, Pacific Grove, CA 93950 •
(800)634-4769 or (408)373-4769

This modern, comfortable motel offers 26 rooms in a variety of sizes, and some units have patios overlooking Spanish Bay. When the weather heats up, you can jump into the swimming pool, which is sheltered from the sea breezes by a glass wall, or dive into the Pacific at nearby Asilomar State Beach (within walking distance). Seafood fans will appreciate having the Fishwife Restaurant right next door. If you're a member of AARP or AAA, ask about room discounts. Unfortunately, the Beachcomber's rates jump way out of *Cheap Sleeps'* price range on summer weekends.

Bide-A-Wee
221 Asilomar Boulevard, Pacific Grove, CA 93950 • (408)372-2330

The genteelly shabby Bide-A-Wee has no doubt seen better days, but it's still a pleasant place to stay, and if you're willing to spend a little more money you can get a room with a kitchenette and fireplace. Set on a quiet, wooded street just one long block from the beach, the 17 fairly large, comfortable rooms are a cut above the motel row–like accommodations so plentiful nearby. This is the kind of place where you could hole up and write your novel—and you can even bring your dog.

Borg's Motel
635 Ocean View Boulevard, Pacific Grove, CA 93950 • (408)375-2406

Borg's would be just another efficient, large complex except for two sterling advantages: location and price. The 60-room motel is situated directly across the street from Monterey Bay and Lover's Point—an ideal spot even if you don't get a room with a view. And unlike the competition, this place has the same nightly rates year-round—positively amazing given the area's ever-changing market. Make your reservations early, naturally.

Butterfly Grove Inn
1073 Lighthouse Avenue, Pacific Grove, CA 93950 • (408)373-4921

The Butterfly Grove Inn is adjacent to the wooded Monarch Grove Sanctuary, where butterflies flock for the winter. You can look out your window and watch people standing around, peering upwards, and saying to each other, "Is *that* one?" without actually ever seeing a *Lepidoptera* (if the temperature is below 55°F, the well-camouflaged butterflies wisely snooze all day). The inn is a bit worn but offers 22 good-sized rooms, a heated pool, shuffleboard, croquet, and volleyball, as well as six family units in a Victorian house. And even if you don't spot a butterfly in the woods, you will see deer, which are remarkably self-confident in Pacific Grove. Unfortunately, the inn's summer rates are a little steep for budget lodgers.

The Larchwood Inn
740 Crocker Avenue, Pacific Grove, CA 93950 • (408)373-1114

The 27 rooms at the Larchwood are larger, newer, and more tastefully furnished than many others within its price range, which is probably why you can get a room at budget rates only during the off season. But this is a great place to stay even in the winter, especially if you book a room with a fireplace. And you certainly can't complain about the location: an attractive, quiet neighborhood two blocks from Asilomar State Beach. A continental breakfast is included.

P. G.'s Painted Ladies

Pacific Grove is famous for its Victorian houses, inns, and churches, and hundreds of them have been declared historically significant by the Pacific Grove Heritage Society. Every October, some of the most beautiful and artfully restored are opened to the public on the Victorian Home Tour ($10 per person); (408)373-3304. If you can't make the tour, you can admire many of the faces of these lavish lovelies clustered along Lighthouse Avenue, Central Avenue, and Ocean View Boulevard.

Olympia Motor Lodge
1140 Lighthouse Avenue, Pacific Grove, CA 93950 • (408)373-2777

Many of the 38 rooms in this modern two-story motel have large sliding-glass doors that open onto the outside hallway, meaning you'll need to keep the curtains shut for privacy. Still, some rooms have balconies and ocean views. There's also a heated pool and a free continental breakfast.

Pacific Grove Motel
204 Grove Acre Avenue (at Lighthouse Avenue), Pacific Grove, CA 93950 • (408)372-3218

A family kind of place, this 30-room motel has a little bit of everything: a playground and barbecue area with picnic tables, a pool and a hot tub, and even water bottles conveniently set outside for cleaning the salt spray off your car windows. Scuba divers often stay here, and an area for rinsing off wet suits has thoughtfully been provided. Each room is equipped with a refrigerator, and moderately priced two-bedroom units are available, too.

Sunset Motel
133 Asilomar Boulevard, Pacific Grove, CA 93950 • (408)375-3936

The recently remodeled Sunset Motel works hard to please. The 20 one- and two-bedroom units offer either a kitchen or a fireplace or both, and rates include a complimentary breakfast of muffins, sweet rolls, and orange juice. You can soak your weary body in the new hot tub, take a walk on the nearby beach, or tee off at the Pacific Grove Municipal Golf Course 1½ blocks away.

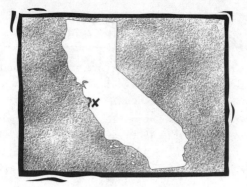

Monterey

If you're looking for the romantically gritty, working-class fishing village of John Steinbeck's Cannery Row, you won't find it here. Even though Monterey was the sardine capital of the Western Hemisphere during World War II, overfishing forced most of the canneries to close in the early '50s, and Monterey began trawling for tourist dollars instead. The low-slung factories of Cannery Row and Fisherman's Wharf have been turned into tacky clothing boutiques, knickknack stores, and yogurt shops. But the town itself, set on the south end of Monterey Bay, still has more than its fair share of breathtaking seacoast vistas, pretty Victorians, historic adobes, and secret gardens full of succulents, herbs, and native plants. It's also the home of a world-famous aquarium. To catch the town at its best, come in the spring or during the sunny Indian-summer months; other times, expect it to be foggy and slightly cool—and expect hotel rates to drop accordingly.

ON THE ROAD

The glory of the town is the amazing, high-tech 221,000-square-foot **Monterey Bay Aquarium**, which features thousands of fascinating fish and other denizens of the (local) deep—not to mention one of the world's largest indoor, glass-walled aquariums (it's three stories high and holds 335,000 gallons of sea water!). The bat-ray petting pool (not to worry, their stingers have been removed) and the two-story sea-otter tank will thrill the kids (and adults), particularly when the sea otters get to scarf down a mixture of clams, rock cod, and shrimp at 10:30, 1:30, and 3:30 every day. Try to visit midweek, to escape the crowds that consistently flock to this beloved institution; reservations are recommended in the summer and on holidays (886 Cannery Row, Monterey; call (408)648-4888 for general information, (800)756-3737 for tickets).

Near the aquarium are some excellent places to eat breakfast and lunch—places that won't break the family bank. At **First Awakenings**, just a jaunt away, even the most finicky eater will find something to order off the large menu. All of the dishes are made from fresh ingredients, and at breakfast you can't go wrong with the gourmet pancakes (125 Ocean View Avenue, in the American Tin Cannery Outlet Center, Monterey; (408)372-1125). The **Bagel Bakery** makes—you guessed it—good bagels and has every kind of filling you could want, from pastrami to peanut butter and jelly (201 Lighthouse Avenue, Monterey; (408)649-1714).

To get the flavor of Monterey's heritage, follow the 2-mile "Path of History," a walking tour of the town's most important historic sites and splendidly preserved old buildings—remember, this city was thriving under Spanish and Mexican flags when San Francisco was still a crude village. Free tour maps are available at various locations, including the **Custom House**, California's oldest public building (at the foot of Alvarado Street, near Fisherman's Wharf, Monterey; (408)649-7118) and **Colton Hall**, where the California State Constitution was written and signed in 1849 (on Pacific Street, between Madison and Jefferson Streets, Monterey; (408)646-5640). Nautical history buffs should visit the **Maritime Museum of Monterey**, which houses ship models, whaling

🎵 *Jazz It Up*

For a terrific, toe-tappin' time in Monterey, visit on the third weekend in September, when top talents like Wynton Marsalis, Etta James, and Ornette Coleman strut their stuff at the Monterey Jazz Festival, one of the country's best jazz jubilees and the oldest continuous jazz celebration in the world. Tickets and hotel rooms sell out fast—so plan early (diehard jazz fans make reservations at least six months before showtime); (800)307-3378 or (408)373-3366.

relics, and the two-story-high, 10,000-pound Fresnel lens used for nearly 80 years at the Point Sur lighthouse to warn mariners away from the treacherous Big Sur coast (5 Custom House Plaza, in Stanton Center, near Fisherman's Wharf, Monterey; (408)373-2469).

The landmark **Fisherman's Wharf**, the center of Monterey's cargo and whaling industry until the early 1900s, is awash today in mediocre (or worse) restaurants and equally tasteless souvenir shops. Serious shoppers will be better off strolling **Alvarado Street**, a pleasantly low-key, attractive downtown area with a much less touristy mix of art galleries, bookstores, and restaurants. Alvarado Street is also the site of the popular **Old Monterey Farmer's Market and Marketplace**, a good spot for free family entertainment and picnic-basket treats; it's held Tuesdays yearround from 4pm to 7pm in winter and 4pm to 8pm in summer.

If your shopping sprees have left you feeling a mite peckish, pull up a chair at **Papa Chano's**, a local favorite known for its big, fresh tacos, quesadillas, enchiladas, and, best of all, delicious burritos (462 Alvarado Street, Monterey; (408)646-9587). Or just around the corner is the **Paris Bakery**, with excellent pastries, clam chowder, calzones, sandwiches, and strong coffee (271 Bonafacio Place, Monterey; (408)646-1620).

CHEAP SLEEPS

The Arbor Inn
1058 Munras Avenue, Monterey, CA 93940 • (408)372-3381

This white country inn, within walking distance of downtown and landscaped with bright, beautiful flowers, offers 55 spacious guest rooms bathed in pale colors, with pretty floral-print bedspreads and matching drapes. Some units are billed as "diver's rooms," complete with hoses for rinsing off the diving gear. Each room has cable TV, phone, and a private bath with tub and shower; some have fireplaces. There's a hot tub on the property, too. The friendly staff serves a large complimentary continental breakfast of fruit, baked goods, cereal, juice, and coffee or tea in the wood-paneled dining room, and during the day, free refreshments are set out in the lobby. Off-season rates are reasonable, although the inn's new managers plan to spruce up the place, which could mean an eventual price increase.

Casa Munras Garden Hotel
700 Munras Avenue, Monterey, CA 93940 • (800)222-2558 (nationwide), (800)222-2446 (California only), or (408)375-2411

The large, sprawling Casa Munras is one of the best of the affordable

Honey, I Packed the Kids

Your kids will love the Dennis the Menace Playground, designed by cartoonist Hank Ketcham himself (at Camino El Estero and Del Monte Avenue, near Lake El Estero). He created enough climbing apparatuses to please a monkey. For fun on the water, take your Curious Georges on a paddleboat—only $5 per half hour—and pedal around Lake El Estero; (408)375-1484. Families with older kids can rent bicycles and in-line skates at the Monterey Bay Recreation Trail, which runs along the Monterey shore for 18 miles to Lover's Point in Pacific Grove. More adventurous sorts should get a sea kayak at one of the rental outlets along Del Monte Avenue and explore the coast. And what could be more thrilling to a little *Free Willy* fan than embarking on one of the whale-watching trips that sail from Fisherman's Wharf in the winter and spring?

upscale accommodations along busy Munras Avenue (also known as motel row). The 151 individually decorated rooms feature pretty armoires, comforters, and white wooden window shutters; some of the pricier rooms have fireplaces. A lovely flower- and tree-filled garden surrounds the hotel, and there's a heated swimming pool, a cafe and bar, and conference rooms. Unlike some of its neighbors, the place is set back from the street, so it doesn't get much traffic noise, though the downtown and wharf areas are just a short walk away. Although the hotel looks quite modern, parts of the original adobe residence built in 1824 have been incorporated into the dining area.

Casa Verde Inn
2113 N Fremont Street, Monterey, CA 93940 • (408)375-5407

The Casa Verde offers some of the most competitive rates on Fremont Street. Eighteen comfortable, newly wallpapered rooms are equipped with cable TVs (with HBO), VCRs, and phones. Vibrant flower beds give the grounds a cheery feeling, and a little restaurant on the property serves Italian dinners. Guests also may pick up free maps of Monterey.

Cypress Tree Inn
2227 N Fremont Street, Monterey, CA 93940 • (408)372-7586

Monterey's budget motel row is on Fremont Street, where basic, no-frills, clean rooms start as low as $29. The Cypress Tree is one of the least tacky, and rates start at about $36 on winter weekdays. The tidy inn offers 55 rooms with salmon-colored walls, queen-size beds, telephones, TVs,

Rate du Jour

Ask a Monterey innkeeper what his or her nightly rates are and you'll likely get six or more quotes for the same room—depending on a variety of factors. Most Monterey hotels have room rates for winter weekdays, winter weekends, summer weekdays, summer weekends, bad-weather days, post-earthquake weeks, and those we-know-you're-desperate-for-a-room periods when the Monterey Jazz Festival, Laguna Seca race days, and other popular events come to town. The bottom line is that the price of a room can triple during peak periods.

For the best bargains, travel on weekdays and always ask about special rates (such as AAA, student, government-employee, and senior-citizen discounts) and package deals, which may include dinner or tickets to the Monterey Bay Aquarium. Also look for hotel-discount coupons at the Monterey Visitors Information Center on 380 Alvarado Street in Monterey; (408)649-1770. If you're visiting from December 1 to January 31, call the Monterey County Holiday Bounty program at (408)649-6544, and the staff will gladly help you find a cheap sleep during this holiday period.

and tiny desks. The Cypress Bakeshop serves coffee, juice, and muffins until noon, with takeout box lunches available on weekdays. Other on-premises amenities include a tourist information and referral center, and a sauna and hot tub.

Del Monte Beach Inn
1110 Del Monte Avenue, Monterey, CA 93940 • (408)649-4410

True to its name, this small 19-room inn is very near Del Monte Beach, though it's also on a busy street in a business district. Still, the comfortable rooms, with period furniture, quilts, and fresh flowers, are a real find, and breakfast is included in the bargain. Most rooms share a bath. Entertainment is limited to board games in the lounge (there are no TVs or phones), but if you brought the kids along, you can take them to the nearby Dennis the Menace Playground and El Estero Lake.

Del Monte Pines
1298 Munras Avenue, Monterey, CA 93940 •
(800)633-6454 or (408)375-2323

The attractive Del Monte Pines motel has 19 large, pleasant rooms with color cable TVs (with HBO), VCRs (movie rentals are available), and coffee makers. Room rates include continental breakfast and, in summer, use of the heated swimming pool. In the off season, midweek rates are low, but they skyrocket when the weather heats up and on weekends and holidays, just as they do at the other lodgings on Munras Avenue. The Del Monte Shopping Center is across the street, and Monterey's major attractions are a 10-minute drive away. You can even buy tickets to the Monterey Bay Aquarium here, which will save you a long wait in line.

Monterey Hotel

406 Alvarado Street, Monterey, CA 93940 • (408)375-3184

This refurbished 1904 Victorian is conveniently located in the middle of downtown Monterey, and it boasts an enchanting European ambience. In the off season, chances are the historic full-service hotel will quote you some equally enchanting weekday rates. The 45 guest rooms are impeccably furnished with reproductions of late-Victorian furniture, including armoires, and they have queen-size beds, TVs, telephones, and private baths with tub showers. Fisherman's Wharf, the Old Capital buildings, restored adobes, and a variety of restaurants and shops are a short walk away. Pampered guests are treated to a continental breakfast, afternoon tea, and cookies and milk in the evening.

Carmel-by-the-Sea

About 35 years ago, Carmel was a quaint little seaside town
with a relaxed Mediterranean atmosphere conducive to such artistic
pursuits as photography, painting, and writing. Luminaries like
Robert Louis Stevenson, Robinson Jeffers, Mary Austin, Sinclair
Lewis, Edward Weston, Upton Sinclair, and Ansel Adams at one
time called Carmel home. Today, though, the very name of this
city has become synonymous with a spectacular fall from grace, and
antidevelopment folks up and down the coast use the term
"Carmelization" with their lips curled in disgust. The charmingly
ragtag bohemian village (which once banned skateboards, high
heels, and ice-cream cones) has long since given way to a cute but
uptight, conservative, and very wealthy coastal tourist village filled
with frozen-yogurt stands, T-shirt stores, and shops hawking out-
rageously overpriced paintings of waves breaking on sandy shores.

As a result, many turn up their nose at the town, irritated by
the relentless traffic—both vehicular and pedestrian—and the too-
darling doodads sold at exorbitant prices. But come to Carmel on
the right day—preferably midweek in the off season, when the sun
is shining and a good, stiff breeze is blowing in from the sea—and
you'll discover all the charm that made this burg so famous. Stroll
the streets in the early morning or early evening to avoid the

crowds and admire the varied, eccentric architecture: Hansel-and-Gretel cottages abut Italian villas, and Spanish haciendas nudge tiny Tudor-style houses. Flowers abound in every place and in every season—in window boxes, on traffic islands, in pretty little courtyards furnished with benches for weary wanderers. And then there's the setting: Even the city's firmest detractors have to admit that Carmel boasts one of the most beautiful beaches on the Central Coast.

Part of Carmel's charm lies in the unusual city ordinances that ban sidewalks, streetlights, franchises, billboards, and even residential addresses. That's right, no one living within the city limits has a numerical street address. Instead, people have homes with names like Periwinkle and Mouse House, and residents go to the post office to pick up their letters and magazines, gossiping all the while about local celebrity citizens like former mayor Clint Eastwood, Kim Novak, and Doris Day.

ON THE ROAD

Carmel is a little bit o' heaven for shoppers with hefty disposable incomes. But even if you can't afford a lizard-skin gym bag or a Waterford crystal birdbath, it's still fun—and free—to window-shop (and people-watch) among Carmel's oh-so-chic boutiques. Some of the more interesting downtown spots are the **Carmel Bay Company**, purveyors of a large, classy collection of California-style gardening tools and house-hold furnishings (Ocean Avenue at Lincoln Street, Carmel; (408)624-3868); **GJ's Wild West**, which sells Western-style clothes and accessories (San Carlos Street, between 5th and 6th Avenues, Carmel; (408)625-9453); **Dansk Designs**, a housewares outlet store (Ocean Avenue at San Carlos Street, Carmel; (408)625-1600); and the **Secret Garden**, which offers unique gardening gadgets (Dolores Street, between 5th and 6th Avenues, Carmel; (408)625-1131). Just outside of town are two luxe sub-urban malls also worth a stroll: the **Barnyard** (Highway 1 at Carmel Ranch Lane, Carmel; (408)624-8886) and the **Crossroads** (Highway 1 at Rio Road, Carmel; (408)625-4106).

Johann's Bach in Town

The annual monthlong Carmel Bach Festival, now led by internationally famous conductor Bruno Weill, offers numerous concerts, recitals, lectures, and discussion groups—many of them free. In addition to Bach masterpieces, you'll hear scores by Vivaldi and Scarlatti, and even some by those young whippersnappers Beethoven and Chopin. The classical-music celebration starts in mid-July; series tickets are sold starting in January, and single-event tickets (ranging from $10 to $30) go on sale in April. Call (800)513-BACH for a list of free events and additional festival facts.

If your sprees have left you shopped out, visit one of the town's two great beaches. **Carmel Beach City Park**, at the foot of Ocean Avenue, tends to be overcrowded in summer (even though its chilly aquamarine water is unsafe for swimming), but the beautiful white sand and towering cypresses are worth the price of sunbathing among the hordes. Or head a mile south on Scenic Drive (the street running alongside the beach) to spectacular **Carmel River State Beach**, where the locals go to hide from the tourists. The Carmel River enters the Pacific here, and you'll see a bird sanctuary frequented by pelicans, hawks, sandpipers, kingfishers, willets, and the occasional goose. There's also a fantastic view of Point Lobos (for more information on this popular spot, see the Big Sur chapter). But beware: Swimming at the Carmel River Beach is dangerous when the surf is high.

A half-mile up the river is the restored **Mission San Carlos Borromeo del Río Carmelo**, better known as the Carmel Mission. Established in 1770, this was the headquarters of Father Junípero Serra's famous chain of California missions, and it was his favorite (Serra is buried in front of the altar in the sanctuary). The vine-covered baroque church with its 11-bell Moorish tower, completed in 1797, is one of California's architectural treasures. The mission houses three extensive museums, and its surrounding 14 acres are planted with native flowers and trees. The cemetery has more than three thousand graves of native Americans who worked and lived in the mission; in place of a gravestone, many plots are marked by a solitary abalone shell (3080 Rio Road at Lasuen Drive, several blocks west of Highway 1, Carmel; (408)624-3600).

Other interesting structural landmarks include the storybook cottages Hugh Comstock constructed in 1924 and 1925 to indulge his wife's love of dollhouses and fairy tales. For a free list of the cottages, stop by or call the Carmel Business Association (on San Carlos Street, above Hog's Breath Inn, between 5th and 6th Avenues, Carmel; (408)624-2522). **Tor House**, the former home of poet Robinson Jeffers, is a rustic granite building that looks as though it were transplanted from the British Isles. Constructed over several years beginning in 1914, today it's the residence of one of Jeffers's descendants. Even more intriguing is the nearby four-story Hawk Tower, which Jeffers built for his wife, Una, with huge rocks he hauled up from the beach below. Guided tours of the house and tower are available for a fee on Friday and Saturday by reservation only (no children under 12; 26304 Ocean View Avenue at Stewart Way, Carmel; (408)624-1813).

Carmel has an active theater scene, perhaps best represented by the **Pacific Repertory Theatre** company, which puts on an outdoor Shakespeare festival each summer and performs other classics such as *The Madness of George III* and *Death of a Salesman* in its indoor theater year-round. Tickets are reasonably priced; call (408)622-0700 or (408)622-0100 for details. A number of quality art galleries are located between Lincoln and San Carlos Streets and 5th and 6th Avenues. Particularly noteworthy is the **Weston Gallery**, which showcases 19th- and 20th-century photographers' works, including a permanent display featuring such famous Carmelites as Edward Weston, Ansel Adams, and Imogen Cunningham (6th Avenue at Dolores Street, Carmel; (408)624-4453).

There are many first-rate restaurants in Carmel, but finding a bargain bite takes some searching (remember, franchises are banned from Carmel, so forget about that Big Mac with cheese). **Katy's Place** is the best stop in town for breakfast, though you'll probably have to wait in a long line before you can dive into her hearty portions of comfort food. Katy offers numerous variations of pancakes, waffles, and eggs, including a dynamite eggs Benedict. Breakfast and lunch are served in the pretty dining room or on the patio under the redwoods (Mission Street, between 5th and 6th Avenues, Carmel; (408)624-0199). Across the street is the cozy little **Carmel Cafe**, which also serves excellent breakfasts—the regulars order the five-grain apple pancakes—and traditional salads and sandwiches for lunch; don't pass up the killer Cafe Meatloaf Sandwich with a glass of fresh-squeezed lemonade (Mission Street, between 5th and 6th Avenues, Carmel; (408)624-1922).

For the perfect picnic-basket ingredients, go to the **Mediterranean Market**, which stocks a large selection of meats, cheeses, and wines (Ocean Avenue at Mission Street, Carmel; (408)624-2022). The **Fabulous Toot's Lagoon** is a local hangout popular for its large portions, and the diverse menu features everything from barbecued ribs and pasta to pizzas, burgers, and fresh fish (Dolores Street, between Ocean

🚲 Gridlock in Paradise

Parking in Carmel can be as tricky as cornering Clint "make my day" Eastwood for an autograph—and the parking tickets are priced high enough to keep the city's coffers overflowing. Avoid the "Carmel crunch" by finding a motel where you can stash your car; then walk, ride a bus, or, better yet, bike through the tiny town. If you didn't pack your two-wheeler, you can rent a mountain bike for about $20 a day (cheaper than a parking ticket!) from Bay Bikes, on Lincoln Street, between 5th and 6th Avenues, in Carmel; (408)625-2453.

and 7th Avenues, Carmel; (408)625-1915). Seafood fans should eat dinner at the moderately priced **Clam Box**, another longtime local favorite (Mission Street, between 5th and 6th Avenues, Carmel; (408)624-8597). If you're craving authentic Italian pizza and pasta, try **Cafe Napoli**, where most dishes are in the $5-to-$10 range (Ocean Avenue at Lincoln Street, Carmel; (408)625-4033).

CHEAP SLEEPS

Carmel Fireplace Inn
4th Avenue and San Carlos Street, Carmel, CA 93921 •
(800)634-1300 or (408)624-4862

Just off the 17-Mile Drive at the north end of town, the colonial-style Fireplace Inn offers 32 rooms individually decorated with hardwood furniture, overstuffed chairs, and fresh flowers. The more expensive units have fireplaces. A patio covered with bougainvillea, geraniums, and hanging baskets of fuchsias offers a pretty place to settle back with a book or a glass of wine.

Carmel River Inn
Highway 1 (at the Carmel River Bridge), Carmel, CA 93922 •
(800)882-8142 or (408)624-1575

The Carmel River Inn is set along the banks of the Carmel River on the southern edge of town, about 1½ miles from the heart of the city. Brilliant flower gardens and cypress and pine trees dot the 7-acre property, and there's a heated pool. The main building's 19 guest rooms are priced out of budget travelers' reach, but 3 of the 24 cottages qualify as cheap sleeps. Each accommodates two and has log cabin–style furnishings as well as a refrigerator, a coffee maker, cable TV, and a phone. The popular Barnyard and Crossroads shopping centers are nearby.

Carmel Wayfarer Inn
4th Avenue and Mission Street, Carmel, CA 93921 • (408)624-2711

This country inn is distinguished by its small tiled patio with a gorgeous brick fireplace that's fired up in the evening. A well-tended garden of colorful flowers (a Carmel trademark) rings the property, and the beach is 8 blocks away. The 15 guest rooms feature color-coordinated English country-style furnishings, including armoires containing TVs. Each room also has a VCR, and there's a large library of videos to choose from. A large continental breakfast with homemade bread and muffins comes with the room. Unfortunately, the inn's rates soar in the summer, especially on weekends. AAA members get a 10 percent discount.

Colonial Terrace Inn
San Antonio Avenue, between 12th and 13th Avenues (P.O. Box 1375),
Carmel, CA 93921 • (800)345-1818 or (408)624-2741

The Colonial Terrace is located in a peaceful residential neighborhood, just a block from the southern (and less populated) end of Carmel Beach. The inn has seven buildings (with a total of 25 guest rooms) set among terraced gardens bordered with flagstone walkways and a white picket fence. The least expensive rooms are two small units that aren't even listed on the inn's rate card. They're both equipped with a private bath, queen-size bed, refrigerator, TV, phone, and coffee maker. The standard rooms have a fireplace and some boast an ocean view, but you'll pay for the extras.

The Homestead
8th Avenue and Lincoln Street, Carmel, CA 93921 • (408)624-4119

This well-maintained turn-of-the-century inn sits in a quiet corner of town, yet it's only a couple of short blocks from Ocean Avenue's shops and restaurants and 6 blocks from the beach. The Homestead has been run by Betty Colletto and her family for 50 years, and they've covered the grounds with gardens of roses and succulents. The barn-red inn offers eight comfortable guest rooms with early-American decor and private bathrooms. Four cottages—complete with maple furniture and lace curtains—are scattered around the property, and each sleeps up to four. Some have fireplaces and kitchens, too.

Horizon Inn

Junípero and 3rd Avenues, Carmel, CA 93921 •
(800)433-4732 (reservations only) or (408)624-5327

Horizon Inn is an upscale facility with 23 rooms ranging from $100 to more than $200 a night; however, three bargain-priced units are located in an annex across the street. These spacious "value rooms" (and they are a good value indeed) offer queen-size beds and private baths, and two have little balconies overlooking the street. A refrigerator, TV, and coffee maker are in each unit, too. A continental breakfast is left outside your door at 7:30am, along with the *Monterey Herald*. The inn also has a swimming pool that's heated to a toasty 87 degrees. Ask the staff about rate discounts, especially between October and May.

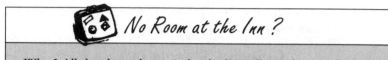

No Room at the Inn?

What? All the cheap sleeps are booked? Well, maybe not all. At no cost to you, the staff at the Tourist Information Center will help you find an affordable place to stay—*if* one exists. They're located on Mission Street, between 5th and 6th Avenues, in Carmel; (800)847-8066 or (408)624-1711.

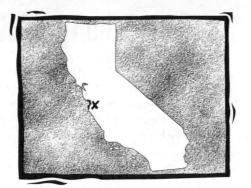

Big Sur

There isn't exactly a Big Sur in Big Sur...not a town by that name, anyway. Originally El Sur Grande *(Spanish for "the Big South")*, Big Sur encompasses 90 miles of rugged, spectacular coastline stretching south from Carmel to San Simeon. A narrow, twisting segment of Highway 1 (built with convict labor in 1937) snakes through this coastal area, and the mist-shrouded forests, plunging cliffs, and cobalt sea bordering the road make the drive one of the most beautiful in the country—if not the world. The region is so scenic that some folks favor giving it national park status; others, however, recoil in horror at the thought of involving the federal government in the preservation of this untamed land and have coined the expression "Don't Yosemitecate Big Sur."

Despite Big Sur's popularity, the area miraculously has remained sparsely populated, and most people journey here for only a few days to camp or backpack—or to luxuriate in the elegant (and exorbitantly priced) resorts hidden in the hills. The bumper-to-bumper traffic on summer weekends is reminiscent of LA's rush hour; to avoid the crowds, come midweek or in the spring, when the gold, yellow, and purple wildflowers brighten the windswept landscape.

ON THE ROAD

Whether you're cruising through for the day or plan to disappear with your sleeping bag somewhere in the vast Ventana Wilderness, spend some time in the gorgeous 1,276-acre **Point Lobos State Reserve** (on Highway 1, 4 miles south of Carmel; (408)624-4909). More than a dozen trails lead to ocean coves, where you might spy sea otters, harbor seals, California sea lions, large colonies of seabirds, and between December and May, migrating California gray whales. Some trails will even take you to one of the two naturally growing stands of Monterey Cypress trees remaining on earth (the other stand is in Pebble Beach on the 17-Mile Drive). Wherever you trek through Big Sur, however, beware of poison oak—it's as ubiquitous as the sea gulls hovering over the coast.

Farther south, Highway 1 crosses over Bixby Creek via the 268-foot-high, 739-foot-long **Bixby Bridge** (also known as the Rainbow Bridge), a solitary, majestic arch that attracts lots of snap-happy photographers. Nearby is the **Point Sur Lighthouse**, built in 1889 and situated 360 feet above the surf on Point Sur, a giant volcanic-rock island. Inexpensive (though physically taxing) 2½-hour guided lighthouse tours, some under spectacular moonlight, are offered on weekends year-round and on Wednesdays in summer (off Highway 1, 19 miles south of Carmel, Big Sur; (408)625-4419).

Hikers and bicyclists often head farther south to navigate the many trails zigzagging through the sycamores and maples in 4,800-acre **Andrew Molera State Park**, the largest state park on the Big Sur coast. A mile-long walk through a meadow laced with wildflowers leads to a 2-mile-long beach harboring the area's best tide pools. The park also offers 50 primitive walk-in tent campsites (on Highway 1, 21 miles south of Carmel, Big Sur; (408)667-2315).

Cheap eats are scarce in Big Sur, but you'll find some good spots in the Big Sur Village area, 3 miles south of Andrew Molera State Park. **The Pub** serves pizza, fish 'n' chips, burritos, and burgers; on weekends there's a barbecue and occasionally live acoustic music (on Highway 1, in the Village Shops, 24 miles south of Carmel, Big Sur; (408)667-2355). Across the highway, the pretty **Ripplewood Cafe** serves breakfast (don't miss the cinnamon French toast or the sticky buns) and lunch (on Highway 1, Big Sur; (408)667-2242).

A few miles down the road on the inland side is one of California's most popular parks, **Pfeiffer–Big Sur State Park**. Here, 810 acres of madrone and oak woodlands and misty redwood canyons are crisscrossed with hiking trails, and many of the paths provide panoramic views of the

Check It Out

Pick up a copy of the free *El Sur Grande* newspaper for maps of the Big Sur coast, names and telephone numbers of commercial services and campgrounds (including free campsites), and hunting and fishing guidelines. It's available in Big Sur stores and ranger stations, or write to *El Sur Grande*, P.O. Box 87, Big Sur, CA 93920.

sea. The Big Sur River meanders through the park, too, attracting anglers and swimmers who brave the chilly waters. Pfeiffer–Big Sur's ultracivilized camping facilities include showers, a laundry, a store, an amphitheater for ranger-led campfire talks, and (bless 'em) even flush toilets (make reservations through Mistix at (800)444-PARK). Nearby, the unmarked Sycamore Canyon Road (the only paved, ungated road west of Highway 1 between the Big Sur Post Office and the state park) leads to beautiful but blustery **Pfeiffer Beach**, with its white-and-mauve sands and enormous sea caves (follow the road until it ends at a parking lot, about 2 miles from Highway 1).

If your idea of communing with nature is a comfy chair in the shade, grab a seat on the upper deck of the fabled **Nepenthe** bar and restaurant, perched 800 feet above the roiling Pacific (Highway 1, 3 miles south of Pfeiffer–Big Sur State Park, Big Sur; (408)667-2345). The food isn't worth the steep prices, but the view merits a pit stop at the bar, particularly at sunset. Sit back and ponder the days when Orson Welles bought this lot in 1944 for his wife, Rita Hayworth.

Four miles south of Nepenthe is the **Coast Gallery**, a showplace for local artists and craftspeople featuring pottery, jewelry, and paintings, including watercolors by author Henry Miller, who lived nearby for more than 15 years. The gallery's casual **Coast Cafe** has a great view of the ocean and offers serve-yourself lunches of soup, sandwiches, baked goods, wine, and espresso drinks (Highway 1, Big Sur; (408)667-2301).

At the southern end of the Big Sur area is beautiful **Julia Pfeiffer Burns State Park**, with 4,000 acres to roam. You'll find some excellent day hikes here and two very popular (i.e., always booked) walk-in environmental campsites (Highway 1, Big Sur; (408)667-2315). If you just want to get out of the car and stretch your legs, take the ¼-mile-long Waterfall Trail to the 80-foot-high **McWay Waterfall**, one of the few falls in California that plunges directly into the sea. Keep an eye open for the silly sea otters that play in McWay Cove.

CHEAP SLEEPS

Big Sur Campground and Cabins

On Highway 1 (about 3 miles south of Andrew Molera State Park), Big Sur, CA 93920 • (408)667-2322

The 14 "cabins" here range from fully equipped mobile homes to wooden A-frames with sleeping lofts and kitchens; many sit along the Big Sur River. Each unit has a private full bath and a fireplace, too. In summer, four tent cabins are also rented (beds and bedding provided). If you're willing to rough it and have brought your sleeping bag, there are about 80 year-round campsites set in a large redwood grove. Guests often while away the day swimming or fishing in the river (steelhead season runs from November 16 through February 28 on weekends, Wednesdays, and holidays only). Amenities include a store, laundry, playground, basketball courts, and inner-tube rentals.

Ripplewood Resort

On Highway 1 (1½ miles north of Pfeiffer–Big Sur State Park), Big Sur, CA 93920 • (408)667-2242

Many of Ripplewood's 16 spare but comfortable cabins are equipped with kitchens, decks, fireplaces, and queen-size beds. Cabins 1 through 9 are on the Big Sur River, far below the highway, where the air is sweet with the scent of redwoods. Cabins 10 and 11 hug the highway, and the others are set at the edge of the woods behind the resort's store. Cabin 12, a knotty pine duplex, is the most affordable. During summer most cabins are booked months in advance, so plan ahead.

Fernwood Motel

On Highway 1 (about ½ mile north of Pfeiffer–Big Sur State Park), Big Sur, CA 93920 • (800)244-7871 (California only) or (408)667-2422

The funky Fernwood offers the least expensive lodging rates in the area. The dozen plain-Jane rooms have a double bed, a little desk and lamp, and a private bath. Guests can kick back in front of the large open-hearth fireplace or watch TV in the lounge. The motel also has a bar that pours drinks till midnight, and a restaurant serving reasonably priced ribs, chicken, burgers, chili, and sandwiches. If sleeping outdoors sounds better than staying indoors, the Fernwood has a campground with 60 sites (most have water and electric hookups) just steps from the motel. A gift shop, gas station, and small grocery store (open every night till midnight) are also on the premises.

Deetjen's Big Sur Inn

On Highway 1 (3 miles south of Pfeiffer–Big Sur State Park), Big Sur,
CA 93920 • (408)667-2377

During the '30s and '40s, travelers making the long journey up and down the coast used to drop in and stay the night with Grandpa Deetjen, a Norwegian immigrant who'd constructed a cluster of redwood buildings with 20 rooms to accommodate his guests. Most of Grandpa's rustic but charming rooms are out of *Cheap Sleeps'* price range, but three of them— a room with a single bed that costs about $50 a night, and two doubles for $70—are worth the splurge: small but comfortable, with bright down comforters, a table and chairs, and a shared bath with a shower. Rates go up $15 on Friday and Saturday.

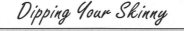

Dipping Your Skinny

Most folks pay over a hundred bucks each to soak their bods in the hot springs overlooking the ocean at Esalen Institute, a world-famous New Age retreat popular for its self-help workshops and body massages. But you can pay a mere $10 for the privilege if you're willing to visit in the wee hours. How wee? Between 1am and 3:30am, any day of the week. Reservations are recommended—even at those hours; (408)667-3023.

GENERAL INDEX

227

U–Z

LODGINGS BY TYPE

Beachfront (or close enough)

APTOS/CENTRAL COAST
Rio Sands Motel, 202

BODEGA BAY/NORTH COAST
Bodega Harbor Inn, 101

JENNER/NORTH COAST
Lazy River Motel, 102

LITTLE RIVER/NORTH COAST
Fools Rush Inn, 109

MOUNT TAMALPAIS STATE PARK/NORTH COAST
Steep Ravine Environmental Cabins, 93

PACIFIC GROVE/CENTRAL COAST
Asilomar Conference Center, 205
Borg's Motel, 206

STINSON BEACH/NORTH COAST
Stinson Beach Motel, 94

Brewery (with rooms)

CALISTOGA/WINE COUNTRY
Calistoga Inn, 82

Cabins

BIG SUR/CENTRAL COAST
Deetjen's Big Sur Inn, 225
Ripplewood Resort, 224

CARMEL/CENTRAL COAST
Carmel River Inn, 218

COLUMBIA/GOLD COUNTRY
Columbia Gem Motel, 190

MIDDLETOWN/WINE COUNTRY
Harbin Hot Springs (see "Hiding Out at Harbin Hot Springs"), 76

MILL CREEK/CASCADE RANGE
Mill Creek Resort, 133

OLD STATION/CASCADE RANGE
Hat Creek Resort, 132
Rim Rock Ranch, 132

ST. HELENA/WINE COUNTRY
White Sulphur Springs Resort & Spa, 79

TAHOE CITY/SIERRA NEVADA
Tamarack Lodge, 144

YOSEMITE NATIONAL PARK
Curry Village, 158
Tuolumne Meadows Lodge, 159
White Wolf Lodge, 159

College Dorm

ARCATA/NORTH COAST
Arcata Crew House, 118

Country Stores (with rooms)

BIG SUR/CENTRAL COAST
Fernwood Motel, 224

DAVENPORT/CENTRAL COAST
New Davenport Bed & Breakfast Inn, 200

Family Oriented

CALISTOGA/WINE COUNTRY
Calistoga Village Inn & Spa, 82

PACIFIC GROVE/CENTRAL COAST
Pacific Grove Motel, 207

PESCADERO/CENTRAL COAST
Pigeon Point Hostel, 199

SACRAMENTO/GOLD COUNTRY
Sacramento Hostel, 175

Farmhouse

CASPAR/NORTH COAST
Jug Handle Creek Farm, 109

237

Fishing Retreats

FORT BRAGG/NORTH COAST
Coast Motel, 110

OLD STATION/CASCADE RANGE
Hat Creek Resort, 132
Rim Rock Ranch, 132

Free (or almost)

ANGEL ISLAND/SAN FRANCISCO BAY AREA
Angel Island Environmental Campsites (see "Escape to Angel Island"), 33

ARCATA/NORTH COAST
Arcata Crew House, 118

CASPAR/NORTH COAST
Jug Handle Creek Farm, 109

CLEAR LAKE/WINE COUNTRY
Clear Lake State Park Campgrounds (see "Clear Lake"), 81

MAMMOTH LAKES/SIERRA NEVADA
Kitzbuhel Lodge, 165

MARIN HEADLANDS/SAN FRANCISCO BAY AREA
Marin Headlands Hostel, 37
Marin Headlands (see "No-Cost Camping") 29

MIDDLETOWN/WINE COUNTRY
Harbin Hot Springs (see "Hiding Out at Harbin Hot Springs"), 76

MOUNT SHASTA/CASCADE RANGE
Alpenrose Cottage Hostel, 127

PESCADERO/CENTRAL COAST
Pigeon Point Hostel, 199

POINT REYES STATION/NORTH COAST
Point Reyes Hostel, 94

SACRAMENTO/GOLD COUNTRY
Sacramento Hostel, 174

SAN FRANCISCO/SAN FRANCISCO BAY AREA
Hostel at Fort Mason, 25
Pacific Tradewinds Guest House, 23

SANTA CRUZ/CENTRAL COAST
Santa Cruz Hostel at the Carmelita Cottages, 202

Gamblers' Choice

KINGS BEACH/SIERRA NEVADA
North Lake Lodge, 144

SOUTH LAKE TAHOE/SIERRA NEVADA
Chamonix Inn, 151

SOUTH LAKE TAHOE/SIERRA NEVADA
Lamplighter Motel, 152

Groups

MAMMOTH LAKES/SIERRA NEVADA
Davison St. Guest House, 164
Kitzbuhel Lodge, 165
Ullr Lodge, 165

MARIN HEADLANDS (SAUSALITO)/SAN FRANCISCO BAY AREA
Marin Headlands Hostel, 37

PACIFIC GROVE/CENTRAL COAST
Asilomar Conference Center, 205

PESCADERO/CENTRAL COAST
Pigeon Point Hostel, 199

SACRAMENTO/GOLD COUNTRY
Sacramento Hostel, 175

SAN FRANCISCO/SAN FRANCISCO BAY AREA
Grant Plaza Hotel, 22
Hostel at Fort Mason, 25
Hostel at Union Square, 21

SANTA CRUZ/CENTRAL COAST
Santa Cruz Hostel at the Carmelita Cottages, 202

ST. HELENA/WINE COUNTRY
White Sulphur Springs Resort & Spa, 79

Homestays

MARIN COUNTY/SAN FRANCISCO BAY AREA
Bed & Breakfast Exchange of Marin (see introduction to Cheap Sleeps), 37

Hostels

ARCATA/NORTH COAST
Arcata Crew House, 118

CASPAR/NORTH COAST
Jug Handle Creek Farm, 109

238

Houseboats

Hunting Lodges

Indian Sweat Lodge

Lakefront

Pet Friendly

Remote

PESCADERO/CENTRAL COAST
Pigeon Point Hostel, 199

POINT REYES STATION/NORTH COAST
Point Reyes Hostel, 94

ST. HELENA/WINE COUNTRY
White Sulphur Springs Resort & Spa, 79

Riverfront

GLEN ELLEN/WINE COUNTRY
Jack London Lodge, 65

JENNER/NORTH COAST
Lazy River Motel, 102

ST. HELENA/WINE COUNTRY
White Sulphur Springs Resort & Spa, 79

Scuba-diving

MONTEREY/CENTRAL COAST
The Arbor Inn, 210

PACIFIC GROVE/CENTRAL COAST
Pacific Grove Motel, 207

Ski Bunks and Hotels

ARNOLD/GOLD COUNTRY
Ebbetts Pass Lodge, 190

KINGS BEACH/SIERRA NEVADA
North Lake Lodge, 144
Northwood Pines Motel, 145

MAMMOTH LAKES/SIERRA NEVADA
Davison St. Guest House, 164
Kitzbuhel Lodge, 165
Mammoth Budget Inn, 165
Ullr Lodge, 165

NORDEN/SIERRA NEVADA
Donner Spitz Hütte (see "High-Altitude Hostels"), 165

SOUTH LAKE TAHOE/SIERRA NEVADA
Chamonix Inn, 151
Lamplighter Motel, 152

SQUAW VALLEY/SIERRA NEVADA
Squaw Valley Hostel (see "High-Altitude Hostels"), 145

TAHOE CITY/SIERRA NEVADA
Family Tree Restaurant & Motel, 144
Rodeway Inn, 144

Spa Resorts

CALISTOGA/WINE COUNTRY
Calistoga Village Inn & Spa, 82
Golden Haven Hot Springs, 83
Nance's Hot Springs, 83

MIDDLETOWN/WINE COUNTRY
Harbin Hot Springs (see "Hiding Out at Harbin Hot Springs"), 76

ST. HELENA/WINE COUNTRY
White Sulphur Springs Resort & Spa, 79

Tent Cabins

BIG SUR/CENTRAL COAST
Big Sur Campground and Cabins, 224

BOULDER CREEK/CENTRAL COAST
Big Basin Redwoods State Park Tent Cabins, 200

YOSEMITE NATIONAL PARK
Curry Village, 150
Housekeeping Camp, 158
Tuolumne Meadows Lodge, 159
White Wolf Lodge, 159

Trailers

MENDOCINO & FORT BRAGG/ NORTH COAST
North Coast Trailer Rentals (see "Comfort Camping"), 110

Train

YOUNTVILLE/WINE COUNTRY
Napa Valley Railway Inn, 81

Vacation Home

TWAIN HARTE/GOLD COUNTRY
Gables Cedar Creek Inn, 191

Zen Retreat

MUIR BEACH (SAUSALITO)/ NORTH COAST
Green Gulch Zen Center, 93

LODGINGS BY REGION

San Francisco

The Adelaide Inn, 19
The Amsterdam Hotel, 20
Brady Acres, 20
Golden Gate Hotel, 21
Grant Plaza Hotel, 22
Herbert Hotel, 21
Hostel at Fort Mason, 25
Hostel at Union Square, 21
Hotel Astoria, 22
Marina Motel, 25
Pacific Tradewinds Guest House, 23
Pension San Francisco, 19
The Red Victorian Bed & Breakfast
   Inn, 26
San Remo Hotel, 24
Temple Hotel, 23
Twin Peaks, 26
Van Ness Motel, 24

Marin County

MARIN HEADLANDS
Marin Headlands Hostel, 37

MILL VALLEY
Fireside Motel, 38
Fountain Motel, 38
Tamalpais Motel, 39
Travelodge, 39

Berkeley

BERKELEY
Campus Motel, 49
Flamingo Motel, 50
The French Hotel, 50
Golden Bear Motel, 50
Travel Inn, 51
Travelodge, 51

OAKLAND
Travelodge, 53

Sonoma Valley

GLEN ELLEN
Jack London Lodge, 65

SONOMA
Sonoma Hotel, 64
Sonoma Valley Inn, 65

Napa Valley

CALISTOGA
Calistoga Inn, 82
Calistoga Village Inn & Spa, 82
Golden Haven Hot Springs, 83
Nance's Hot Springs, 83

MIDDLETOWN
Harbin Hot Springs, 76

NAPA
The Chablis Lodge, 78
Napa Valley Budget Inn, 78

ST. HELENA
El Bonita Motel, 79
Hotel St. Helena, 79
White Sulphur Springs Resort & Spa, 79

YOUNTVILLE
Napa Valley Railway Inn, 81

Stinson Beach and Point Reyes National Seashore

INVERNESS
Motel Inverness, 95

MOUNT TAMALPAIS STATE PARK
Steep Ravine Environmental Cabins, 93

MUIR BEACH
Green Gulch Farm Zen Center, 93

POINT REYES STATION
Point Reyes Hostel, 94

STINSON BEACH
Stinson Beach Motel, 94

Bodega Bay and Jenner

BODEGA BAY
Bodega Harbor Inn, 101

JENNER
Lazy River Motel, 102

241

Northern California Cheap Sleeps
Report Form

Got a tip? A find? A gripe? A fact? A comment?
Send us your Cheap Sleep suggestions. Please include the
address and phone number, if convenient.

Name of place _____

Address _____

Telephone _____

Comments:

I am not affiliated, directly or indirectly, with the management or
ownership of this establishment.

Name _____

Address _____

Telephone _____ Date _____

Send to:

Northern California Cheap Sleeps
Sasquatch Books
1008 Western Avenue, Suite 300
Seattle, WA 98104

Northern California Cheap Sleeps
Report Form

Got a tip? A find? A gripe? A fact? A comment?
Send us your Cheap Sleep suggestions. Please include the
address and phone number, if convenient.

Name of place _____

Address _____

Telephone _____

Comments:

I am not affiliated, directly or indirectly, with the management or
ownership of this establishment.

Name _____

Address _____

Telephone _____ Date _____

Send to:
      Northern California Cheap Sleeps
      Sasquatch Books
      1008 Western Avenue, Suite 300
      Seattle, WA 98104